Kierkegaard on Sin and Salvation

Continuum Studies in Philosophy
Series Editor: James Fieser, University of Tennessee at Martin, USA

Continuum Studies in Philosophy is a major monograph series from Continuum. The series features first-class scholarly research monographs across the whole field of philosophy. Each work makes a major contribution to the field of philosophical research.

Kierkegaard on Sin and Salvation

From *Philosophical Fragments* through the *Two Ages*

W. Glenn Kirkconnell

continuum

Continuum International Publishing Group

The Tower Building
11 York Road
London SE1 7NX

80 Maiden Lane
Suite 704
New York, NY 10038

www.continuumbooks.com

British Library Cataloguing-in-Publication Data
A catalogue record for this book is available from the British Library.

ISBN: HB: 978-1-4411-2083-0

Library of Congress Cataloging-in-Publication Data
A catalog record for this book is available from the Library of Congress.

Typeset by Newgen Imaging Systems Pvt Ltd, Chennai, India
Printed and bound in Great Britain by the MPG Books Group

Contents

Chapter One

Introduction

During his lifetime, Kierkegaard lamented that the world 'took with its right hand what I offered with my left;' that is, readers took his indirect and pseudonymous works at face value, while ignoring his signed books and discourses.[1] His task, he wrote, had been that of a religious writer; but he was taken to be merely a clever, witty philosopher. None had even noticed the questions raised by his publishing *Either/Or* and the *Two Upbuilding Discourses* virtually simultaneously. Nevertheless, he continued his strategy of pairing signed, direct discourses with pseudonymous and esoteric philosophical works through the *Concluding Unscientific Postscript*. This final work had been intended as the capstone of his professional literary activity; and while he in fact remained an author until his death, the *Postscript* does represent the end of the first major phase of his professional authorship.

Even within this first phase, it is possible to see a major division. The *Philosophical Fragments* was unique in that Kierkegaard's name appears as 'editor,' the first time he had so acknowledged one of his pseudonymous works. Also, it is the first pseudonym to discuss 'decisively Christian' concepts, something Kierkegaard did not do under his own name until considerably later. In fact, after the *Fragments* Kierkegaard backs away from discussing Christianity for awhile, returning to it later in his *Postscript* to the *Fragments*. Thus we have an entire section of his authorship which is set apart by two major works under the same pseudonym, Johannes Climacus. Kierkegaard's signed works also change during this period, in ways that link the two tracks of the authorship even more tightly together. Even Kierkegaard's earliest commentators took notice of the questions raised, at least sometimes. Still, the general trend remained to read the pseudonymous works and largely ignore the signed ones; or if the upbuilding discourses were read at all, they were read through the filter of the pseudonyms rather than the other way around.

Kierkegaard's pseudonymous authorship is particularly devoted to exploring the concepts of the ethical, the religious and the relationship between them. With the Climacus writings, this general discussion is made more specific as an analysis of sin and salvation. Sin represents the breakdown of the ethical, as Kierkegaard said as early as *Fear and Trembling*; salvation is the recovery, the religious solution to a problem ethics can only discover. While the upbuilding discourses never quite reach the level of a 'decisively Christian' discussion, they do throw light on the discussion of sin and salvation being pseudonymously presented simultaneously. Reading the signed and pseudonymous works together gives us a clearer view of these important concepts than reading either alone could, as well as revealing an underlying unity of Kierkegaard's authorship that would otherwise remain invisible.

Chapter Two

Faith and Sin Prior to the *Fragments*

In *Concept of Anxiety*, the pseudonym Vigilius Haufniensis claims that the earlier works *Fear and Trembling* and *Repetition* are in fact covert discussions of the problem of sin.[1] However, in the *Concluding Unscientific Postscript*, Johannes Climacus claims that, 'Sin was not brought up in any of the pseudonymous books' prior to *Concept of Anxiety*.[2] Which is true? While *Either/Or* does discuss sin repeatedly, I will concede to Climacus that this book does not give it a decisively religious, coherently developed presentation. The later works, however, require more scrutiny. I believe that by examining Kierkegaard's works together we can develop a clearer understanding of the concept of sin, resolve which of these pseudonyms has correctly interpreted the others, and also resolve the analogous debate between commentators over the meaning and significance of these writings.

On October 16, 1843, Kierkegaard published three books under three names on the exact same day. Usually there was at least a day's spacing, which suggests that a particular book is intended to be read first; but in this case we are given no clue. We cannot possibly read all three simultaneously, but the one we pick to read first will influence how we see the others. In *Point of View for my Work as an Author*, Kierkegaard writes that his signed works are intended to be read more directly than his unsigned ones; therefore, let us start with *Three Upbuilding Discourses* of 1843.[3]

The first describes itself as addressed 'to the perfect'—that is, the morally and religiously blameless. It assumes the worthiness of the reader, and presents a religious ethic to guide how one should live in an admittedly sinful and imperfect world. One should love; one should be loving. This is more of a virtue-based ethic than an ethic of commands and rules. The perfect one lives in a sinful world, but should not look on the sins of others; instead, one should love, and thus hide the multitude of sins around one from oneself. Furthermore, a loving response can actually evoke a loving response in return, whereas anger or suspicion can stir up more sins; so by loving one helps to lessen the sins and increase the love in the

world, making it a little more perfect. And the sins of the world undoubtedly deserve punishment, but a loving person in the midst of the world
may save the rest as Paul's presence on a pagan ship saved the crew from
death by shipwreck. And finally, it discusses how God's love for us hides a
multitude of sins.[4] This is really a different notion; it doesn't seem quite so
applicable to 'the perfect' who have no sins to hide, nor does it really give
instruction to the reader since it is God and not the reader who is doing
the loving. But it does offer God's love as an ideal for the perfect to try to
emulate. The end effect is to urge the reader to remain loving, even when
circumstances do not immediately seem to warrant it. Having faith that
one's own love is not deceived by this hopeful stance, not only does one
become God's coworker making the world more loving, but one becomes
an imitator of God as well.

The second discourse, by contrast, is addressed to the 'imperfect.'[5] Here
the multitude of sins which love hides are the lover's own. It begins with
an individualistic interpretation of apocalyptic themes; these are the 'end
times,' in that each individual has only a limited time before 'the end.'
In such a time of urgency, one needs a sense of assurance of one's own
salvation, before death comes. If one loves much, one does not have time
to dwell on one's own sins, for one is too busy loving. Furthermore, God
sees the love in one, and out of love will ignore the sin to look on the love,
so love hides sins even from God. And one who loves (God) does not care
about the judgment of others, but only about God's judgment, so the judgment of others becomes irrelevant; thus love can be said to hide one's sins
from others as well.

This discourse in particular is aimed at the one who has already morally
slipped, and therefore must find a way beyond the ethical to be restored to
some sort of wholeness. Further underscoring this point, both discourses
end with a New Testament story of an encounter between Jesus and a sinful woman. The first, the woman caught in adultery, has her sins hidden
by Christ's love, whereas the sin in her accusers had quickly discovered her
sin; the second, the sinner who weeps at Christ's feet while he dines in the
house of a Pharisee, has her love hidden both by her love and by his. The
first says, 'The punishment of sins breeds new sins, but love hides a multitude of sins:' the second, that Christ's love and forgiveness enabled her to
love even more.[6]

In both discourses, 'sin' is discussed primarily as moral failure. The
sinner is someone who has done something wrong. This creates a gulf
between the sinner and God. In *Either/Or*, William thought that to 'know
oneself' or 'choose oneself' as guilty was a necessary condition for ethical

righteousness; to choose oneself as guilty was to repent of one's own sins and even the sins of one's parents, and thus one repents of individual and social sins.[7] And this 'choosing' seems to be not only a necessary but also a sufficient condition for ethical righteousness, since to 'choose yourself' truly is to take oneself as an ethical task, and thus to become ethical. But Kierkegaard is saying that when you know yourself as guilty, you know yourself as unworthy to approach God and are repelled. To know others as guilty is to be repelled from those others. So to know oneself as guilty is an obstacle to one's ability to live in community or to accept oneself and take up the life one knows one ought to live. From God's side, sin is an obstacle, but God overcomes this by loving the sinner more and not imposing the deserved punishment. But from the human side, the sinner needs a way beyond the ethical command to 'Be good!' in order to take up the life of goodness, since the sinner knows already that he or she is guilty. Thus, in order to live as one ought, one must love enough to hide one's own sins from oneself, not in order to deserve God's love but just in order to accept it as part of the mutually loving relationship. And by loving others and God, one is also able to live in a more (and improving) moral community as well, where sin and sin's divisiveness are both weakened.

The third discourse, 'Strengthening in the Inner Being,' does not seem to completely connect up with the other two, as there is little discussion of sin. In this third discourse the state of bondage to the world does not seem to be due to anything the person has done; rather, it seems to be the natural or default state, which the individual is now called upon to rise above. One point on which all three agree is that the individual does not act alone, but only with God's help. Without God's love, the human's love cannot hide the multitude of sins; and without God's grace, one cannot find strengthening in the inner being. More significantly, in all three discourses the challenges of the ethical life, as presented in *Either/Or*, are being addressed and solved with the resources of God's gracious love. *Either/Or* is not even really aware of the full problem of sin and can offer no solution to the guilty person. The ethical can only condemn the individual sinner; forgiveness requires other categories. Kierkegaard's discourses here begin to provide those other categories, though they only begin. And it is through God's grace within one, and not one's own resources alone that one is able to be free of bondage to the world and to live in free response to God's love.

The mention of 'spiritual trials' in the third discourse leads naturally to either of the two accompanying pseudonymous works, since both Abraham and Job are famously tried men. Let us start with *Repetition,* if for no other reason than because it doesn't get nearly the attention of *Fear and Trembling.* In Part One, the pseudonymous author Constantin develops the notion of 'repetition,' by which he basically means the fulfillment in the future of the possibilities and intentions of the past. However, his own attempt at repetition fails miserably, and in fact seems to fail by design, since it is not in fact a genuine repetition at all. He seeks to repeat a past trip to Berlin, which seems more like an attempt to relive a recollection than any genuine repetition as he himself has described it. Part Two likewise begins with a presentation of repetition, in this case a melancholy young man's hope for a repetition that will allow him to make a new and successful start of his broken engagement; and likewise it also ends in a failure that seems to call the whole concept of repetition into doubt. In both cases, the goal seems to be to create a text that will point beyond itself. By presenting the breakdowns of false notions of repetition, the book reveals them as false; and by not fully presenting the true notion, the book leaves the reader to continue the search personally.

Part Two of *Repetition* is more overtly religious, so if we are to find a connection with the discourses it is the logical place to look. This consists primarily of a series of letters to Constantin from his young friend. This young man got engaged, then concluded that he was psychologically unsuited for marriage. Constantin advised him to pretend to be a two-timing cad, so the girl could break up with him and find happiness with someone else. Unwilling to reject her by breaking his promise of marriage, but also unwilling to deceive her into dumping him, he instead flees to Stockholm without a word. From there, he sends a series of letters to Constantin, obsessing over his guilt as a deceiver and promise-breaker, and hoping for a miraculous repetition that will somehow allow him to start over with his beloved, marry her and become the husband he ought to have been. His role model is Job, who was innocent even though all his friends believed he was a sinner, and who received all he had lost back from the hand of God. The most obvious connection is when 'Strengthening in the Inner Being' addresses 'the person who was *tried,* who was tested in the distress of spiritual trial.'[8] When *Repetition* speaks of Job, we cannot help but recall this phrase, and of how Job certainly was 'tried.' Job suffered or enjoyed all the possible temptations mentioned in the discourse: prosperity, adversity, being wronged, even feeling abandoned by God. Job's friends have a ready theodicy, to restore their confidence that life has meaning and God still reigns: all who suffer have sinned, so Job must have sinned. Job has no explanation, since he knows he has not sinned; the Sabeans have not robbed him merely of his flocks, but more of his sense of meaning. But as Kierkegaard says, one who is strengthened in the inner being finds that the meaning is to wait for meaning, that God's purpose is that one should wait for purpose to be revealed.[9]

Job has strengthening in the inner being, so when adversity and trial come to him he receives them as he did prosperity and good fortune: from God. And because of this, he receives his repetition. How about Constantin's melancholy young friend? He starts well by rejecting Constantin's advice. Constantin is not himself religious, and believes that while religion can help, one should only resort to it when sagacity has failed.[10] Kierkegaard, on the other hand, tells us that strengthening in the inner being comes from God.[11] The young man has chosen to await a 'thunderstorm' from God, to passively sit and expect that God will somehow appear to him and make everything right in the end. And this watchful waiting is in fact the necessary condition for experiencing the thunderstorm at all. If the man had followed Constantin's elaborate plan to deceive the girl into breaking the engagement, he would not have experienced her later marriage as a thunderstorm from God but rather as the result of his own cleverness.

Why did the young man not attain a full repetition? Constantin writes, 'If he had had a deeper religious background, he would not have become a poet.'[12] His young friend's entire problem is that he was so 'melancholy' that he relates to everything abstractly, detachedly. His fiancée is not a real, concrete girl to him, but rather his muse, though he only half realizes this.[13] He does realize it enough to conclude that he would be an unfit husband, and therefore flees to Stockholm. There he turns to Job; but here too his love is too abstract. As Kierkegaard says, for one who loves much, one's multitude of sins are hidden; but for the young man, the question of his own sin or righteousness becomes an obsession.[14] Religion for him is more a mood than a concern, or even object of attention, just as the girl is more an occasion than an individual. His real concern is for himself.

In *Fear and Trembling*, we find the story of another lover who concludes that he is unfit to marry his beloved: the story of Agnes and the Merman.[15] The merman spies Agnes walking on the beach, and decides to seduce and abduct her. However, he finds that her innocent trust instead seduces him, and he falls in love with her.[16] He no longer wishes to seize Agnes as his prize, but she still loves him. If he simply abandons her, she will be heartbroken, and again deceived. He therefore must choose: 'repentance, or Agnes and repentance.'[17] He can confess his original intentions to her, hope she can forgive him and that they can share a genuine love; or he can deceive her again, this time for her own good, hiding his love for her and attempting to convince her to give up her love of him. He may insult her, ridicule her, whatever it takes for her to give him up; and the more it hurts *him*, the better, since he knows his own guilt and accepts this as his just punishment. De Silentio labels this option 'the demonic.'

Looking at *Repetition*, there are some clear parallels to the young man's case. While his unfitness for marriage is not said to be due to guilt, like the merman he does find himself loved by a girl who, he feels, he cannot marry without deceiving and wronging her. In this situation, Constantin's advice appears to fit de Silentio's description of the demonic: to deceive the girl 'for her own good' so that she freely gives up her love and can go on to find another. But the young man's refusal to join in this plot is still deficient. Had he chosen 'Agnes and repentance,' he would have told his fiancée directly of his worries and concerns. Then, as the merman should have done, he can marry his beloved, trusting in the divine paradox to allow them to rise above the condemnation of the ethical.[18] The young man has neither demonically resorted to sagacity, nor faithfully repented and gone ahead with the marriage; instead, as de Silentio says, he takes the more medieval way; he trusts 'the divine counterparadox' to care for the girl he has abandoned, and gives up all hope of saving her himself. While the young man's way is certainly superior to Constantin's by this standard, it is still not complete; he may have been waiting for a miracle, but was unable to disclose himself to his beloved and to marry her in anticipation of a miracle. And when we read de Silentio's description of this approach as akin to monasticism, it makes perfect sense that the young man should in his turn wind up as a religious poet, who renounces all worldly joys in his love for the pure infinite.

Fear and Trembling's 'third problema' contains the closest link between the pseudonymous works and the discourses, and illustrates the advantages of the elegant approach perhaps better than any other passage. Following the discussion of Agnes and the Merman, de Silentio begins a lengthy discussion of sin. In the context of a discussion of Abraham, this seems like a digression; de Silentio says as much, when he concludes his discussion of sin by saying that 'nothing of what has been said here explains Abraham, for Abraham did not become the single individual by way of sin—on the contrary, he was a righteous man, God's chosen one.'[19] But when we read this book in the light of the discourses, the discussion of sin seems perfectly relevant. De Silentio writes that, 'Sin is not the first immediacy; sin is a later immediacy.'[20] Sin removes the individual from the universal, and moves the individual toward the paradox of the demonic. The universal (i.e. the ethical) cannot demand the individual be good, since the individual is starting from guilt already; but if the universal acknowledges sin, it is already looking for a way out that escapes the judgment of the ethical, and thus exceeds itself. And this is what the discourses address. The individual who loves much escapes his or her own guiltiness, and can live in the 'new immediacy' of faith. The individual who loves much also escapes living in a guilty world, and can see the world anew. The religious offers a new beginning, whereas the ethical cannot even get started since all it can do is condemn the guilty. Reading the discourses and *Fear and Trembling* together draws our attention to the point where they intersect: the problem of sin.

This portion of *Fear and Trembling* is arguably the key to understanding not just the connection between the books, but also *Fear and Trembling* itself. It is not primarily about how the individual should will to be an individual no matter what. It is not, as one author called it, 'absurd spiritual heroics.' It is not a call to criterionless choice, to choosing 'the absurd' in the sense of the meaningless and giving it meaning by one's own choosing of it. It is an analysis of faith, as it says of itself; but more, it is an analysis of the problem of sin. Abraham is 'the father of faith,' and by him all nations are blessed; but Abraham's story is not my story, and if the story ended with his faith I would be lost. The merman's story is my story. The story of the sinner is my story.

Because the bulk of *Fear and Trembling* discusses faith in relation to Abraham, it creates the impression that this is something that applies to extraordinary individuals, or those who will to be extraordinary. But the merman's story is everyone's story, for all have sinned and fallen short. The demonic, sagacious response is the one that Constantin recommended to his young friend. The hidden but unsagacious approach is the one the young man chooses, and he winds up lost to the world. The 'greatest human being' de Silentio can imagine is the knight of faith, who repents of his or her sin and then finds the way through 'by virtue of the absurd,' beyond all human power and understanding.

Conclusions: Either/Or raises the concept of sin several times, but by design it fails to clearly define it or to address the problem fully. The three books of October 16, 1843 raise the problem of sin directly, although they still do not solve it completely. In isolation, these pseudonymous works rank as Kierkegaard's most controversial and obscure, and that is saying a lot. When viewed together with the three discourses, some of the controversy and confusion can be cleared up. It becomes more obvious that, whatever else the pseudonymous books achieve, their primary task is to explore the problem of sin and redemption.

Kierkegaard's upbuilding discourses after this date become increasingly paradoxical and stringent, but continue to move within what he called later 'the sphere of immanence.' The next major development of the concept of sin in his writings comes in his pseudonymous exploration of Christianity, the *Philosophical Fragments.*

Chapter Three

Sin and Salvation in the
Philosophical Fragments

The *Philosophical Fragments* develops Kierkegaard's understanding of the problems of sin, repentance, and redemption: questions that, as de Silentio said, are both beyond the ethical and essential to it. Climacus is often interpreted as arguing that salvation occurs through faith in the God-Man, the Absolute Paradox, a logical contradiction on a par with square circles. Arguments then revolve around whether it is morally permissible to assent to something which one knows to be false, or believes might be false, or knows to be supported by little or no evidence; whether there are beliefs which one morally *ought* to have, and whether one should thus somehow strive to believe; and so on. When read in isolation from Kierkegaard's signed works, *Fear and Trembling* is often interpreted as the call to do any crazy thing, as long as it is done with passion as an expression of one's individuality.[1] Likewise, *Philosophical Fragments* has been interpreted as the call to believe any crazy thing with passion, 'by virtue of the absurd,' transcending reason the same way Abraham is said to have transcended the ethical.[2] What is left out of both interpretations is the nature of the problem: sin.

While the *Fragments* was released within days of the *Concept of Anxiety*, it seems even Kierkegaard had trouble remembering which was published first.[3] An original reader of Kierkegaard's authorship would have had time, just barely, to finish the *Fragments* before *Anxiety* appeared. Furthermore, the way for the *Fragments* was prepared by another collection of upbuilding discourses. Therefore, to try to set the pseudonymous books in a wider context, let us begin with the discourses which introduce this collection of writings.

The Three Upbuilding Discourses of 1844: These were published five days before the *Philosophical Fragments,* which would lead one to suspect they are intended to 'accompany' the *Fragments,* as the discourses that appeared on October 16, 1843 reinforced and commented upon themes raised in the pseudonymous works they accompanied. In some ways, these discourses seem particularly close to the Climacus writings, not just chronologically but also in shared topics and phrases that appear in both the discourses and the Climacus writings.[4] However, the third discourse in particular demonstrates just how different the discourses in general are from the *Fragments*, and how no upbuilding discourse could be said to 'accompany' Climacus' writings. This discourse, 'He Must Increase; I Must Decrease,' draws on the words attributed to John the Baptizer by the fourth Gospel. What will really strike any Christian reader about this discourse is what is missing. Kierkegaard uses the Baptizer's experience as a model for any individual and for all who must learn 'in humble self-denial' and 'genuine joy' to accept being superseded by another.[5] There is no mention of Christ's name directly, and while Kierkegaard does acknowledge that the Baptizer's situation was unique because the 'he' who 'must increase' was truly unique, he repeatedly turns attention back to 'how the single individual is to fulfill something similar in lesser situations.'[6] Kierkegaard could have written something about how the Baptizer had to step aside for Christ's mission, and the individual must likewise 'decrease' so that Christ can be born into his or her life; but Kierkegaard assiduously avoids anything of the sort. In a curious way, then, this discourse does lead into the *Fragments* and yet does not. The *Fragments* is to be a discussion of Christ, revelation and salvation, and it makes sense that the Baptizer would be forerunner to this as in all four Gospels; but the discussion itself seems to deliberately and even with difficulty turn aside from any discussion of the Baptizer that would actually qualify as 'Christian.'

There is an implied progression in this collection of discourses. The first is addressed to 'youth,' the second to both youth and experience; and the third, by referencing John, points beyond all the discourses even as it stops short of any content or argument that would go beyond a general religiousness. There are multiple parallels to passages from Climacus' books. An original reader would have had difficulty distinguishing between Kierkegaard and Climacus, or knowing how many of these connections are intentional and informative rather than coincidental. What is clear is that the discourses are continuing to approach the problem of sin, but have not broached it. While there is discussion of what might separate the individual from God, there is also the assurance that the recollection of the youthful thought of the Creator and the expectancy of an eternal salvation can help one overcome that separation. Sin is not treated as so decisive that anything as extreme as the Incarnation would be necessary to overcome it; so it makes sense that the Baptizer is treated not as the forerunner of a unique Teacher but rather as a role-model for any of us.

The Philosophical Fragments: Johannes Climacus is unusual in the pantheon of Kierkegaardian pseudonyms, in that 'S. Kierkegaard' appears as editor to the two books listing Climacus as author. This is the first time Kierkegaard publically associates himself with a pseudonymous work. Still, there are characteristics that Climacus shares with other pseudonyms. Like Constantin, he is deliberately obscure, so that the reader must excavate the meaning from the pseudonym's words, separating grain from chaff before she or he can even begin asking what Kierkegaard himself might have intended. Like de Silentio, Climacus discusses something he himself claims not to understand first-hand: in this case, Christianity, or what it is to be a Christian. This means that at times the pseudonym is deliberately misleading, and at other times may be unintentionally misleading. Sometimes he deliberately and obviously jokes with us, other times he subtly leads us astray, and still other times it seems that perhaps he is trying to explain himself and it is his thoughts that have become too subtle.

'*Can the truth be learned?*' Climacus begins the first chapter of his *Philosophical Fragments* with subtle misdirection. He begins with an epistemological question, first asked by Plato: how can the truth be learned? If one already knows the truth, then of course there is no reason to learn it; but if one does not know it, how will one recognize it when he or she encounters it?[7] Climacus hints that this is primarily a moral and religious question, when he cites Platonic dialogues that deal with the moral question, 'Can virtue be learned?' But this is only a hint, and a vague one, as he quickly turns it back to a question of knowledge rather than action. Climacus proceeds to describe what he calls the Socratic position: recollection. In a previous life, the individual knew the truth; but in coming into this life, she or he forgot it. Now the individual must be reminded of the truth again. However, once reminded, she or he recognizes the truth. The Socratic solution basically solves the 'pugnacious proposition' by denying it. One in fact does have at least a latent knowledge of the truth, and need only have that knowledge awakened. This, Climacus says, is the essence of all philosophical notions of learning, including the Hegelian attempt to 'go beyond' Socrates.[8]

Climacus next suggests that we see if it is possible to really 'go beyond' Socrates, in the sense of proposing a concept of learning that is truly different.[9] This 'beyond' accepts the pugnacious proposition that the learner is in fact in total ignorance of the truth, and yet somehow learns it. In this case, says Climacus, the learner does not seek the truth, for she or he does not know what to seek or even that there is anything

to seek. Such a learner believes she or he has already found the truth
and is living in its light; but in fact, the learner is untruth, not only
ignorant but actually moving away from the truth and reflexively hostile
toward it. In this case, the learner will not come to the truth, so the truth
must be brought to the learner. To understand the truth is an essential
human condition; so the teacher who gives the truth is giving the human
learner back his or her own human nature. Only the god can create a
human nature where there was none; so the teacher must be the god. It
is a contradiction to suppose that the god first creates the learner in the
truth, then deprives the learner of the truth, then bestows it again; so
the original loss of the truth must be due to the learner's free choice to
reject the truth. 'But this state—to be untruth and to be that through
one's own fault—what can we call it? Let us call it *sin*.'[10] This is the first
direct statement that we are really dealing with more than an epistemological dispute.

Climacus quickly reverts to more philosophical terms like 'untruth' and
'teacher,' but only after identifying the untruth as sin, and the teacher
as a savior and judge who comes in the fullness of time. Furthermore,
his description of untruth/sin is fairly familiar to those acquainted with
Pauline Christianity: the learner is bound and cannot free herself or
himself, totally dependent on God to even recognize how bound she or
he really is. Even the notion that the learner/sinner is 'polemical against'
the truth echoes Paul's claims that 'the flesh' wars against 'the Spirit.' But
Climacus is actually very vague regarding the nature of sin, just what the
individual did to become a sinner, how it separates one from the god, and
so on. He says that the learner has chosen 'unfreedom' and thus is no
longer free to again simply choose freedom; it must be given by the god.
But he doesn't say why this is, except that to claim otherwise would refute
the whole idea that the learner chose unfreedom in the first place.

What he does say in his 'thought project' is that the teacher must be the
god, and that the truth the teacher gives is the god's own self. And in the
'poetical venture' that follows, Climacus argues that the god must become
a human to accomplish this.[11] In this way and only in this way can the
learner be enabled to see the truth, while still retaining the integrity of her
or his own human nature.

The Absolute Paradox: The third chapter retraces much of the progress
of the first two, with some additional insights of its own. One difference
is that the third chapter is much denser than the others, and the argument much harder to follow. The first chapter presents a hypothetical
experiment: If A=recollection, what would not-A be? The entire rest of the

chapter purports to be an elaboration of this 'not-A.' The second likewise is a fairly straightforward disjunction: If the god from love wishes to become a teacher, how can this be done? Ascent of learner or descent of the god; not ascent, therefore descent. This is not to say that everything about these chapters is indisputable, but the basic logical structure is clear enough. Commentators who debate the merits of the arguments at least tend to debate the same points. The third chapter by contrast seems to be more nebulous; despite or because of its more 'philosophical' manner, its actual argument is more subtle and tortuous. It is therefore particularly in order to begin with a sketch of the apparent argument underlying Climacus' dialectical meanderings:

1) We assume recollection achieves its fondest goal; 'we know what a human being is.'
2) Reason, not content to sit on its laurels here, 'seeks its own downfall' in a 'collision' with 'something thought cannot think.'
3) We may name this unknown 'the god.'
4) The god (=unknown) really is irremediably unknown; it is absolutely different from reason, and cannot be described or understood in any way.
5) We only know what anything is in distinction from its opposite; so we only know what a human being (the known) is by comparing this concept to its opposite, the unknown. But we cannot do this, since we have no concept of the unknown.
6) Therefore we cannot know what a human being is without knowing the god.
7) We cannot even grasp the nature of the difference between ourselves and the god; since we lack any clear conception of the god beyond being 'unknown,' any attempt to further define this difference only generates confusions of the known and the unknown.
8) Therefore reason is 'self-ironizing' or self-negating; it can only know itself in opposition to the unknown, which it then confuses with itself; so that from the initial assumption that reason knows itself, we conclude that it cannot.
9) To know the unknown (the god), a human being must first know it as different. Even this information must be given by the god, since the understanding is unable to conceive of the absolutely different and confuses it with itself. But if the god does give this knowledge, the understanding cannot understand it and hence cannot know it. 'We seem to stand at a paradox.'

10) This absolute difference could not come from the god, since anything deriving from the god constitutes a relationship; so the difference must derive from the human being himself or herself. This difference we have already named as 'sin.'

This seems to me to be the argument of the chapter; but even granting this formulation as correct and the logical connections as sound, many of the premises would remain controversial. The main areas of debate need to be considered in more detail.

First, the claim that reason seeks its own downfall has inspired more than one objection. I don't start thinking with the hope of failure but of success, and what I seek are not paradoxes but answers. On the other hand, unless I run into a paradox, why should thought stop? Why should it not continue until checked by something it cannot think? Reason always seems to strive to push limits back, unless held in check by the laziness of the thinker. Any earlier halt seems arbitrary. So if the passion of reason is at its 'ultimate potentiation,' a collision with the unknown is inevitable. Within the philosophical world which Climacus and Kierkegaard share, this claim should appear far less controversial. The *Critique of Pure Reason* is virtually devoted to the proposition that reason, in its desire to know everything and how everything relates to everything else, inevitably posits metaphysical concepts such as God, the soul, and the universe: concepts which it cannot *know*, although it may *think* it knows (whereupon it falls into fallacies and self-contradictions). Likewise, the *Phenomenology of Spirit* is driven by the unstoppable compulsion of Spirit to find and embrace its opposite, time and again, even though this means the downfall of the understanding—although Hegel goes on to claim that Reason, having discovered its opposite, then goes on to reunite itself with that which 'thought cannot think' in a higher synthesis.

Perhaps the most notable point here is the description of reason as passionate.[12] It is not some 'dialectic' of a pure, impersonal Reason driving thought toward its collision with the paradox; rather it is the passion of the thinker to carry thought through to its end. Plato certainly writes of thought in this way; the motive force in the *Symposium* or *Phaedrus* is not Reason, but Love. And while these might be taken as poetic metaphor, there is certainly nothing metaphorical about Hamann's protest against the idea of abstract, disembodied Reason. He says as clearly as he says anything that it is the whole, concrete, flesh-and-blood-and-passion person who thinks, and that any attempt to free thought from its place in the whole person undermines both the thinker and the thought.[13] Climacus draws on these sources in his rebellion against the universal, passionless, 'objective' Reason which Hamann saw as imperiously directing the Enlightenment, and Climacus sees as the idol of the 'speculative philosopher' or the 'professor.' It is a peculiar disease of all species of intellectuals to tend to forget that they are also human beings, with needs and appetites and passions; and this fact means that their achievements are not the acts of Reason but of one person's reasoning. This fact becomes important in the later discussion of offense; while it is in fact individuals who are offended at the paradox of the god-teacher, it is always tempting to believe it is impersonal and universal Logic or Science or History which rejects the paradox.

The next move, 'let us call this unknown *the god*,' purports to be merely definitional; however, the sudden and apparently arbitrary introduction of such a philosophically and emotionally loaded term certainly arouses suspicion. It is also not immediately clear what Climacus intends by this. Is he trying to smuggle in some religious import; or is he trying simply to draw attention to the fact that the god *is* unknown; or are there once again hidden assumptions underlying his logic? On reflection, one sees that there are compelling historical reasons for this identification. Aquinas' five proofs for the existence of God all follow the basic pattern of establishing the existence of some frontier concept, such as a 'first cause' we 'must suppose,' which is then named 'God.'[14] More recent is the practice of examining the concept 'Being,' which is described as either so transcendent or so primordial that it escapes direct experience and hence exists only as a frontier concept, which is then identified with 'God.' Kant's uses of the concept 'God' all likewise use this as a designation for some idea which reason is driven to assume, rather than for something known. Hence the name could be said to be arbitrary, though sanctioned by common usage; Climacus is not merely being flippant to designate the unknown as 'the god,' although he is being coy to suggest that this definition is arbitrary. In fact, it is a common and significant identification, which Climacus is concerned to demonstrate as the cause of the chief ills of philosophical theology. Reason, he says, continues in its efforts until it runs into a brick wall. The unknown something beyond this wall it then labels 'God.' Having now got a name for the unknown, reason begins to suppose that it can deduce all sorts of other attributes of the unknown something beyond the wall; but this supposition is false. One simply cannot deduce from the premise that 'the unknown=the god' that therefore 'the unknown is known.' However, thinkers have been attempting to do just that for thousands of years.

It is within this context that Climacus places his extensive discussion on the subject of proving the existence of God.[15] Climacus begins by objecting that there is something insincere about the attempt to demonstrate the existence of the god. If the god does not exist, then of course it is impossible to *prove* otherwise; therefore the whole exercise of 'proving' the existence of the god presumes that the god does in fact exist, and now we will prove it. In fact, of course, most if not all so-called proofs come from believers trying to persuade, not from doubters seeking to establish the facts. This is not so much a logical investigation as rhetoric. While there may be other, legitimate purposes to the practice of 'proving the existence of God' which Climacus overlooks, his discussion does establish his point: that the unknown/god really is and remains unknown. The understanding has no route to the god, no bridge to cross from the known (*ex hypotheosi*, its own nature as human) to the unknown. It is not merely temporarily unknown, awaiting further investigation and discovery; it is irremediably unknown. This is also to say that it is 'absolutely different,' since any similarity would provide a point of contact between the understanding and the unknown so that it might be, to some extent, known. But simply to say that the unknown is the frontier of understanding, that it is beyond the reach of the thinker's passion for reason, and that it is absolutely different, still does not give this 'concept' any distinguishing characteristics. Even our categories for distinguishing the unknown from the known are drawn from reason itself. Always we think in terms of the general rules of thought and reality: we may think of something that fits the normal rules, or that violates them, but we cannot think without reference to them. But the *absolutely* different is not just something that violates this or that rule; it is something to which such rules are totally irrelevant. Climacus says that the understanding cannot preserve a sense of the absolutely different, and that in specifying the difference and thus bringing it under the categories of thought, it erases the absoluteness. This specification thus generates its own conceptions of the difference(s), creating the various arbitrary and fantastic notions of the god which history has known. From the crudest mythologies to the philosopher's more refined definitions, each is arbitrary and each equally false. What is worse, each is a confusion of the understanding with the unknown, as it projects its own nature and categories upon the unknown, until it can no longer tell the difference between itself and the unknown. But if the understanding cannot tell the unknown from itself, it cannot be said to know either; since if it knew either it would certainly be able to tell what it knows from the unknown. This is what Climacus means by the 'self-ironizing of the understanding.'[16] The understanding negates itself; beginning with the assumption that we know what human nature is, we have arrived at the conclusion that we cannot, for reason pursues thought to the frontier of understanding, only to confuse what is on one side of the frontier for the other, and hence undermines whatever knowledge it might have had to begin with. The irony becomes evident when Climacus undertakes a little thought-experiment.[17] Suppose there was this guy, a regular ordinary Joe, a family man and a good citizen. Suppose he was also the god. How would I know it? 'Well, I cannot know it, for in that case I would have to know the god and the difference, and I do not know the difference, inasmuch as the understanding has made it like unto that from which it differs.' I do not know *the* difference between the god and myself; although I may have a whole list of 'differences,' these are all human inventions only, and are all based on some relation between my nature and the unknown god. They never comprehend the difference, and in describing it make it only a degree of dissimilarity, perhaps a great one; but at the base of any dissimilarity is still a point of contact, a similarity, even if a minute one. This is obvious in the case of a *via eminentiae,* but is even the case with *via negationis,* except that here the 'similarity' consists in the god's being on the negative end of the scale, while the conceptual scale remains the same for both parties in the comparison.

So even if the god/the unknown should come ever so close to me and my place, I cannot recognize it. It is the nature of human understanding to tend to generate false differences and false similarities when confronted with such an intangible concept as 'the unknown,' so that if the true unknown did appear before me seeking to become known, I still could not recognize or understand it. If I were to understand anything, the first thing I would have to understand is that it is the unknown, the different, the absolutely different. But to say that it is absolutely different is to say I cannot understand it and hence cannot know it. The god's act of seeking the learner (to return to the material of the first two chapters) simply succeeds in pushing the understanding further away, showing it to be absolutely shut out. In short, if the god should come seeking the learner in order to be known by him or her, the god reveals that the god is the unknown and unknowable; if the god becomes a suffering servant in order to become equal to the beloved so that they may understand one another in love, the first thing revealed to the beloved is the absolute inequality. This seems to be the absolute paradox; 'absolute' in the sense that it is absolutely insoluble by the understanding, because it is based on the absolute difference between the unknown god and the known. In its general form, it is similar to the paradox which began the first chapter: how can the truth be learned, since if it's known we don't need to learn it; and if it's unknown, how would we know to look for it, or recognize it if we found it? The Socratic position makes this a relative paradox, by abolishing the absolute ignorance in the doctrine of recollection. This relative paradox is resolved when one recognizes that one in fact knows the truth one seeks already, and must merely bring it to full consciousness. The absolute paradox, by contrast, is only 'resolved' when one recognizes that one does not posses the truth, and must in fact lock everything out of one's consciousness in order to think it.[18] Or rather, since this is impossible, it cannot be thought at all, and the paradox can only be resolved by other means.

So the 'absolute paradox,' as presented in the *Fragments*, has little to do with the logical anomalies posed by the concept of an infinite God incarnate in a finite, historical man. These would only be a real problem if we in fact knew the unknown, and knew what rules actually apply to the god; but we don't. The problem is rather that we *think* we know what the god can and should do, and even tend to insist on the validity of our standards in the face of something truly novel like the Incarnation. Not only does this seem to violate the usual rules of thought, as we see in the first chapter; it also violates our rules of propriety. The love shown by the god for the individual is too extravagant. The problem is that it cannot occur to any human that the god would do such a thing, or might actually consider the individual worth so much effort and sacrifice. The paradox is thus a violation of human expectations, and our limited ability to comprehend something so novel—and even that it *is* so novel. The supposed miscegenation of the opposed concepts divine/human is just a smoke screen.

The fact that the real breach between the god and the human is not a question of eternity, infinity, invisibility, or whatever becomes even clearer when Climacus postulates on the nature of the difference.

> But if the god is to be absolutely different from a human being, this can have its basis not in that which man owes to the god (for to that extent they are akin) but in that which he owes to himself or in that which he himself has committed. What, then, is the difference? Indeed, what else but sin, since the difference, the absolute difference, must have been caused by the individual himself. . . . Thus the paradox becomes even more terrible, or the same paradox has the duplexity by which it manifests itself as the absolute—negatively, by bringing into prominence the absolute difference of sin and, positively, by wanting to annul this absolute difference in absolute equality.[19]

The 'difference,' then, is that one 'is untruth, and that through one's own fault.' It is not that the god appears to violate human standards, for in seeking the unknown reason is in fact (perhaps unconsciously) seeking just such a violation. Nor is it the fact that the Creator is so different from the creature as to be incomprehensible, for the relation of Creator to creature *is* a relation. If not for sin, I would be able to look at myself, and reason to the god as from effect to cause: The god is something which would create a thing like me. But because of sin, I cannot do that, for my will is too warped and my knowledge therefore too distorted. That sort of reasoning could, if laid bare, resemble: 'I am a manipulative, autocratic bastard; therefore God must likewise be a demanding patriarch.' Or, 'I hate my enemies, foreigners, or other threatening strangers; God created me and gave me this hatred, and therefore must hate them too.' Even our knowledge of the 'objective' world is distorted by sin. As one person I talked to appeared to reason, 'My law school program has convinced me that we live in a cold, impersonal universe;' or, 'My program seems cold, impersonal, and ruthless towards me; I accept this as my world; therefore "the god" must likewise be cold and impersonal—not a "person" at all, but only a blind originative source.' Many other people, looking at the same universe, see it as either supportive and nurturing, or at any rate benignly neglectful rather than actively threatening. And under the hypothesis that each individual is in untruth, no one can really *know* which if any is correct. The optimist might be in the grip of a narcissistic illusion, and the paranoid might misinterpret the universe out of her or his own fear and insecurity. Both persons will have very different notions of 'the god,' the unknown source of themselves and the universe; but both derive their views from their own untruth. Sin makes it impossible to reason accurately from God's *vestigia* in Creation (i.e. in us), since these are largely effaced by sin, and since our attention is in fact turned away from the true *vestigia* and toward our own chosen untruth.

We have seen, therefore, that the passion of reason drives it toward a collision with the unknown. It seeks to find its limit, and to push at this frontier with all its might to see if it really is so impenetrable; and if it is to know anything, particularly itself, it must also know this opposite, the unknown. So reason's deepest impulses and needs would be met by some sort of reconciliation with the unknown, i.e. the god. And this is also the god's desire, both to be known by the individual *qua* learner and to be loved by the individual *qua* beloved. But on the other hand, the first thing the individual must know if he or she is to know the god is that there is an absolute difference between them, and that this difference is due entirely to the individual's sin, and that this sin has so totally corrupted the individual that he or she is now unable to know the god, or even to recognize the god if encountered. The individual's deepest need is for the god, but the understanding simply cannot take the god in. There are two possible responses to this situation: The individual can 'set the understanding aside' and choose to relate to the god in a 'happy passion' which Climacus does not yet name; or the individual can cling to the understanding with its limits, and thus renounce any further attempt to relate to the unknown beyond understanding's limits. This second option Climacus terms 'offense.'

A Word about Offense: Climacus devotes an appendix to this chapter to the topic of offense.[20] In detail he argues that offense is an 'acoustic illusion,' wherein the understanding claims to sit in judgment upon the paradoxical manifestation of the unknown while all the time it is the paradox which judges the understanding. Offense is thus passive and reactive, and not even original in its reactions. Its terms of criticism are drawn from the paradox itself. The problem, from the point of view of the paradox, is why being 'improbable' or 'absurd' should count as an objection, since it really is nothing more than a recognition that this is indeed the paradox, an encounter with the unknown. Offense is an act, says Climacus, not a state; and hence to that extent it is active. One is not forced by the unreasonableness of the paradox to be offended; rather, one chooses to be offended when one prefers to let reason define the limits of possible truth, rather than letting the paradox show that there is truth beyond the limits of reason. But the paradox is the truth, at least according to the thought-experiment, and hence is the true measure both of itself and of the false; so any attempt to condemn, reject, or redefine the paradox only reveals the fact that the judge is still in untruth.

The purpose of this section seems to be to emphasize the primacy of the paradox as the truth (*ex hypotheosi*), and all other stances not just as mistakes or compromises or open-minded agnosticism, but as active rejection of the truth. Reason does not judge the paradox, but the other way around; and no one is unable to will the paradoxical truth unless that one wishes to be unable. This of course does not consider persons for whom the 'moment' of encounter with the god has not occurred, for it is only with the appearance of the paradox that the possibility of offense came into existence—and thus only when the paradox comes into my life does the possibility of offense come to me.

In all of this, there is no question of believing nonsense, or embracing logical contradictions. The paradox comes about because the god is the unknown, as a result of the learner's own guilt, and yet desires to establish a relationship to the learner. The paradox is thus not the logical anomaly of the Incarnation, but the difficulties in overcoming sin. It is only offense that claims to find anomalies in the god's actions and declares that these refute the paradox. Reason can choose to continue to function within the limits marked by the unknown, and Climacus uses such reasoning in his own work. Not only does Climacus not reject the principle of contradiction, but in fact he relies heavily on it in his criticism of idealism.[21] A reason disciplined by its encounter with the unknown god can serve to refute arrogant presumptions of reason elsewhere, or at least demonstrate that these are presumptions and not valid reinterpretations of the paradox; and it can clear out mistaken interpretations so that the true paradox may be more clearly seen.

If this still-unnamed hypothetical advance upon the Socratic position is true, and the reason we are in untruth is through our own guilt, then the wounded pride of offense is the reason one might remain in untruth even after the god has become teacher and savior. It is *not* because we are mere temporal, finite beings that we are initially separate from the god, nor is it the apparent absurdity of the paradox which keeps some from embracing it; after all, people choose to ignore dissonant information all the time, if they are convinced that the apparent discrepancy is refuted by other knowledge. If someone you love does something disturbing, you might describe this action as 'out of character,' not a true accounting; in the absence of love, the very same act might seem to reveal a deeply flawed character. There is nothing in either option that demands one ignore the act or the fact that it was disturbing, even wrong; but whereas love seeks to understand the act in a wider context or seeks an explanation to reconcile the apparent wrongness with the perceived lovableness of the other, a judgmental lack of love condemns according to its own adopted stance of superiority. The reason of the unnamed 'happy passion' adopts the strategy of love, recognizing that while the paradox is paradoxical, it also meets the deepest needs of reason and is just what was sought. It chooses to admit that its standpoint might be limited, and that there might be another explanation for the apparent absurdity, in response to the love the god has shown. The offended one, by contrast, adopts the stance of aloof and superior judge, and rejects the god as absurdly paradoxical without considering whether this might in fact have another explanation—one which might reveal that the paradoxical is just what one needs if one is to reach the truth. The question, then, is not about the paradox or whether it is a paradox; it is whether one responds with love and humility, or with pride and egoism. It is character and choice, not logic or metaphysics, which determine whether one accepts the truth or takes offense.

The happy passion: Only after discussing offense does Climacus begin to discuss the 'happy passion' of faith. Parts of his discussion are scattered in the more transparent portions of the text; other essential elements are discussed in the most obscure and controversial passages, which yield only reluctantly to determined exegesis.

This much seems clear: The learner has become untruth, by his or her own fault. The learner has 'bound himself,' and cannot 'now set himself free.'[22] The god loves the learner, and wishes to become teacher to save the individual from untruth (sin). Since to know the truth (that is, to know God) is an essential human condition, this is not just giving the learner knowledge; it is restoring the individual's human nature after it has been lost through sin.[23] It is thus appropriate to say the learner is 'reborn' and that the teacher is 'Savior,' and 'Redeemer.' The god can only redeem the individual by becoming a human, even a servant; any other theophany would fail to establish the equal, loving relationship the god desires to have with the learner.[24] As we have seen in our analysis, the learner may not respond positively; he or she may respond with offense, rejecting the claims of the god-teacher as too paradoxical and absurd, and too extravagant to be believed. The absence of offense does not itself mean the learner has learned, either; it could be that the individual has failed to recognize the nature of the god's self-revelation, and confused this utterly unknown with what is essentially known (as when the Incarnation is misinterpreted as a myth of the unity of human spirit with Absolute Spirit). But when the revelation is recognized and accepted, it is received in a 'happy passion' that corresponds to the 'unhappy passion' of offense. This 'happy passion' is called 'faith.'[25]

Other claims seem clearly stated, though controversial. Climacus claims that faith is not a form of knowledge. It is not historical knowledge, because the historical details of the god's life as a human are insufficient and unnecessary. One can know every detail of the teacher's life in exquisite detail, and still lack faith. Or one can know every iota of the teacher's doctrine and every word he uttered, and still have no faith. And one can know nothing more than the fact that this teacher was also said to be the god, and respond with the sense that this claim is decisive for his or her eternal happiness, and thus have faith.[26] What Climacus means is clear enough: faith is not knowing either the facts of the teacher's life or details of his teaching, but is rather an attitude in response to the claim that the teacher is also the god. But this claim suggests that the entire New Testament could have been reduced to one sentence without any loss.[27]

Climacus also says that faith is not an act of will, since (*ex hypotheosi*) the learner's will is not free to respond positively to the truth; yet he is often understood to have said the very opposite.[28] To understand why this is, it is necessary to try to untangle the book's other Gordian knot: the 'interlude' between chapters four and five.

Some Themes from the 'Interlude': C. S. Evans sums up the challenge of the 'Interlude' about as well as possible:

> The 'Interlude' between chapters 4 and 5 of *Philosophical Fragments* rivals chapter 3 for the honor of being the most difficult and obscure section of the book. The difficulty here, however, is of a different type. In chapter 3 the chief problem lay in determining the overall point of the chapter and its place in the book as a whole. The individual sentences and paragraphs were, with some exceptions, clear enough, but the purpose of the chapter was not. The problem with the Interlude is just the reverse. The place of the Interlude in the structure of the book is not too difficult to determine, and its overall point is likewise accessible. The prose is, however, easily the most philosophically dense of the book.[29]

The general purpose of the 'Interlude' is to challenge the Hegelian notion that the appearance of the Christ can be understood in retrospect to have been a necessary event in the development of Spirit. In Hegelian philosophy and theology, the appearance of the Christ might well have seemed novel and unheralded to contemporaries, as it represented a new relationship between humanity and God. The individual might well have not known how to respond properly to such an event, and been without adequate guidance from reason or society to properly interpret the signs of the times. In such an anomalous situation, the individual's response would be just that: individual and free. But now, with 1843 years of historical consequences plus the fruits of speculative philosophical analysis of that history to draw on, we can see that the appearance of Christianity was in fact necessary and rational. Therefore, while the contemporary follower was forced to respond from his or her own resources, the follower at second hand can draw on reason and his or her cultural history to see how to respond to the Christ.

If, however, it is a mistake to believe that the past is somehow more necessary than the present or future, then it will share in the contingency and uncertainty they have. If, as Climacus argues, belief is underdetermined by reason regardless of whether the event in question is past or present, then there can be no purely rational certainty; certainty must be derived from another source. In attacking the description of the past as necessary, and belief that history is rationally determined, Climacus is plugging a potential bolt-hole for his opponents. Climacus wants to argue that, if Christianity is true, salvation comes by faith alone, and this choice of faith is the same for the individual today as it was when Christ first taught. This understanding of Christianity differs radically from that offered by the Hegelian Christians of nineteenth-century Denmark, and by the populists led by N. F. S. Grundtvig, who in different ways shifted attention away from the original situation of the first believers and more to the confidence the modern person could have based on the effects and successes of Christianity through the millennia. If the past is as uncertain as the future, then no historical knowledge (either of Christianity's doctrines or its social institutions) can make its truth certain; we all must 'believe what is not seen,' as the New Testament itself defines 'faith.'

Because the prose is so 'dense,' there is considerable debate over just how Climacus pursues this goal, much less whether he attains it. To adequately deal with all these issues would require a commentary devoted entirely to Climacus alone. Even attempting to discuss just those elements most relevant to the questions of sin and salvation requires some extensive analysis, as Climacus here gives careful argument to lay the foundation for understanding such concepts as faith and repentance. Some of his argument, however, is more definitional, and can be condensed without too much distortion. The argument of the first portion of the Interlude seems to be as follows:

1. The possible is that which is not, but could be.
2. The necessary is that which is, by definition. It is, and must be, and must be just as it is always.
3. The actual is what is, but does not have to be. If something has come into existence, then at one time it was not; therefore, it was not necessary then and is not so now.
4. Therefore, the actual is a realized possibility. Both the possible and the actual are contingent; by definition, they do not have to be. The necessary, by definition, must be and cannot be other than it is; it is entirely different from both the possible and the actual.
5. The 'historical in the strictest sense' is not essentially different than the coming into existence of nature. It contains a dialectical element that nature does not; nature is the actualization of its possibility, while human history involves the 'relatively free causes' of individual choices to actualize some possibilities and not others. But both are examples of

the possible becoming actual, and thus neither occurs by necessity. All coming into existence happens by way of a free cause, not a necessary ground.

6. The past is no more necessary than the future. The unchangeableness of the past has nothing to do with necessity. The past is an actualized possibility, the future is a possibility to be actualized.

7. Thus there is no place where necessity intervenes in the historical. If either the past or the future were necessary, then there would be no freedom at all; but in fact the causes that actualize some possibility point back to a first, absolutely free cause.

8. Because the past, present and future are contingent rather than necessary, all historical knowledge is likewise contingent and uncertain.

9. Therefore, uncertainty is not overcome by knowledge of actuality alone; doubt can be terminated only by an act of will.

The definitions of the possible, the actual and the necessary are fairly straightforward. It is fairly obvious what Climacus means, and his implications follow from his definitions. The claim that all coming into existence occurs as a result of a freely acting cause is far more controversial. If Climacus meant this to apply only to 'the historical in the strictest sense,' it would be clear enough; but in fact it is clear that he means that even natural events occur by way of a free cause, not a 'ground' or necessity.[30] Climacus is making a claim about the whole realm of causality: that everything which happens points ultimately to some human or divine agency, and finally to a divine agency as the first uncaused and absolutely free cause. [31] But this seems to make hash of the arguments in chapter three that the god could not be known. However, the notion of 'unconditioned causality' does not necessarily yield 'person'; it could be that the first cause is still simply 'unknown.' This would mean that every causal string would have an end—somewhere—in an uncaused cause, which defies further rational(ist) analysis. This claim would be reconcilable with the rest of Climacus' claims in the *Fragments*. He writes:

All coming into existence occurs in freedom, not by way of necessity. Nothing coming into existence comes into existence by way of a ground, but everything by way of a cause. Every cause ends in a freely acting cause. The intervening causes are misleading in that the coming into existence appears to be necessary; the truth about them is that they, as having themselves come into existence, *definitively* point back to a freely acting cause. As soon as coming into existence is definitively reflected upon,

even an inference from natural law is not evidence of the necessity of any
coming into existence. So also with manifestations of freedom, as soon
as one refuses to be deceived by its manifestations but reflects on its coming into existence.[32]

It is unclear whether Climacus intends this as argument or simple asser-
tion. If there is an argument, it would seem to be as follows: Hegelianism
claims that existence arises from its ontological ground due to the necessity
of its own logic. But an analysis of possibility and necessity shows that the
two are essentially opposite: the one is not but could be, the other is and
could not not be. So necessity cannot have anything to do with the change
from possibility to actuality; some other mechanism must be supposed,
which we call a *cause*. As to the origin of the cause, a chain of intermediary
causes suggests the possibility of an infinite chain, linked by necessary laws
of nature; but in fact this explains little. We still don't know why this chain
rather than another, whether it really is infinite, and so on. The only conclusion to this reflection can be that there is a freely acting cause, which
has no cause and in fact remains invisible to our investigation, which is
responsible for anything coming into existence.

In so understanding Climacus, I am treating 'freedom' as equivalent to
'unknown' in the realm of causality, just as Climacus treats 'the god' as
'unknown' in the realm of truth. Whether freedom applies more appropriately to the consciously chosen actions of persons, or the apparently spontaneous swerving of subatomic particles, I leave undecided for now. Even
assuming freedom to reside in the chaotic behavior of subatomic particles,
this still does not explain where they came from, which seems to lead back
to an absolutely free cause, the unknown cause of all, the god. So the most
likely assumption is that Climacus is thinking about the god and persons
when he writes of 'free causes.'

At the same time, he recognizes a distinction between the history of
nature, which merely has come into existence and now is, and the historical 'in the stricter sense.'[33] Unlike nature, it is 'dialectical with respect to
time,' something nature only intimates by having a past and present. What
nature lacks is a 'future,' in the peculiar sense of a currently conceived
range of anticipated possibilities, some slated for actuality while others are
not. This area of coming into existence contains a further coming into
existence within itself, so that within the actualized possibility of nature
there is another sort of possibility. Persons can conceive of possibilities and
freely act to cause certain of these to come into existence; nature does
not anticipate, and hence is not dialectically related to time as persons

are.[34] The crucial point Climacus wishes us to grasp, however, is that this unique coming into existence of persons is part of the larger coming into existence of nature. And just as nature, through its chains of intermediate causes, definitively points back to a freely acting cause of it all, so too history, which comes into existence through the agency of 'a relatively freely acting cause,' points back to an 'absolutely freely acting cause.' Climacus will shortly argue that belief in the god-teacher is a peculiarly paradoxical species of belief, but still a species of the same passion of belief involved in any perception of coming into existence. Evidently, for this reason Climacus also wishes to establish the basic identity of all past coming into existence, whether it applies to nature or humanity.

We get the payoff to all these dialectics in a somewhat obscure reference to 'repentance':

> The unchageableness of the past is that its actual 'thus and so' cannot become different, but from this does it follow that its possible 'how' could not have been different? But the unchangeableness of the necessary— that it is constantly related to itself and is related to itself in the same way and excludes all change—is not satisfied with the unchangeableness of the past, which, as shown above, is not only dialectical with regard to an earlier change, from which it results, but must be dialectical even with regard to a higher change that nullifies it. (For example, the change of repentance, which wants to nullify an actuality.)[35]

This passage is interesting partly because of the jarring language about 'nullifying' a past actuality despite its unchangeableness, and partly because of the ethical and theological implications of the passage. Repentance is mentioned in the course of this discussion of the contingency of the past for good reason: if the past were necessary, repentance would be absurd. If sin were really an inevitable part of the necessary development of either the individual or Spirit itself (as it is treated by Hegel[36]), then it would not really make sense so much to *repent* sin as to *renounce* it, rather as one outgrows a variety of undesirable habits as one matures. One need not feel guilty over what could not be avoided; but if it could have been avoided, then it makes sense to ask if it ought to have been avoided, and whether one is guilty because it was not. The past cannot be changed, and one cannot do anything about the fact that one sinned in the past; nevertheless, just as the past is 'dialectical' in regard to the change that brought it into existence, so it 'must be dialectical even with regard to a higher change that nullifies it. (For example, the change of repentance, which wants to nullify an actuality.)'[37] I cannot logically repent for the utter lack of social and hygienic graces I exhibited as an infant; it is an essential part of the human condition that we begin with the necessity to have certain behaviors which we later outgrow—we become toilet trained, learn not to drool, and so on. To repent is to say that, even though my past sin is an ineradicable part of my historical actuality, it is not an inevitable or essential part, and I now desire to change my life and abandon the values and behaviors I once embraced. Repentance 'seeks to nullify' a past actuality—namely, that I have become untruth by my own guilt. It is this actuality which the follower seeks to flee at conversion, with sorrow and haste.[38] Presumably, the 'higher change' that can truly nullify a past actuality would be forgiveness of sin, which does not change the fact that one has been a sinner, but which undoes the effects of that past actuality so that one need not be bound by sin any longer.[39]

The section on the apprehension of the past contains perhaps the most controversial themes of the Interlude: the nature of skepticism and the role of the will in belief.[40] These themes are themselves derived from the foregoing discussion of necessity, as well as epistemological considerations. Climacus writes:

> The distinctively historical is perpetually the past (it is gone; whether it was years or days ago makes no difference), and as something bygone it has actuality, for it is certain and trustworthy that it occurred. But that it occurred is, in turn, precisely its uncertainty, which will perpetually prevent the apprehension from taking the past as if it had been that way from eternity. Only in this contradiction between certainty and uncertainty, the *discrimen* [distinctive mark] of something that has come into existence and thus also of the past, is the past understood . . . Knowledge of the present does not confer necessity upon it; foreknowledge of the future does not confer necessity upon it (Boethius); knowledge of the past does not confer necessity upon it—for all apprehension, like all knowing, has nothing from which to give.[41]

Climacus declares himself for empiricism, in the radical distinction he draws between essence and factual being.[42] In his criticism of Hegel, he likewise equates idealism with tautology.[43] Idealism seeks to derive knowledge of facts from the internal content of concepts and categories themselves; but Climacus insists that all such exercises only show what the object described would be, *if* it exists. It is blatant circularity to argue that something exists necessarily, because one has defined it as necessary—whether a necessary being or a necessary historical progress. In rejecting idealism, Climacus has in turn uncovered the ugly philosophical secret previously exposed by Hume: knowledge of the world is inherently uncertain. As Hume claimed in his discussion of causality, much of what we claim we 'know' we can only assume. We know what is because we perceive it; we cannot perceive the necessary connection between cause and effect, for example; therefore, we do not *know* that it exists. What we observe is that whenever *A* is present, *B* turns up afterward, with such a high degree of consistency that we confidently predict that *A* will always be followed by *B*. When we have thus become sufficiently used to this conjunction, we presume to call it a 'necessary connection,' or to say '*A* causes *B*.' This is not knowledge, however; when we stop to examine the set of things which we know, which we cannot be mistaken about, of which we have true and certain belief, we find that set to be vanishingly small, primarily concerned with mathematical propositions and other purely mental concepts. Regarding 'matters of fact' in the real world, what we have are degrees of probability and habitual assumptions about things in the world being the way we have always perceived them to be.[44] Intellectual honesty would demand that we therefore desist from claiming certainty about any matter of fact; we should grant assent to beliefs only in proportion to which we are compelled to do so to function as human beings; and even where we must act as if something was certain, we need never grant any more credence than necessary. For example, while we may leave the building by the door rather than an upper window, this does not mean that we *know* that the earth will necessarily attract our bodies to itself at a rapid and injurious rate of speed; it only means that life has wrung this concession from us, that it generally works better to fear gravity than to tempt it.[45] This is Hume's famous 'mitigated skepticism' in practice.

Kierkegaard is heir to two of Hume's intellectual descendants: Kant and Hamann. Both of these accepted Hume's skeptical judgment regarding empirical knowledge, though they reacted in opposite ways. Kant argues that for knowledge to be certain, it had to concern itself primarily with the categories and concepts which made human thought possible. Causality, for example, is one of the defining principles of reality. We organize experience in terms of causal connections between phenomena, to the extent that if we had an intuition of a phenomenon which had no cause or caused no effect, we should label it an hallucination or dream. We may not perceive necessary connection, but we can see that it is necessary to think it. Certain knowledge, therefore, concerns these pure, synthetic *a priori* concepts, which though they deal with the empirical world, derive their certainty not from being observed, but because rational thought is impossible for us without them.

Hamann takes the opposite tack; if knowledge is derived from and concerned with empirical fact, then it cannot be certain.[46] He embraces Hume's skeptical conclusions as truly reflecting what human reason, apart from revelation of some sort, is actually capable of: a complete lack of knowledge. For Hamann, knowing is receptive; truth must bestow itself. His model for this is the Incarnation: human reason could not find the truth of God, so God had to give the knowledge by sending the Son. This Son, in turn, has to be accepted by faith alone, since he does not conform to the expectations of reason and is not derivable from its principles. But even though a folly to reason and a scandal to human expectations, the Son really did come; and to deny the Incarnation happened is not to love truth but to resist it. Human knowledge must yield to reality, not attempt to impose false standards of neatness or certainty upon it. Hamann generalizes this receptive approach to reason, arguing for example that historical and communal resources are as valid sources of knowledge as those deriving from the individual's own experience—both are uncertain, but indispensable. This reflects the difference between Hamann and Hume, and how he is closer to Hume than to his colleague Kant. Both Hamann and Hume have basically the same understanding of human reason, and the same standards for 'knowledge.' The difference between them is that where Hume urges a stance of suspicion, Hamann urges openness, even at the risk of error. Hume's skeptical stance leads him to withhold assent to religious revelation; since we lack compelling evidence as well as any compelling need to assume the legitimacy of religious claims, we are better off holding to the common-sense, materialistic assumptions which serve us so well the rest of the time. Hamann argues that this fear of being deceived has in fact deceived itself, by denying legitimate cause for accepting these as true. The skepticism Hume advocates not only rules out religious insights, but whole realms of legitimate insights regarding facts, history, and so on. Kant seems to accept Hume''s destruction of empirical knowledge, and therefore retreats into the realm of pure reason. Hamann doubted such a retreat was possible; and further, he did not see it as necessary.[47] True knowledge might not be as certain or clean as Kant might want, but that does not mean that it is illegitimate; it may just mean that Kant's and Hume's standards are flawed. Hamann's position might loosely be titled 'mitigated belief.' Humans simply do not have access to certainty about most of what really matters, whether empirical, metaphysical, or religious reality; but rather than pretend to a false certainty, it is better and even necessary to accept uncertainty and possible error as the price of actual knowledge of reality.

Climacus—like Hume and Hamann and against Plato, Kant and Hegel—accepts the conception of knowledge as primarily receptive: it 'has nothing from which to give.'[48] And Climacus also accepts the notion that certainty must mean necessary; if it is only possible, it is also possibly not. So the historical may be a past actuality, and in that sense 'certainly' true; but at the same time it is not necessary, and therefore not certain. No necessity forces the mind to accept an actuality, no logic compels assent. If Hume or the Greek skeptics choose to withhold assent, and insist on calling it only highly probable rather than certain, they are certainly within their rights. Only the illusion spawned by temporal distance can lead one to mistakenly take for necessary and certain what was, at its birth, only an actualized possibility, a coming into existence, and hence inherently uncertain.

Coming into existence is *illusive,* according to Climacus. One can perceive *A,* and then *B,* but one does not immediately perceive that *B,* which was once a nothing (a 'mere possibility'), has become a something, or that countless alternative nothings have now been ruled out from ever becoming something. The issue Climacus raises is again parallel to Hume's discussion of causality—all the more so, as coming into existence is said to occur by way of a *cause.* For Hume, one can perceive that *A* follows *B,* but not that *A* causes *B;* for Climacus, one can perceive *B,* but not that *B* had some cause—*A,* which brought it into existence. So the historical, as coming into existence, is not immediately perceivable; nor is it necessary, so as to compel assent as might a logical proof. The problem is therefore that there is a gap between the knowledge of the past, which is presumed to exist, and the nature of the past, which is inherently uncertain and illusive. If one is to limit knowledge to the nature of the evidence, and if 'knowledge' is understood (as it usually is) as certain and true, then how is one to attain certainty regarding the past? The evidence does not appear to warrant certainty, and certainly cannot compel it. He writes:

Immediate sensation and immediate cognition cannot deceive. This alone indicates that the historical cannot become the object of sense perception or of immediate cognition, because the historical has in itself that very illusiveness that is the illusiveness of coming into existence. In relation to the immediate, coming into existence is an illusiveness whereby that which is most firm is made dubious. For example, when the perceiver sees a star, the star becomes dubious for him the moment he seeks to become aware that it has come into existence. It is just as if reflection removed the star from his senses. It is clear, then, that the organ for the historical must be formed in likeness to this, must have within itself the corresponding something by which in its certitude it continually annuls the incertitude that corresponds to the uncertainty of coming into existence—a double uncertainty: the nothingness of non-being and the annihilated possibility, which is also the annihilation of every other possibility. This is precisely the nature of belief [Tro], for continually present as the nullified in the certitude of belief is the incertitude that in every way corresponds to the uncertainty of coming into existence. Thus, belief believes what it does not see; it does not believe that the star exists, for that it sees, but it believes that the star has come into existence. The same is true of an event. The occurrence can be known immediately but not that it has occurred, not even that it is in the process of occurring, even though it is taking place, as they say, right in front of one's nose. The illusiveness of the occurrence is that it has occurred, and therein lies the transition from nothing, from non-being, and from the multiple possible 'how.'[49]

Only the necessary or the immediate are absolutely certain and cannot deceive. To say something has come into existence is to make it mediate and contingent, and therefore to say that it is something less than absolutely certain. No matter how little uncertainty the perceiver may actually feel, even if the thing seems completely certain, there is still some small gap between the perception and the certainty of knowledge. Therefore, 'the organ for the historical' must in some way overcome or 'annul' the uncertainty; it must bridge the gap between the perception and the certainty of the judgment that A has come into existence. The name for this organ is 'belief.' Belief judges between uncertainty and assent, and nullifies the uncertainty in order to give assent to what is unable to absolutely compel assent. In this context, 'belief' is the organ for accepting both the probable and the improbable; any time one moves beyond the suspended judgment of the skeptics to accept some matter of factual existence, one believes.

    Although Climacus is not here using 'belief' in any sort of religious manner, it is worth noting that he is adopting a religiously originated concept as a basis for a general epistemology. Just as Hamann used the Incarnation as an image for truth in general and how the truth comes to an individual, so too does Climacus take the religious conception of belief as a model of how the individual overcomes doubt in order to receive the historical in general. That he is doing this is shown by his adaptation of Hebrews 11:1: 'Now faith is the assurance of things hoped for, the conviction of things not seen.' The religious believer moves beyond what can be immediately perceived in order to establish a relationship to the eternal; as long as one clings only to the obvious, one can never reach faith. The religious believer must therefore move beyond what is considered certain, and must take some risk by breaking with the usual, the 'granted as given' in the world, to see another level of truth. Climacus sees the same essential process at work in any encounter with the historical. Although some 'facts' may be granted as given in the world, because they are actualities rather than necessities or immediacies they are to a greater or lesser degree uncertain, by definition. No matter how carefully one may weigh the probabilities, there is still some measure of uncertainty left, some risk of error, which one must deal with. 'Belief' is the giving of assent to what cannot be immediately perceived, bridging the gap between uncertainty and assurance whether that gap be great or little.

This is the real lesson of Greek skepticism (as opposed to Hegelian, i.e. affected skepticism). The Greeks never doubted immediate sense perception and immediate cognition, but they refused to draw conclusions from these. In order to preserve a tranquil, detached frame of mind, they simply refused to draw conclusions, or to assert any knowledge. They would not even assert a theoretical skepticism; their arguments were only a tactic to help resist coming to a conclusion about anything beyond the immediate. It is not as if they were merely unsure, or lacked evidence, or were driven by some necessity (logical or psychological) to doubt. They chose not to draw conclusions, even where others would almost universally do so; they chose to doubt. And in this they illustrate the nature of doubt in general. Doubt is the passion of uncertainty, just as belief is the passion of certainty. Doubt, rightly or wrongly, does not give assent; belief does. Faced with the same evidence and the same inherent uncertainty of all contingent things, the skeptic withholds assent which the believing person gives. In doing so, the believer naturally risks error; the tower turns out to be square close up. And if skepticism is treated as some sort of sin or disease of philosophy by some, credulity is twice so. But to want to believe without risk, says Climacus, is like wanting to know one can swim before ever attempting to enter the water.[50] As soon as one begins drawing any conclusions about the real world of existence, one risks error. But on the other hand, belief is sometimes right, and withholding of assent mistaken and even willful stubbornness. Climacus gives no help here determining when belief is or is not justified; his interest here is only to examine the process of belief itself, whether 'warranted' or not. Even warranted belief is not knowledge; it is an act of will, whereby one annuls the uncertainty and assents to the thing as certain—because it meets the standards one has assented to.

Seen in the context of the chapter, Climacus' claim that 'belief . . . is an act of freedom, an expression of will,' does not seem like willful or arbitrary volitionalism.[51] His point here seems to be almost the opposite: to establish a familial relationship between all beliefs, even the most certain. And given that nothing happens of necessity but from a cause, and every cause harks back to a freely effecting cause, it would be rather odd if Climacus didn't say that belief is rooted in freedom. He writes:

> Insofar as that which by belief becomes the historical, and as the historical becomes the object of belief (the one corresponds to the other), does exist immediately and is apprehended immediately, it does not deceive. The contemporary does, then, use his eyes etc., but he must pay attention to the conclusion. He cannot know immediately and directly that it has come into existence, but neither can he know with necessity that it has come into existence, for the first mark of coming into existence is specifically a break in continuity . . . Belief is the opposite of doubt. Belief and doubt are not two kinds of knowledge that can be defined in continuity with each other, for neither of them is a cognitive act, and they are opposite passions. Belief is a sense for coming into existence, and doubt is a protest against any conclusion that wants to go beyond immediate sensation and immediate knowledge.[52]

In describing belief as a 'sense for coming into existence,' Climacus is assigning belief a similar role to that played by imagination in Hamann's thought. In both cases, there is a gap between what can be said to be 'known,' i.e. certainly true, and the richness of reality. If the individual is not to lose touch with reality, he or she must open up to receive it in its variety. To do this one must move beyond what can be certainly known, the necessary or immediate; and to make this move, some 'organ' besides pure reason is needed. Both Hamann and Climacus would say that this sense can be stifled by the individual's preconceptions and stubbornness, but Climacus is more straightforward in describing the organ for perceiving reality as a function of will. Hamann seems to consider it more a sensitivity, which can be distorted or shut off by will; Climacus describes it as will, which serves as a sense for coming into existence. It is significant that belief incorporates both willing and sensibility; it is neither wholly passive nor arbitrary. Whether the doubter or the believer is more justified is not rationally demonstrable, since they are defined by opposite passions and not degrees of knowledge. The one risks missing out on the given reality, while the other risks error and even delusion. Practically speaking, even Hume admitted that strict skepticism could not be lived, and hence had to be 'mitigated;' so it is not surprising that belief generally has the upper hand.

Belief of the strictly historical involves several levels of uncertainty. First, as it has come into existence, it is inherently uncertain, and belief must annul that uncertainty even for the contemporary. Second, it may involve the duplexity of the coming into existence within coming into existence, when humans conceive of a possible future and bring it into existence. Third, as the historical is past, it is likely that the individual is not in fact a contemporary at all, but is totally reliant on second-hand reports.[53] In this case, says Climacus, the later believer stands in the same relationship to the report as the contemporary to the immediate perception; neither can give the crucial element of coming into existence, that this has come into existence—that it has come from the nothingness of possibility, has become the only truth out of a range of admitted alternative possibilities, and none can say how. Both the contemporary and the later believer must believe, must overcome doubt by will and not knowledge, for knowledge cannot guide. The former may think that he or she has immediate knowledge, while the latter is more likely to think that historical consequences show the necessity of the event, but both are mistaken; both annul the uncertainty by will and not knowledge.

In his appendix to the Interlude, Climacus returns 'to our poem and to our assumption that the god *has* been,' in order to show the application of this investigation to his main project.[54] As the appearance of the god as servant is an historical event which has come into existence, it cannot be immediately perceived any more than any other coming into existence could. But furthermore, the fact itself 'is based upon a self-contradiction.' The unknown has become a fact, a perfectly ordinary fact as a perfectly ordinary human, without therefore being any less the unknown; it has come to give truth to the individual, first by revealing that he or she is alien to truth by his or her own guilt. So the risk attached in assenting to this fact is much greater than is the case in ordinary belief, so much so that this belief becomes something else: 'faith . . . in the wholly eminent sense.' So faith in the God-Man bears a family resemblance to faith that I myself have come into existence; but at the same time, the former faith in the absolute paradox entails an absolute risk and hence can be said to be absolute faith, while the latter has a good degree of probability on its side, so that the risk in assenting to it is virtually negligible and the faith required to believe it virtually unnoticeable. In both, however, there is still an element of will—whether the grand passion to struggle to grasp faith across the yawning chasm of offense, or the scarcely conscious, tiny step across the gap of uncertainty between the mountain of evidence and the plateau of certainty. Both of these are contrasted with the Socratic knowledge of the god-which significantly *is* called 'knowledge.' Socrates gained his knowledge by recollection, by the eternal connection of the god to the human being. He thus knew (in the more precise language of the *Postscript*) that the god is, but of course not that the god has come into existence—for in the Socratic scheme, the god hasn't, needn't, and couldn't. This knowledge is not the passion of faith, but simply the inevitable result of properly executed recollection and investigation.

'So, then, that historical fact remains.' The god has come into existence, and thus must remain an object for belief, and more specifically 'faith in the eminent sense.' It never becomes necessary, neither because of its historical consequences (such as the present existence of the Church, in which Grundtvig placed such stock) nor its philosophical consequences (as for the Hegelians). The immediate contemporary has immediate sensation, which is not enough to give certainty as the crucial elements (the coming into existence, and the presence of the unknown) are not immediately available but must be believed. The later believer has only the contemporary accounts, which can do no more than present one with the same uncertainty the contemporary faced, and the historical consequences of the event, which themselves are derived from that first uncertainty and therefore at least as uncertain as their cause. The contemporary follower and the follower at second hand are therefore once again seen to be in essentially the same relationship to the paradox.

Conclusions: Climacus rarely takes a straight line, so it was perhaps inevitable that any attempt to explore his thought would likewise meander. After a lengthy examination of selected portions of his book, we are perhaps in a position to draw some conclusions regarding his views on sin and salvation.

Climacus does not say much about sin as an act, except that it was a choice, and was the sinner's own fault. He says more about the fallen state, as sin corrupts the knowledge and the will so that the sinner has chosen unfreedom and now cannot free herself or himself. The salvation that undoes this fallen state is described as a sort of teaching whereby the god/teacher reveals first of all that the god still loves the learner enough to become a teacher, a servant, even to suffer. When this teaching is received in 'the happy passion' of faith, the individual can set aside all the sin-spawned preconceptions of God's nature and fears of God's wrath, and learn to receive and return this love.

Climacus says faith is not an act of will, but rather must be received from the god alone. At the same time, the will clearly plays a strong role in faith. First, Climacus clearly rejects predestination. God does not choose to give faith to some and leave others to be offended; the choice between faith and offense is the learner's own. Second, faith in the Incarnation is still a form of belief, and has all the uncertainty and will that all belief have. What the god must give the learner is what the learner has lost through sin: freedom. The learner cannot choose faith, or offense, until the god gives the learner the ability to choose.

Chapter Four

Anxiety and Beyond

Philosophical Fragments raised the problem of sin, and argued that faith through the Incarnation was the only solution to the problem (short of denying the reality of sin). Still, this book is highly algebraic; it presents everything as mere theory, avoiding direct discussion of Christian history or beliefs. Its discussion of sin is likewise undefined. Later works begin to give more content to Kierkegaard's understanding of sin and salvation.

A. *The Concept of Anxiety*: This work often seems to be treated as something apart from the bulk of Kierkegaard's authorship. *Either/Or* through the *Fragments* seem to follow the 'stages (or "spheres") of existence' theory quite well, as this is presented by Frater Taciturnus and Johannes Climacus. One starts in the esthetic stage, but this ultimately breaks down; if one so wills, one acknowledges this and moves on to the ethical and then the religious stages, and finally by the grace of God one may enter Religiousness B, or Christianity. *The Concept of Anxiety* doesn't seem to fit in that tidy theory. Adam is said to have had anxiety: does that mean it is a phenomenon of the esthetic? But it is a sign of freedom, and the esthetic is said to be unfree. Is it an ethical category? This book deals with sin, and de Silentio has said that an ethics that attempts to discuss sin has *eo ipso* gone beyond its proper bounds. Often commentators seem to opt for the path of least resistance, by simply setting the book aside and treating it as independent of the rest of the authorship. It is evident, though, that Kierkegaard did not view it this way, and that his wish was that his reader would see it in the context of the other works he had produced. To properly understand this seminal yet perplexing book, it is necessary to see it in relation to the works Kierkegaard wrote, with attention to the chronological order in which these works were first published.

In any attempt at comparative exegesis of Kierkegaard, however, one must face the question of pseudonymity. While both the *Concept of Anxiety* and the *Prefaces* were published four days after the *Fragments*, in the *Postscript* Climacus mistakenly claims they preceded it. This suggests that these works do in fact represent something of a retreat from the viewpoint of the *Fragments*. After all, the *Fragments* deals with salvation, a topic that the pseudonymous author of *Anxiety* claims is beyond his competence and transcends his categories. *Concept of Anxiety* is written by Vigilius Haufniensis, 'the Watchman of Copenhagen;' unlike the *Fragments*, Kierkegaard's own name does not appear anywhere on the title page, even as editor. This seems to imply a retreat to greater indirectness, a distancing from the work and its views. On the other hand, Climacus is purposefully obscure and ironic, whereas Haufniensis is much more straightforward and didactic. While undoubtedly a talented psychologist and dialectician, he does not show the literary artistry of Climacus. Still, it may be that his personal standpoint really is less true, although more direct and honest. It has been argued that Climacus may in fact be more of a Christian than he initially lets on, using feigned ignorance and irony to trap his opponents and educate his audience as Socrates did. On the other hand, the entire standpoint of Haufniensis as the detached psychological observer is inappropriate to consideration of the problems of guilt and sin.[1] This is largely why he must content himself with discussing anxiety, which is really more of a psychological reflection of sin than the thing itself. While he may present the truth as best he is able, he has definite limits; one of these is that sin is most appropriately treated not by psychological observation and reflection but by ethical-religious action, by repentance and resolution. 'Sin' properly does not even exist from a psychological perspective; it is a religious/dogmatic concept.[2] Psychology and ethics can both help reveal aspects of the nature of sin, as concepts within their own proper purviews relate to it, but they only approximate sin; they do not reach it. Thus, the standpoint of Haufniensis obscures certain aspects of the concept of 'sin,' even as it clarifies others.

First and second ethics: Kierkegaard put his name on the *Fragments*, but did not acknowledge *Concept of Anxiety* even as its 'editor'; so in a sense it seems to be a retreat into greater indirectness and away from 'the truth.' But in another sense, it begins a new phase in the pseudonymous authorship. Earlier pseudonymous works seem primarily concerned with drawing distinctions, defining the esthetic, ethical, religious and Christian, and drawing the borders between them. Either you are the esthete using the world and others for your own enjoyment, or you are the ethicist realizing the universal, or you are the knight of faith climbing Mount Moriah to murder the ethical for the sake of your absolute relationship to God, or you are the bound sinner being freed by the God-Man as Teacher. Haufniensis begins something new: reintegrating these different spheres after they have been separated. He begins by arguing for the importance of clarity. 'Philosophy' (by which he means primarily Hegelianism) has confused the different sciences, to the detriment of all. When the different branches of knowledge are confused, the concepts are confused. When the sciences are clearly distinguished, then it is possible to bring them into conversation with one another, to contrast and compare how they use the concepts and see what each can reveal from its own perspective. It is not enough to use the same word; if it is not used correctly, with the proper mood, it is fundamentally distorted and any 'knowledge' gained is fundamentally false.[3] This is important to Haufniensis, as he believes the concept of 'sin' is particularly confused. Hegel has discussed it in logic as 'the negative,' implying that one's sin is not really a personal failing but only an inevitable development of spirit. Or sin is discussed metaphysically, with a mood of disinterestedness, or psychologically in an observational mood, and so on. In each case sin is falsified in that its seriousness is denied, for the proper mood for understanding sin is earnestness. It is my sin which concerns me, and yours which concerns you, and it is a mortal threat. Ethics seems to be the most appropriate science for dealing with sin, but ethics presents ideality, what you ought to do; it cannot understand sin or reconcile the sinner, but only condemn it as what ought not to be.

Haufniensis echoes de Silentio's claim that sin is the shipwreck upon which ethics founders.[4] Ethics deals in ideality, in what ought to be; but actual people are sinners. Dogmatics starts with this actuality, and has the concepts of repentance, grace, and salvation to respond to it. In this context Haufniensis says that faith is the true repetition that Constantin hinted at but obscured behind various false conceptions.[5] When the first immediacy (innocence) has been lost, the only return is through repentance leading to faith. The ethical can only condemn, and if the ethical is all there is then life ends when one falls. Only through the religious can the individual start again.

The ethical fails, and fails by design. It is the ideal, and seeks to move from ideality to actuality: it presents the good and declares that the individual ought to do this, ought to actualize this ideal in his or her life. But this cannot work; Haufniensis says you cannot start with ideality and reach actuality. In this he argues in a completely Pauline-Lutheran way.[6] The purpose of ethics is not to make one good, any more than the Law was intended to save; rather, its purpose is to drive one to the religious. When one has failed ethically and is ready to repent, then dogmatics can begin, and with the transcendent categories such as hereditary sin, faith, and grace it enables a 'second ethics.'[7] The first ethics failed in that it required the ideal from actual individuals. Dogmatics comes to the rescue with new concepts, and can start with the individual where he or she actually is, and from there hold up the ideal as an ideal to be striven toward, a goal rather than an impossible burden. Dogmatics starts with sinners, and aims to start them moving toward righteousness, recognizing that they will never actually attain the full ideal.[8]

Up until now, the pseudonymous works have aimed at distinguishing, with a series of either/ors: esthetic/or ethical, ethical/or religious, Socratic/or Christian. Haufniensis affirms the importance of this work, saying that until the different perspectives are clear to themselves and clearly distinguished from one another they cannot do their own jobs or meaningfully converse. But with the appearance of the second ethics after the religious, that seemingly strict opposition is broken down. Now, the ethical is not just that which condemns Abraham; having left the first ethics for faith, he now lives in the second ethics. This really is a 'repetition,' a return of what was lost, but at the same time something new. Dogmatics, the religious, fulfills the aspirations and promises of the earlier pseudonyms and their competing philosophies. But Haufniensis is not doing dogmatics; he is only a psychologist. Thus, even in describing this second ethics he is only distinguishing again, pointing out the territory and borders of his own chosen domain. He does not himself explain sin or salvation; he only seeks to present the psychological concepts and facts that make sin possible, or salvation necessary.

Views of Adam, Innocence and the Fall: Haufniensis is a serious, yet also detached, observer of the human condition—a stance neatly summarized in his chosen title of '*watch*man.' He shows considerable acquaintance with the other pseudonymous works, but little or none with Kierkegaard's direct, upbuilding discourses. This is unfortunate for him, since these works emphasize the sort of resolution and active participation that his own stance tends to overlook.

One nagging question left by the *Fragments* was, how does 'being in untruth' relate to the traditional notion of sin as related to moral guilt? Climacus describes the learner as 'in error, and that by his own guilt,' but he never presents any sort of description of how the individual actually moved into untruth, or how the individual is now bound in untruth. *The Concept of Anxiety* fills this gap, by examining the transition from innocence to sin, relating it specifically to wrongdoing before God, and furthermore by indicating how this guilt can become an estranging force between the individual and God. It is particularly helpful in this regard to examine Kierkegaard's first discourse on the theme 'Every Good and Perfect Gift

is from Above' from December 1843, which resembles *Concept of Anxiety* in
that both discuss the prelapsarian state, the Fall, and its results.

The Concept of Anxiety agrees with the earlier discourse in equating
Adam's prelapsarian innocence with an absence of the knowledge of
good and evil.[9] The *Fragments*, in apparent disagreement, implies that
the prelapsarian state to be 'in the truth,' since the learner is said to have
been created in the truth and to have become untruth later through a
free choice to sin.[10] Ordinarily, one would think that to be 'in the truth'
was to possess some kind of knowledge; but in this case, ignorance really
does appear to have been bliss. Haufniensis pictures Adam as living in
easy unity with the decrees of God, until the moment when he conceived
of the possibility of doing something else, something 'forbidden,' and
gaining the knowledge of good and evil. Adam cannot really conceive
of just what this is, since in innocence he is still ignorant of these categories. He only knows that this possibility to do what he should not do
is here, and this possibility is both frightening and compelling. This is
the 'sympathetic antipathy or antipathetic sympathy' which Haufniensis
labels 'anxiety,' and which he considers the paradigmatic psychological
expression for temptation. Only when he has exercised his freedom in
opposition to the divine prohibition does he learn, and at the same time
he knows himself as evil, since he has done this evil thing. In just the
same way, every individual moves from a state of ignorance to knowledge,
where knowledge of the difference between good and evil can only be
gained by having done wrong.

The earlier discourse supports both pseudonymous works at this point;
before Adam's sin there is 'truth in everything,' yet there is not knowledge.
Instead, there is an immediate unity of God and Creation, with the latter
a perfect mirror for the former. God, the good, is not sought, asked for,
or known, because God is so immediately omnipresent that Adam has no
time or cause to wonder. But when knowledge comes in, reflection comes
in as well, so that the good is not something that is invisible by being so
immediate and pervasive; now it is something that must be sought, something that is now distinct from the rest of Creation and is to be sought in it.
But because the good is now a matter for reflection, it is prey to doubt. The
immediate certainty of prelapsarian innocence is lost, and the world that
once expressed God's immediate presence is now something alien from
the person, a threat to one's being in innumerable ways.

Haufniensis also discusses how the later situation differs from that faced
by Adam. Before the first sin, the notion of a cleavage between God and
any part of Creation was only an unarticulated possibility, a nothing, until

Adam's sin made sin an actuality in the world. Consequent humans inherit a world where sin is 'a fact of life,' in that it is in the world all around us-although not in the sense that it is an inevitable fact of any one person's life that he or she must sin. One becomes a sinner only by sinning, and one loses innocence only by abandoning it. One does wrong only by choice; it would be a contradiction to say one could sin of necessity, or that it could be an essential part of human nature to sin. It may be an essential part of human nature to have the possibility, as Adam did, but not to realize it. But whereas Adam started with 'a clean slate,' consequent humans start with the history of the race behind them, with the present of the race around them, and sin everywhere in these. What for Adam could only have been an indefinable nothing, a mere possibility to do I-don't-know-what, is for successive generations a concrete possibility which tempts them in their anxiety to make it a part of their own existence. Even if I do not know what sin is until I have sinned, I am surrounded by any number of examples of sin which may attract and repel me in my anxiety, until I succumb to temptation in the 'dizziness' of anxiety, or reach out through my anxiety and lay hold of the power to stand in the midst of anxiety through faith.

Likewise, the upbuilding discourse stresses that one does not check doubt by pursuing more knowledge, or anxiety by controlling finitude around one; one only stands firm through hearing the word of God and living in it through faith.[11] Reflection only feeds doubt, and the pursuit of power only feeds anxiety, as one finds more and more clearly the limits of one's own abilities and the magnitudes of the threats one faces. Only the infinite power of the eternal is able to face those threats, and only faith is able to believe that there is an eternal power that is both benevolent and capable of sustaining the self against the threats of finitude.

The sin of spiritlessness: Haufniensis goes further than Kierkegaard's discourse in describing the state of the individual who has sinned. Some traditional discussions have implied that after the first sin, the individual has so lost his or her freedom that it is impossible to avoid further sins. While Haufniensis agrees that the individual sinner is unable to free himself or herself from the effects of sin, he denies that any act of sin is inevitable. Each sin enters by the qualitative leap, the free choice of the individual.[12] But at the same time, the individual now lives in an anxiety-filled world. All people subsequent to Adam live in a world where sin is an actuality; it may be that it is only actual for me when I sin, but it exists in the world as possibility that others have actualized for themselves. We are all related, and as descendents of Adam we inherit the anxiety of seeing his sin before us as a possibility we ourselves could realize. When we do sin, we know that it was nevertheless not inevitable; we sin not because Adam sinned but because each of us chose to sin. There is no explanation beyond this; sin comes into the world by a sin. As Climacus said, there is no necessary ground; there is only a free cause.[13] So we now have anxiety over the possibility of sin, anxiety over the objective world (which has become an object of reflection and hence doubt due to sin), anxiety over having sinned personally, and anxiety over the possibility of sinning again. The most the individual can do is repent.[14] In repentance the individual acknowledges that his or her sin was freely chosen and he or she is solely responsible; the individual sorrows over the past sin; but in sorrowing over the sin still cannot forget the sin, cannot annul it or cease reflecting on it, and hence cannot help but have still more anxiety over sin. There are only two possible routes to escape this anxiety: faith, or spiritlessness.[15] Haufniensis describes spiritlessness as the state of 'paganism within Christianity,'[16] Paganism lacks the full consciousness of guilt and hence of sin, but in Christianity the eternal is fully present. The ethical is not (as in Greek philosophy) aimed at a finite teleology (eudaimonia), but is fully ideal, so the person who is less than ideal has failed and thus becomes anxious over his or her guilt. So while the pagan could not fully experience anxiety but was moving toward the fullness of spirit, the pagan within Christianity is moving away from spirit by fleeing anxiety. Spiritlessness is not just the immersion in immediacy, which was in a sense unavoidable for the pagan; it is the sin of choosing immersion in immediacy as an escape from anxiety and the pain of repentance. This is the most effective escape from anxiety that the human can find apart from faith. Anxiety is a manifestation of freedom; to be rid of anxiety one must merely be rid of one's sense of freedom and selfhood.

The demonic: If choosing to seek after knowledge of good and evil is what got Adam into trouble in the first place, then what should we make of William's advice to A that he 'choose good and evil?' While this advice seems to contradict what has been said above regarding the true nature of the relationship between the individual and the good (i.e. God), it is important to remember that the judge is not writing to an innocent but a sinner, one who has turned from the immediacy of innocence and made the good an object of reflection. In fact, he is what Haufniensis terms 'demonic': he fears becoming free, realizing his true human nature. While a repentant sinner is anxious about the evil, whether it might again gain some triumph over him or her by tempting the individual into a new sin, a demoniac is anxious over the good, which threatens to call him or her back to freedom, back to the struggle with anxiety. The demoniac wishes only to remain in unfreedom, unconscious of the possibility of freedom and the anxiety that goes along with it. This spiritlessness becomes the demonic facsimile for the peaceful immediacy of innocence, but in fact it is its opposite; while the prelapsarian immediacy still contained freedom and hence anxiety, and was rooted in God and the good, this flight from anxiety flees from God and the good, flees from its own nature as free, and seeks only to embrace the spiritless (hence anxiety-free) existence of a beast.[17] While William lacks a full understanding of the nature of sin or God, evil or good, he does correctly see that the esthete's claim to moral neutrality is a sham, a rebellion against the good. For one who has indeed lost innocence, it is necessary to choose good and evil, for this means to accept one's true nature as spirit to which moral qualifiers are relevant, rather than attempting to pass oneself off as a mere animal living beneath such standards.

Much of the attention directed toward *The Concept of Anxiety* has centered on the earlier passages, which describe anxiety in general and the workings of freedom. Similarly, much of the commentary on *Fear and Trembling* have left the last problema out of the picture, concentrating instead on de Silentio's discussions of the absurd, the limits of the ethical, and the stark individuality of Abraham on the mountain, knife in hand. There has simply been too little attention given to Kierkegaard's discussions of the demonic in these two works.[18] This is really too bad, for an examination of the demonic easily reveals that much of the criticism directed at Kierkegaard's understanding of the religious has been misdirected.[19]

According to Haufniensis, anxiety arises from the self's ambiguous reaction to possibility. The fallen self fears sin, fears the possibility of the evil that threatens to undermine it, but nevertheless cannot totally free itself from the temptation to sin further and fall deeper. The demonic self, by contrast, fears the good, freedom, the possibility of becoming a fully self-conscious self. It longs for the continued unfreedom and loss of self-responsibility which sin represents, and sees the promise of the good to liberate and integrate it as frightening. At the same time, it remains tempted by the possibility of the good just as the other self is tempted by the possibility of evil. While it fears the good, it cannot totally shut this possibility out of its consciousness. The most remarkable facet of the demonic self is its 'shut-upness' or 'inclosing reserve.' The demonic self does not express itself; in fact, it seeks to conceal its own nature. While it may talk, it does so not to communicate but to deceive; when something of its own true inner state does break out, it is by compulsion rather than intent. The last thing the demoniac desires is to speak and be healed. Rather than let the light shine in and dry up the inner corruption, the demoniac conceals the inner disorder from the potentially curing power of self-revelation, thus allowing the infection to grow further. The repentant, faithful self by contrast knows it must be clear to itself, to God, and so far as possible to its neighbor. It must become concrete, which it can only do by living in the actual, external, social world in which it finds itself.

This sort of demonic introversion is also the theme of the story of Agnes and the Merman in *Fear and Trembling*.[20] In this story, the merman sees Agnes on the beach and decides to seduce and betray her; but instead he is moved by her innocent trust and genuinely falls in love with her. Now he faces a choice: he can abandon his evil plan, return her to the shore and swim away, or he can confess and ask her forgiveness. The faithful response of the merman to Agnes is to confess his earlier evil intentions, and to seek a new, honest relationship with her. The silent merman, who superficially seems to most resemble Abraham in his silence before his household, is in fact a demoniac. His self-imposed silence, his solitary repentance, his arrogant resolve to keep silent 'for her sake,' his self-martyrdom which leads him away from the society of others and from the world of responsible relationships, leads him also away from faith, and is a fundamental dysfunction of spirit. Likewise as we shall see, Quidam of the *Stages* is demonic precisely because he is silent, even deceptive. While he seeks to be good, and to do right by his jilted beloved, he avoids the one thing that would allow him to heal the fracture in his psyche: disclosure. Everything he does works the poisoned arrow of his shut-upness deeper into his spirit. And his own comments on the redemptive power of disclosure reflect the very sort of self-contradiction Haufniensis attributed to the demoniac; his own words condemn his actions.[21]

Comparing Kierkegaard's pseudonymous works is always questionable; the pseudonyms have such distinctive perspectives that it is impossible to be sure that they even understand each other, or use key terms in the same way. Still, the discussions of the demonic in different books can help to mutually explain each, despite different perspectives of the pseudonyms involved. Kierkegaard clearly thought the concept of the demonic was important, not just to understanding anxiety but to understanding faith as well. And it is clear from even this brief examination that the cliché of Kierkegaard the isolationist is wrong; the sort of voluntary withdrawal often identified with the Kierkegaardian ideal has more in common with his description of the demonic.

Anxiety and Christianity: While Haufniensis does not discuss *Philosophical Fragments*, comparing *The Concept of Anxiety* to *Philosophical Fragments* is encouraged by Kierkegaard's releasing both within days of each other. My governing hypothesis has been that works that were released together should be read together, as they are most likely related to each other. At any rate, we will never know unless we try. Can Haufniensis' discussion of anxiety, original sin, and the demonic be usefully connected to Climacus' exploration of revelation and salvation?

Before the Fall, Adam lived in such intimate connection with God that one can not say he really knew God, any more than one normally knows or is conscious of what is behind one's own eyes: God was just that near, as near as his own self. But he had the freedom to break this immediate unity if he chose, by choosing instead to do what he knew was forbidden—the 'evil.' When he so chose, he gained knowledge and lost innocence, so that now the good and the evil became objects of knowledge to be pursued, reflected upon, doubted, and so on. The immediate unity between God and the individual is shattered when the individual again freely chooses to make Adam's sin his or her own, and gains this knowledge as well. Once God has become an independent object, fit for reflection and concomitant uncertainty, there is no turning back to a simple presumption of immediate unity. One is estranged from God by one's knowledge that God is separate from one, and that because one has chosen to separate oneself from God through sinning. Now Adam, and any human who follows Adam's path by sinning, has only anxiety. Freedom was dizzying when it was only a possibility; when one sins it becomes even more so, as the individual now sees everything as a potential temptation. Temptation to evil is all around the anxious sinner, and he or she can never be free from it. The seemingly surest escape from the anxiety over the evil is spiritlessness. To be free is to be anxious; so to escape anxiety, escape freedom. That road ultimately leads to the demonic. In sin, the individual is unable to do the good he or she wishes; in the demonic, the individual would be free of the determinants of good or evil and the burden of freedom, but cannot be. One in bondage to sin is anxious over his or her guilt; repentance can sorrow over sin but cannot remove it. Everything in existence remains a threat, a temptation to new sin. The demoniac is anxious over the good, fears God and the salvation that would restore the burden of freedom. The sinner needs a new vision, that the sinner cannot give himself or herself.

The only cure for sin is faith, and the only way God (who has become the unknown by the individual's sin) can become present as an object of faith is by God's own self-revelation through the God-Man. By becoming incarnate in the particular person Jesus, God again becomes present for the individual, but in a way that acknowledges the separation from God that the individual has established by turning to sin. When God reveals that God loves the individual, the sinner is freed to respond with love, and in faith to see that 'the proof of God's amazing love is this,' and 'nothing in all creation can separate us from the love of God.'[22] Anxiety is not banished, but it is defanged. And the demoniac can see the possibility of living in freedom, seeing the model for such a life in the God-Man as man, and seeing the salvation possible through the God-Man as God. Any other attempt to escape or even manage anxiety, apart from the proactive revelation of God, will be futile at best and likely lead to the demonic, either as spiritlessness or as offense.

If we would link *The Concept of Anxiety* to the other pseudonymous works, I would say that first one must differentiate between the esthete by choice versus the esthete by immaturity. All people pretty much start out as 'esthetic,' when they are pre-reflective. Kierkegaard's theories generally do not address children, however, and his esthetes are not those who have never encountered good or evil; they are those who choose not to choose. This fits Haufniensis' description of the demonic: they fear to be free and thus are anxious over the good. Those who choose the good, and find themselves bound by anxiety over the evil, are those who would choose to be ethical and are finding the resources of the ethical sphere inadequate. The religious person recognizes the reality of sin, and repents, but cannot be freed from anxiety short of the miracle of the God as Teacher. 'Anxiety' is the psychological perspective on the bondage of untruth, which leads the individual further away from the truth no matter how much the individual seeks to approach it. The solution to anxiety is faith, which can be obtained only by God's saving action in the Incarnation; as Haufniensis says, this is beyond the scope of psychology and properly belongs to dogmatics, which Climacus has begun to analyze in the *Fragments*.

B. *Prefaces*. *Prefaces* was published the same day as the *Concept of Anxiety*, in a completely different style. Whereas the direct discourses are homiletic and practical, and *Anxiety* is dialectical and didactic, this work is a pure exercise in irony and ridicule. Its considerable social and moral commentary relies neither on admonition or theoretical argument but on satire for its force. Perhaps Kierkegaard felt that some positions do not need to be refuted, but to be laughed out of court.

The work consists entirely of prefaces for a variety of other books, journals, or pamphlets; but while a preface is normally intended to recommend the work to a reader, these all have the effect of undermining the work they preface. The preface for a pamphlet by a temperance society praises the society because it is able to raise an act of hygiene to the plane of morality; when one private individual chooses to moderate his drinking as a matter of health it is nothing, but if he should join a society dedicated to moderation it becomes a social movement of world-historical importance, and his formerly self-serving act becomes the highest moral achievement.[23] It is left to the reader to raise the question of just how a whole group of people, each one taking a nonmoral stance for self-serving reasons, can merely by joining together to take the same nonmoral stance suddenly become moral crusaders and paragons; or whether this might not be a fraud, and the banding together in fact a distraction from the only truly moral stance of self-reformation. When the preface ends with the admonition to members to be drunk not with wine but with enthusiasm, again the reader is left to decide whether there really is a significant difference after all between the intoxicants, or if the impairment of the individual's judgment and action are not essentially the same.

The following preface, to an 'edifying work for the cultured,' contrasts itself to the actual contemporary (and very popular) edifying work, a collection of sermons by Bishop Mynster.[24] Mynster's work contains sermons that, while individually edifying to the meditative individual reader or listener, show no systematic conceptual connection with one another. They are suited to 'the masses,' but fail to reach the cultured, who desire a work with more intellectual content and literary style. The prefaced work for the cultured, by contrast, admittedly contains essays which are unedifying when taken separately, but which when seen in their total context are parts of an edifying whole, which suits the cultured person's desire for philosophical maturity and mental stimulation. Again, a sum of things that each lack the desired quality of moral or religious worthiness is said to generate this quality, simply by being added together. That the supposed edifying work is unsuited for most persons, that it resembles paganism's standards of thought and style more than what has generally been regarded as Christian, and even that its views will almost certainly be overthrown in the foreseeable future by contrary views, are all cited as proof of how suited this edifying work is to the needs of the cultured Christian.

The theme echoed throughout the collection of prefaces is the contrast between the easy, glorious, and socially important work of joining and organizing banquets and committees, versus the slow, difficult, and utterly insignificant work of actually improving oneself.[25] This theme is treated as an ethical question, in the preface for the Temperance Society; as a religious question, in the preface for the edifying book; and as a question for the philosopher and author, in the final prefaces of the collection. Unlike the systematizers who explain the whole of world history and thought and only fail to explain how anyone is to understand all this or live in relation to it, the prefaces are offered as the work of a writer who seeks to understand himself and how he is to live, seeking a reader who reads deeply and carefully while always considering how to likewise understand himself or herself. He writes nonauthoritatively and seeks to be read the same way, not as one who knows but as one who seeks, and who even seeks assistance from the reader in this seeking. Like Socrates, the writer freely claims to be both unimportant and stupid—stupid enough to still be unable to understand just exactly how Hegelian philosophy has conquered all doubt, including the doubt whether anyone has actually understood Hegelian philosophy. On the other hand, unlike the philosophers who read ten books and mediate them together into an eleventh, the author claims to write only about what he himself has understood; namely, himself and the struggle to understand himself.

While there is something absurd about a preface which undermines the work it prefaces, and something even more absurd about a whole collections of prefaces designed to undermine works which were never written, perhaps there is something existentially significant about the notion that one should preface one's reaction to philosophy, social movements, religious trends, and so on by the thought that it is your own relationship to the truth which is of sole essential importance. In fact, Notabene has depicted in literary form what Haufniensis has described as the social manifestation of spiritlessness.[26] Notabene produces a book that is not a book but only a collection of prefaces to other books, and he describes cases where collections of people, upbuilding discourses, and so on are said to have qualities that none of the individual parts possess. Likewise, the pagan within Christianity seeks to reassure himself or herself by joining together with other 'respectable' people that he or she is in fact free from sin, by virtue of being part of the group known as 'Christianity.'

C. *Four Upbuilding Discourses* of 1844: This was the last of the series of eighteen upbuilding discourses that Kierkegaard published to accompany the pseudonymous works. The book completes the development noticeable in the others: an ever more radical questioning of the human ability to achieve anything of ethical-religious significance without God's proactive grace. The highest perfection of a human existence, says Kierkegaard, is to know that one is capable of nothing at all, that one relies on God for absolutely everything, and even to realize this one needs God's help.[27] While

a person may be able to achieve much in the world if he or she is willing
to move at the behest of 'inexplicable drives,' determined by the external
world itself, once one resolves to follow the ethicist's advice and be free
from determination by the world, one finds one can accomplish absolutely
nothing. At best, one can be 'courageous' enough to be willing to recognize one's own impotence when God reveals it.

Coupled with all this talk about the individual's utter powerlessness
is other talk, urging the reader to action. One is urged 'against cow-
ardice,' and toward resolution.[28] Or one is urged to indict oneself all
the more fiercely for one's own sin, so that one may learn to rely on
God's mercy all the more.[29] The reader is urged to acknowledge his or
her own inability to do any good, but not to take this as an excuse for
complacency or inaction. All of this implies that the human will is morally relevant after all. Kierkegaard indicates that the person must will to
respond to God's initiative, and that this humility to admit one's need
and accept help further requires courage—two virtues, cultivated by
the individual. Faith, of course, is also urged; it is faith that allows one
to trust that whatever happens is meant by God to be for one's good,
and therefore faith transforms an angel of Satan into an emissary of
God.[30] So one is urged to embrace certain virtues, and to cooperate with
God's activity in one's own life. The strongest activity of human freedom, however, may be the negative; individuals are capable of a variety
of stratagems to avoid or resist God's will, and their own development
of self-consciousness when it threatens to make manifest to them their
own need for God. It is thus not a simple, two-sphere explanation of the
will that is offered, whereby humans can will in the worldly sphere and
not at all in the godly. Rather, Kierkegaard offers a much more dialectical theory, whereby the human will is capable of some nearly intangible
yet significant effects within the godly realm; and conversely, within the
worldly realm an honest appraisal will admit that any belief in human
control or freedom is a delusion, given the strength of the cosmic forces
and inner compulsions aligned against the individual. The 'freedom'
which Kierkegaard assumes is 'enmeshed,' neither unconstrained arbi-
trariness nor total determinism, but morally and religiously significant
within its given parameters so that exhortations, repentance, blame,
self-accusation, praise, and so on remain reasonable.

The paradox of the situation is fairly well summed up in the title to
the last of the upbuilding discourses: 'One who Prays Aright Struggles in
Prayer and is Victorious—In that God is Victorious.'[31] One who struggles
is active, exerting force against some opposition; one who is victorious

in a struggle overcomes the opposition and attains his or her goal; but Kierkegaard says the one who prays aright is victorious in that God is victorious, and conquers in being conquered by God! The effort exerted to overcome God, to persuade God to one's own way of thinking, to assert oneself before God and bring God to concede one's rightness—this effort is fulfilled when God overcomes the praying one, when one is brought to agree with God, when one accepts one's own nothingness before God; as Kierkegaard writes:

> Only when he himself becomes nothing, only then can God illuminate him so that he resembles God. However great he is, he cannot manifest God's likeness; God can imprint himself in him only when he himself has become nothing.
>
> Who, then, was victorious? It was God, because he did not give the explanation requested by the one who prayed, and he did not give it as the struggling one requested it. But the one struggling was also victorious. Or was it not a victory that instead of receiving an explanation from God he was transfigured in God, and his transfiguration is this: to reflect the image of God.[32]

There are several passages or phrases which suggest earlier pseudonymous works, and which cumulatively suggest a retrospective on the earlier authorship. For example, Kierkegaard writes, 'Yes, it would be a uniquely great and exceptional person who in his adulthood accomplished merely half of what he knew in his childhood, of what in his boyhood he knew how to develop in an essay'; indirectly raising the theme of *Repetition*, but even more directly recalling the diapsalm in which A bemoans the fact that he can no longer believe in the immortality of the soul, a subject on which he once won prizes for his essays.[33] Kierkegaard's claim that one can only perceive the benefits of the religious life when one jettisons sagacity and embraces faith without hope of reward reverses the advice of Constantin, who argues that one ought only to take refuge in the religious after one has exhausted sagacity.[34] Kierkegaard also indirectly suggests both Judge William and de Silentio in his discussion of resolution, resignation, and renunciation found on these pages.

Parallels with the *Fragments* are also easy to find. Some, while not particularly significant for their own sakes, do help prove that at least some of the thoughts attributed to Climacus are Kierkegaard's own: for example, his stressing of the Socratic egalitarianism between persons, his description of faith as 'unununderstandable,' or his claim that it was good for the disciples that Christ should leave them.[35] Much more interesting is Kierkegaard's claim that:

> . . . it is the worst and the most revolting blasphemy to say of God that he is inhuman, no matter if it is supposed to be very fashionable or bold to talk that way. No, the God to whom (one) prays is human, has the heart to feel humanly, the ear to hear a human being's complaint; and even though he does not fulfill every wish, he still lives close to us and is moved by the struggler's cry, by his humble request, by his wretchedness when he sits abandoned and as if in prison, by his speedy joy over the fulfill-ment when in hope he anticipates it.[36]

Clearly, there is no way Kierkegaard could claim to know this if God had not actually revealed it; the central theme of the *Fragments* is, after all, that God has come as a human being because only in this way could any attain a true relationship to God. At the same time, Kierkegaard does not explain in this text that this is how he knows that God has human attributes, and hence he avoids discussing the essential Christian doctrine of the Incarnation even as he draws on it. In that respect, the discourse remains (barely) within the sphere Climacus later describes as 'religiousness A,' as opposed to the paradoxical religiousness of full Christianity.

The retrospective aspect of this upbuilding discourse is itself significant on two levels. First, it suggests that Kierkegaard is here already embark-ing on a summation of his entire authorship, a task he will complete with the *Stages* and *Postscript*. And the fact that these retrospective elements can appear interwoven through this discourse illustrates something of the relationship of the spheres to each other in the religious life. First, there is Kierkegaard's claim that 'there has never been anyone who has not assumed the existence of a god, but there certainly have been some who have not wanted to let this thought have any power over them.'[37] While everyone has some sort of basic sense of the transcendent, in 'some' (or better, 'most') this sense is suppressed, evaded, resisted, or otherwise unwelcomed. Whether it is openly warred against or subtly subverted to the service of the ego, for most people it is not something that one wishes to grant too much power. But if this initial sense is granted its due, is allowed to acquire power over one, then one must develop even further such vir-tues as resolve and renunciation for which the ethicist strove on humano-centric grounds alone. Kierkegaard does not indicate here how the spheres integrate with one another, but he does illustrate that they do and must, if the religious life is to exist at all. This is particularly valuable juxtaposed to the pseudonymous authorship, which is largely devoted to conceptually distinguishing the spheres from one another, at times to the point that it becomes difficult to see how they could be reintegrated back together as elements of a single human life.

   D. *Summary*: If Haufniensis focuses on the problem of sin as generated by the infinite ethical demand upon the individual, Notabene depicts the evasion of the demands of individuality, and sin by collectivism. While Hegel's equation of ethics with society and world history is clearly a target here, the preface to the address by the temperance society illustrates that this is a common human tactic.[38] Given the choice between seeing the essential human task as the individual's ethical striving and repentance/or the individual's participation in politics and social movements of great importance, Notabene simply asks, if the parts all lack the essential quality, how can the sum have it? If the individuals are self-centered, so is their Society; if the individual sermons are unedifying, the collection too must be unspiritual; and if all the individuals are spiritless pagans, then a 'Christian nation' can only be pagan. The redemption which Hegel, or anyone else might seek in the progress of Christian history simply cannot be; there is either individual redemption through Christ or there is no relief from sin. The world-historical or Church-historical approaches, or any other sort of collectivism, does not address the problem of sin but simply tries to prevent it from becoming visible, and thus to prevent the need for genuine grace and a real God-relationship from appearing.

   In a different way, this is also what Climacus argues in the *Fragments*. There, he describes sin as 'untruth,' and that the only way for the individual to escape from sin is a direct relationship to the god, who has entered time as a human to reach and teach the individual and free him or her from bondage to sin.[39] One does not gain anything essential from the previous generations; one may hear about the god as Teacher from others, but one is saved only by relating to the god as did any contemporary follower.[40] As the four upbuilding discourses argue, Climacus also asserts that the individual needs God's proactive grace to be freed from sin.[41] When the individual has chosen unfreedom, he or she has no more power left to simply undo that choice. As the discourse on prayer put it, one's will can battle itself, but it cannot overcome itself; God must intervene to tip the balance between the sinful side of the will versus the repentant side. And likewise, Haufniensis argues that the self caught in anxiety cannot free itself from anxiety alone; all its efforts simply dig the hole deeper. The idea that a collection of sinners somehow becomes the People of God simply by joining together, so that I can be assured of my salvation simply by my membership in that group, is a spiritless flight from selfhood, more demonic than divine. I can only escape my anxiety by God's intervention, which is a matter for dogmatics rather than psychology; therefore Haufniensis refuses to discuss how this can happen, and Climacus only discusses it maieutically as the appearance of the god as teacher. Together, these four books discuss the problem of sin from four different angles, but this is still Kierkegaard's 'esthetic' authorship, and he still employs indirect methods to lure his readers in.

Chapter Five

Sin and Salvation from the *Three Discourses* to the Three *Stages*

It is obvious that Kierkegaard's *Stages on Life's Way* is a retrospective summary on the earlier pseudonymous authorship, beginning with the themes and characters of *Either/Or* and continuing through the demonic, a theme explored most completely in the *Concept of Anxiety*. It is also clear that the *Three Discourses on Imagined Occasions* represents a culmination of Kierkegaard's direct authorship to that time; just as the last of the eighteen upbuilding discourses had bumped up against the concept of sin (without quite broaching it) so do the *Discourses on Imagined Occasions* begin with a confession of sin, and proceed from there to explore various aspects of the religious life. The unity between these two books is not always recognized; and when it is, there is disagreement over just what the relationship is. Close examination suggests the *Stages on Life's Way* and the *Three Discourses on Imagined Occasions* form a distinct unity, together serving to summarize and explain Kierkegaard's authorship to that point. Not only do they serve a culminating role in the track of the authorship which each one represents, but they mutually explain each other, and in doing so tie together Kierkegaard's direct and indirect authorships in preparation for what he expected to be the capstone of his entire effort as a writer: the *Concluding Unscientific Postscript*.

A. *Three Discourses on Imagined Occasions*: Kierkegaard released the *Three Discourses on Imagined Occasions* under his own name on April 29, 1845, eight months after the last of the eighteen upbuilding discourses and one day before the massive *Stages on Life's Way*. It seems clear that the three discourses are intended to 'accompany' and comment upon the *Stages*, and the tripartite division of both, coupled with the similarity in subject matter of the second part of each, further suggests a one-to-one correspondence between the chapters of each. In the *Stages*, Kierkegaard pseudonymously recapitulates and represents the three spheres of existence; in each of the *Discourses on Imagined Occasions* he comments on the themes of one of the pseudonymous representations directly and from a religious perspective.

Unfortunately, it is not as simple as that; for it is not in fact clear how the correspondence runs. It might be a straightforward parallel, where the first and third chapters of each book correspond to each other; or it might be an acrostic, with the first chapter of each corresponding to the third in the other.[1] Johann G. Hamann (one of Kierkegaard's favorite authors) is notorious for employing this sort of literary puzzle, so it is certainly possible that Kierkegaard might have borrowed the strategy himself. Furthermore, more recently Andrew Burgess has suggested that the discourses should be read with the first corresponding to the ethical, and the third to the religious; though he admits this theory lacks support from the text. He also proceeds to argue that the most meaningful relationship is not between those two books at all, but between both of them versus the *Concluding Unscientific Postscript.*[2]

If it is truly a misunderstanding to believe the *Stages* and the three discourses relate to each other, it is certainly a misunderstanding Kierkegaard himself has invited his readers to make. As originally published, no one would have been able to compare these writings to the *Postscript* for nearly a year. As to whether or which discourses are intended to comment on which stages, we certainly will not discover any connections unless we provisionally assume there are some, and try to find them. The only way to discover the truth is to try to interpret the content of the discourses themselves, seeking further clues.

The reader expecting to find connections between the first discourse and the esthetic stage of the *Stages on Life's Way* would not be disappointed. The entire discourse is shot through with emotional, passional references—the stillness of the single individual before God, the wonder of the presence of God, and so on—so that the reader gains the distinct impression that what is under discussion is the proper religious mood, how one ought to feel upon entering into the religious experience: 'So, then, the confessor seeks God in the confession of sins, and the confession is the road and is a biding place on the road of salvation, where one pauses and collects one's thoughts and makes an accounting.'[3] '(W)onder is immediacy's sense of God and is the beginning of all deeper understanding . . . Wonder is an ambivalent state of mind containing both fear and blessedness. Worship therefore is simultaneously a mixture of fear and blessedness.'[4] So wonder and the stillness of confession seem to be preliminary to entering the religious stage, not unlike the step of infinite resignation described by de Silentio, or even the repentance described by William in 'Equilibrium.'

The individual steps away from the busyness and distraction of the world, collects himself or herself, feels the wonder of the divine, and then is ready to enter into the life of the God-relationship—beginning most likely with the active life described in the wedding discourse, and culminating in the final break with the world that comes from the meditation upon death described in the funeral discourse. If this reading were valid, it would also loosely parallel the Greek notion that the highest life was primarily a practice in dying, a continuous breaking with the finite and temporal until the soul could finally join with the eternal completely.[5]

But this straightforward progression turns out to be too quick a solution. Upon further reflection, one considers that the first discourse is the one which bumps up against the notion of sin; the other two do not get so far. When one is still in the presence of God, it is largely a sense of one's own guilt that makes one shy to speak.[6] The wonder one experiences in the presence of God comes when one has despaired of finite goals and wonders, turned to seek the true and eternal wonder, and 'suddenly discovered that he has what is sought and . . . that he is standing there and losing it!'—that is, one discovers that God is as near as can be, but one is continually moving further away through sin.[7] This recalls the description Climacus offered in the beginning of the *Fragments* about the learner's state of untruth, as polemically moving away from the truth until the god intervenes. When Kierkegaard remarks that even if the seers in Egypt had performed greater signs than Moses, this would have proven nothing regarding the validity of Moses' God-relationship, he echoes Climacus' comments regarding the irrelevance of the quality of objective evidence in Scripture.[8] Or again, Kierkegaard writes that one must feel oneself to be a nothing before God, even less than nothing, because of one's sin; one has begun badly in guilt and is continuing what was badly begun in sin.[9] When Kierkegaard writes here that one can only become aware of God by becoming a sinner (that is, by becoming one in one's own eyes), this recalls the contention in the *Fragments* that the first thing the learner learns in encountering the god-teacher is the learner's own state of untruth.[10] This talk of being as 'nothing' recalls the last upbuilding discourses, which also speak of being 'nothing' before God, of being built up in being overcome by God, and so on. Relative to these, the *Discourses on Imagined Occasions* picks up where they left off, goes a little further in specifying the continuing state and activity of sin relative to the individual's 'nothingness' before God, and then moves backwards through the rest of the book to consider less decisive themes. When this discourse refers to itself as preparatory, then, it is not in the sense that the esthetic is the starting point for all of us, but rather in the sense that this highest development of immanent religiousness leads to sin-consciousness; to encounter God is first to recognize oneself as a sinner, and if one is to have a continuing relationship with God it must continue with repentance and grace.

This being said, it is certainly significant that one can find so many esthetic elements in this discourse, so much discussion of mood and religious immediacy. Likewise, it is certainly significant that the first discourse compares itself to the subject of the third: 'The person who is making confession is alone—indeed, as alone as a dying person.'[11] The esthetic is clearly active in the developed religious life; there is no Platonic retreat into a purely intellectual, dispassionate eternal.

The second discourse, happily, offers none of these interpretive puzzles. It clearly corresponds to the ethical, as it has been represented in and by Judge William. It even treats the same material as William's essay in *Stages* and the first letter of *Either/Or*: marriage. Furthermore, so much of what Kierkegaard says on the subject could just as easily have been put in the mouth of Judge William that to mention every similarity would end up by quoting almost the whole discourse. The first page opens with a discussion of the 'beautiful assurance of erotic love,' now transformed by setting it into 'a sacred mood'; and then the incongruity that this 'indefinable wealth of moods is to be transformed, given clarity and spoken expression, and finally made a duty—here love is to become a duty.' And this is furthermore 'a resolution in freedom' made by the lovers themselves, a resolution 'for eternity'; the 'eternal resolution and the duty for eternity must remain with the wedded pair in the union of love through time.'[12] Virtually all the Judge's themes are touched on in these passages—the interplay between the esthetic and ethical; the need to make an accounting of oneself before 'God and your conscience'; the struggle to preserve love against the ravages of time, security, habit, and so on; the centrality of freedom and resolution.

The list of points of divergence between the pseudonym's views and Kierkegaard's words, by contrast, is short though significant. First, there is precious little said about realizing some universal or essentially human ideal, about a duty to be married, about social or communal responsibilities, or other positive relations to any third party. Clearly, the wedding is a public ceremony and a social event, but the emphasis is on the individual; the relationship of the lovers to each other and each to God. Having a true conception of oneself before God, or being earnest in one's duty to work out one's own salvation in fear and trembling, without dependence on external guides or advice to reveal one's own unique and personal task;

or the importance of desiring to be built up, so that one can be strengthened even by mediocre assistance from another, taken the right way: these
are the sorts of points Kierkegaard discusses. Each partner in the wedding
must come individually before God and conscience to be made fit and able
to be joined together as they themselves freely desire and resolve.[13]

Second, the lovers to be married must each have a true, definite conception of God.[14] No matter how many times God is mentioned in the service,
it does not follow that God has been truly known, and has not been mis-
construed as 'an enigmatic power, whose intervention prompts one to be
amazed—and to idolize.'[15] And a definite conception of God seems to be
lacking in Judge William's writings. He reveres and invokes God enough,
but his God always remains an eternal power which blesses and undergirds
the universal ethical duty. God is not definite or personal for him; to consult with God is precisely identical with consulting with your conscience in
his thought, so that the standard pastoral charge to the couple (have you
consulted with God and your conscience?) becomes a little redundant. For
Kierkegaard, too, they are identical, but in a very different sense than for
the Judge. To consult truly with one's conscience, one must consult with
God; and to consult truly with God must involve conscience, so that to tell
the couple to 'consult with God' implies 'and your conscience,' while to
'consult with your conscience' alone would be to do neither.

The last discourse, 'At a Graveside,' is concerned to distinguish between
'mood' and 'earnestness.' It is one thing to be in a somber, sober mood
at a funeral; it is quite another to take the thought of death and finitude
to heart, and be built up by it. The reader is invited to consider death, to
meditate upon it; not just in the general sense that all living things die, but
in the quite personal sense that you will die, any time now, and that will be
the end of it. It is quite possible to meditate on death, become melancholy
over it, sorrow cynically or depressedly as the esthetic writer in *Either/Or*
does.[16] It is even possible to reflect on one's own inevitable death, with such
thoughts that one will 'rest from one's labors' or 'finally find peace,' and
thus possibly even anticipate the end of one's life with a certain pleasure.
But in all this, one has not seriously thought through that *you* are going to
die; not just anyone, and not just rest or escape one's burdens, but that *all*
one's hopes and projects and desires will be cut off permanently by death.
As long as there is any abstraction, impersonality, or unclarity in thinking
about death, the awareness of it remains at the level of mood: an esthetic
awareness. But when one considers with stark clarity what one's own death
means, one can become earnest. One can begin to see the ultimate futility
of all the finite attachments one has, which will be cut off by death; and

also to see how urgent it is that one seek the 'one thing needful' while there is still time. One must personally appropriate the thought of one's own death; to learn from another is no use, nor to know everything and never let it apply to one's own life. There is no objective or second-hand consideration of one's own death, unless one has retreated into the unclarity of mood and is avoiding the clarity of earnestness. There is relatively little said in the discourse about God and the God-relationship; by contrast, there is quite a lot said about the many evasions of earnestness one might invent, and how the earnest thought of death can shake one out of any mere mood and impel one to earnest action and decision. This is really a discourse about the break with the esthetic and the move to a higher existence, one which recognizes the final refutation of finitude which death presents; it is also a discourse on decisiveness, which recognizes the fact that death has made temporality precious by limiting the span of time each individual has to decide and act. This is the beginning of the journey to a higher existence, and ultimately toward a mature God-relationship.

Comparing this discourse to *Either/Or*, one can readily see that while A is preoccupied with the theme of death, and alternatively laughs or weeps over it, he never lets it 'get to him' in the sense of actually shaking him out of his apathy. He feels no need to seek a higher goal than his own arbitrary projects; indeed, he does not even feel any urgency to finish one of these. He simply drifts along as if he had forever. When he does reflect upon his own death, it is in the sense of relieving his pain and boredom, as if somehow he would still exist after the suffering had died.[17] He even writes essays and speeches for the 'Fellowship of the Dead,' as if he and the other dead souls could sit around enlightening one another on the truths of existence.[18] A might seem serious to the point of melancholy, a very somber fellow who really understands that all things pass away, but he seems uninterested or unmoved by the notion that he himself is passing away; the thought of death, even his own dying, is still external to himself, like a drug he uses to numb the pain and boredom of his meaningless existence so that he himself may continue, always hoping by his superior insight to have the laugh on his side.[19]

This collection of discourses completes the review of the earlier authorship, preparing the scene for the final commentary of the *Concluding Unscientific Postscript*. The previous pseudonymous works discussed sin; this collection begins with confession without discussing sin itself in much detail, then gives a religious treatment of marriage (William's central concern in his first ethical essay) and of death (a recurring topic for A). In relation to the direct authorship, it begins about where the upbuilding discourses left off, moving back from that point to consider a very basic religiousness and how the religious ought to differ from a religiously colored estheticism or ethicism. To summarize in reverse order the development suggested: the sincere contemplation of one's own death leads to an earnestness which breaks with the finite trivialities which death will end, and the lethargy of a life of mood, giving 'the earnest person the right momentum in life and the right goal towards which he directs his momentum.'[20] Resolution allows one to undertake the ethical task before God and with the definite conception of God. And when one honestly admits the fact to oneself that one has failed in the good one resolved, one finds one's guilt and then one's sin, and in becoming a sinner before God and in one's own conscience one becomes as nothing before God, so that God may become everything in one's life. In the order Kierkegaard follows in this book of discourses, he offers an archeology of faith: excavating from the summit of sin and repentance down until he reaches the earnestness which is the foundation for any spiritually developed life.

One further interpretive question remains: why *Three Discourses on Imagined Occasions*? The other collections of discourses had no title beyond the number of discourses in the book; the discourses themselves were titled by their themes. These last three discourses each have a fictional setting, for which the book itself is named; and the individual chapters are named for the imagined occasions for each discourse, not their actual themes. Clearly, Kierkegaard is communicating something by this creative flourish; and in fact, the occasions he chooses seem to be paradigmatic for the religious life. This becomes clearer in the *Postscript*, but the discourses' original readers would not have had the chance to read that book for another ten months. An original reader of *Three Discourses on Imagined Occasions* might have recalled the death references in the first volume of *Either/Or*, and how important marriage was as a paradigm of the ethical life in the second volume. A reader might also reflect on how sin was the defining characteristic that separated Christianity from all other views, according to the *Fragments*. So the funeral, wedding, and confession are rites that particularly reflect the key transitional moments in the life of the self, as reflected in the pseudonymous works to this point.

This book is the first one published under Kierkegaard's own name that clearly reflects the three-sphere theory he has been developing in the pseudonyms. While the entire work moves within the religious sphere, it offers a religious esthetic, religious ethic, and a decisive religiousness in inverse order. In doing so, it also suggests how an individual could move through the spheres progressively by seriously considering the common biological, social, and religious events of life in Danish Christendom. While Kierkegaard and his pseudonyms generally write as if the truths they present are universally valid, it usually appears that only a highly reflective, introverted, and perhaps insecure personality like Kierkegaard's could really carry out this program, or even make sense of it.[21] This impression is particularly strong when one considers the strategy implicit in the pseudonymous authorship. The pseudonyms are almost universally reflective, introverted thinkers; even the Judge delves more deeply and philosophically into existence than most people can or wish. By tying his esoteric theories to practical events, universal within the culture for which he wrote, Kierkegaard renders his program more accessible. It is not in fact necessary to withdraw from society or devote oneself solely to philosophic contemplation to become a mature personality; all that is required is to think seriously about what one is doing, and consider the implications of death, marriage, and the religious practices one sees around one every day and most likely (at least in Golden Age Denmark) joins in oneself. Not, of course, that serious thought itself is universal or habitual; Kierkegaard's program of maieutically awakening his readers from the illusion that all are Christians is based on his belief that most people are enslaved to frivolity. But this book in particular does make clearer why he thought his proposals were universally accessible and necessary, since they arise out of universal human experiences.

B. *Stages on Life's Way*: This is easily Kierkegaard's most massive work since he opened with *Either/Or*, and like this earlier work, it contains a collection of pseudonymous authors, speakers, editors, and now even a bookbinder who allegedly found the various papers presented, collected them together, and sent them on to be printed and published. The internal structure is thus reminiscent of *Either/Or*, but is even more convoluted; and the task of the work is similarly more ambitious, being a recapitulation not only of the themes of *Either/Or*, but continuing beyond for an intensive exploration of the demonic and religious. Victor Eremita, Johannes the Seducer, Constantin Constantius, and Judge William all appear as writers or speakers. Additionally, there are several other esthetic characters in the first section, and the third is written under a completely new pseudonym, an experimenting psychologist named Frater Taciturnus who in turn authors a pseudonymous work of his own: 'Quidam's diary,' which examines issues of guilt, repentance, and forgiveness. The multilayered pseudonymity and considerable dramatic flourishes, coupled with the absence of Kierkegaard's own name on the title page, indicate his intention to once again distance himself from the views portrayed. The spheres are again being allowed to speak for themselves without 'external' comment or judgment, as distinct viewpoints which stand or fall on their own merits.

Each of the three sections centers around issues of love: erotic affairs, betrothal, marriage. This fundamental interpersonal relationship serves as a touchstone for each of the three stages of existence, as their treatment of these themes reveals the nature of the spheres themselves. The esthetic dialogue, 'In Vino Veritas,' consists largely of speeches on the subject of women, either as objects of love affairs or sources of temptation. The ethical essay, by contrast, consists of 'Reflections on Marriage' by Judge William, and considers the love relationship of commitment over time, the universality of the ethical relationship, and how the two partners are supposed to complement one another in the relationship. The religious essay is the only one of the three written by a character not living the lifestyle he discusses. Frater Taciturnus claims to be only an observing psychologist, who knows what the religious is although he declines to take the step of actually becoming religious. His invention, Quidam, is himself also not religious; he is in fact caught in the demonic. He has broken his engagement, and now tortures himself over whether he is morally justified in doing so; and he furthermore is obsessed with the eventual fate of the girl he jilted, believing that any injury that might eventually befall her will be a new sin for him as well. In his inability to turn over either his own guilt or her fate to God, he fails to fully enter the religious even though he has left the ethical behind in his break with the universal, and the esthetic behind with his acceptance of moral categories. Stuck in the transition between stages, he is used by Taciturnus to illustrate essential religious psychological themes such as suffering and inwardness.

'In Vino Veritas:' The elaborate setting for the speeches of the esthetes is at least as revealing as any of the speeches themselves. Subtitled 'a recollection related by William Afham,' it is introduced with an extensive discussion of the notions of 'recollection' versus 'remembering,' more than slightly reminiscent of the discussion of recollection in *Either/Or.*[22] While Afham allows some importance to accuracy of recall, recollection is much more concerned with the 'essence' of what is recalled, and with putting oneself back in that situation. Thus it is no matter to him when the events actually took place, or other historic details: 'The only subject matter for recollection is mood and whatever is classified under mood.'[23] He does seek to recall the people involved, although he is not so much concerned with names as with their personalities and words as these impacted the mood he wishes to recollect. And for readers of Kierkegaard's earlier pseudonymous works, some of these names are revelatory: Victor Eremita,

Constantin Constantius, Johannes the Seducer. The other two have no names; one is recalled only as 'the Fashion Designer,' while the other is described as 'the Young Man.' The banquet comes about as the result of a conversation about what would make a good banquet, and how impossible it would be to bring this ideal into existence. Eremita offers to present his notion of the ideal banquet 'immediately,' rather than with any reflection or planning. This echoes the idea found throughout *Either/Or* that the esthetic is the immediate, and that when it is reflected on or even put into words it is already spoiled.[24] The problem, of course, is that you cannot plan immediacy; so once Eremita has described the ideal banquet, his work is done. But Constantin seems to see this as his chance to test his powers of repetition, for he undertakes to create precisely the banquet Eremita has described, using sleight of hand and artistry to make it appear to have just happened.[25] Then, when all is prepared, he invites the original plotters to the banquet, giving them as little time as possible to anticipate or plan, but rather immersing them as immediately as possible in the 'spontaneous' party.

Constantin's actions and success seem to validate the concept of repetition; but the banquet itself is bracketed with salutes to impermanence and death. The festivities begin with Eremita, overwhelmed by the scene, giving a spontaneous invocation and thanks to Mozart, 'you to whom I owe everything,' until that time when 'I shall no longer belong to you or to the world, but only to the earnest thought of death!'[26] As in *Either/Or*, Mozart is the patron saint or daimon of esthetic enjoyment; but even in the height of his revelry Eremita recalls the reality of death.[27] But for now, 'earnestness' is far from everyone's mind, and death is recalled only to add to the enjoyment of the moment. Reinforcing this message is the presence of four workmen, who stand prepared to destroy the banquet hall as soon as the party has finished; there will never again be a repetition of any enjoyment here.[28]

The dramatic framing of the banquet thus presents us with an inversion of earnestness. These esthetes regard the planning of a banquet with mortal seriousness, but discuss death and love as objects of amusement. The one demonstrates our innate aloneness, the other our essential community, but neither truly matters to the banqueters; they care only for entertaining themselves as long as they can.

While the pseudonyms and material in the esthetic and ethical chapters of *Stages* largely resemble those in *Either/Or*, there are important differences. The esthetic portion of *Either/Or* contains a strong element of religious polemic. The material contains a mixture of Christian and pagan motifs, as if the author is unsure whether he exists primarily in Christendom or ancient Greece—or as if he sees nothing incongruous in this sort of Christian paganism. Furthermore, his paganism at least has (esthetic) passion and inwardness; the bourgeois religion of Christendom's masses lacks even this. Part of the aim of *Either/Or* seems to be to traffic on this confusion between poetics and Christianity, which it shares with many of Kierkegaard's contemporaries, in order to expose and undermine the religious confusions of Golden Age Denmark.[29] 'In Vino Veritas,' by contrast, is largely devoid of Christian pretenses or references. When religious references appear at all, they are pagan and mythological. Its pseudonyms are so esthetically self-absorbed that women vanish from their speeches as independent human beings at all. They are unfathomable mysteries, to be avoided, mocked, observed, or consumed, depending on the particular character's personal bent. This might be termed 'inwardness' in a manner of speaking, but not in the Kierkegaardian sense; for Kierkegaard, true inwardness seeks to understand itself, not merely to inwardly reflect on external realities. While *Either/Or* seems to build on esthetic-ethical-Christian confusions, *Stages* presents the esthetic in its purity—pure paganism, pure selfishness.

We can expect no true understanding of sin or salvation in the speeches of these esthetes; but in their misappropriation of religious values we might begin to see truth reflected in reverse, as in a mirror. The Seducer's speech features religious themes more prominently than any of the others, and thus warrants particular attention. He begins with the Greek myth that there was originally only one sex: male. The gods had created man as the pinnacle of Creation, but now became fearful of their own handiwork. There simply seemed to be no limits to what man might accomplish, since nothing in Creation could subdue his spirit or reason. Left unchecked, his power might have eventually grown to the point of being able to challenge even the gods, or at least dispense with them; and so they devised a cunning trap. Since man was created to be the height of Creation, he would be trapped by something weaker than himself, for which he would feel such desire that he would voluntarily bind himself to it. So the gods created woman as the bait whereby man would bind himself to the finite, his power forever diverted from the infinity toward which it tended and from which it could have threatened the gods. Man's love for woman bound him to her and to earthly finitude, leaving Heaven to the gods alone. Only the seducers see through the trap which woman represents, and avoid being hooked by any particular woman while they constantly feast on the bait of the gods.[30]

The adversarial relationship between the esthete and the religious, as implied by this myth, is certainly noteworthy. The gods want to subdue and control man; the seducer sees through their trick, and takes their creation for his own pleasure. Man can only be fully great by rebelling against the gods, by taking without gratitude, prescribed right, or fear. This is also reflected in *Either/Or*, where the religious serves the esthete as an intoxicant, rather than the esthete serving the religious as a worshipper. A may write about the religious comfort for guilt, but he neither truly understands it nor desires it for himself; he merely amuses himself writing to fictitious colleagues.[31] Woman, the other, likewise is treated as a threat, as far as any sincere relationship is considered. As an object of desire, deception, and seduction, she is possibility, an ambrosial delight, and her seducer remains free in infinity; in marriage she becomes concrete and temporal, as her husband does through her.

In this myth, the Seducer treats the divine as the source of both esthetic pleasures and ethical bonds; in fact, both are joined in his understanding of woman. The intention of the religious/the gods is that a person should be drawn into the ethical through the pursuit of pleasure; woman tempts to marriage, wealth tempts to vocation, and so on. To be thus ethically bound stifles the infinite freedom to which the esthete aspires, so the esthete seeks to enjoy the world while denying its demands.

The Seducer's speech is only one of several offered here, and the variations on the esthetic offered here are not identical with each other or the views of *Either/Or*. For our purposes here, the differences are not particularly important, although the mere fact that there are differences itself says something about the esthetic *per se*. The esthetic is not a unity; rather, it is any of a wide range of views sharing certain characteristics. All the esthetes are self-absorbed rather than inwardly reflective; they consider the other (here woman) from a selfish point of view, as either a threat or a satisfaction for certain felt needs; they seek freedom from ethical and religious demands, even though they may treat with ethical or religious themes when it suits them.[32] The chapter suits the material; the esthetic is presented as a series of speeches, so there is disagreement and even some discussion without real dialogue. A dialogue would have implied real engagement and cooperation within the group, whereas each one of these men is interested only in his own agenda. While giving and hearing speeches may be amusing, actually teaching or learning would be too serious to remain esthetically interesting.

'*Some Reflections on Marriage:*' Socrates, by contrast, is always depicted in dialogue, reflecting both his serious engagement with the other and his serious striving toward the truth. Even in Plato's *Symposium*, on which this banquet is apparently based, he converses with the other speakers, explores their views, invites their opinions and reacts to them.[33] One may wonder therefore if it might not have been appropriate for Judge William's 'Reflections on Marriage' to have been offered in dialogue rather than monologue. Several possible reasons suggest themselves as explanations of Kierkegaard's choice of style. The Judge lacks the Socratic gift for irony and debate, as he is intended to be an ordinary ethical person. The Socratic dialogues generally present ethical and nonethical views, whereas the Judge's essay is meant to present only the ethical. Or perhaps Kierkegaard means to suggest that the ethical really is one, in a way the esthetic is not. And while the Judge's essay is ostensibly stolen from him and published without his consent, and without his having heard the banquet speeches, it does show some knowledge of the sorts of things esthetes say against marriage as well as a concern to either refute or rebuke their charges; so there is a sort of dialogue contained within his monologue.

The vision of the ethical presented in the *Stages* is virtually identical with that found in *Either/Or*. The Judge continues to hammer home such themes as duty, the universal, freedom, and preserving one's love in the concrete and temporal world, over time and in the face of the thousands of ordinary everyday challenges. And relative to the esthetes, he has a much more healthy relationship to woman, the other, and his wife in particular. While he shares the prejudice of most or all of Kierkegaard's pseudonyms that woman is less 'reflective' than man, he has no doubt that woman is 'as good as' man; he consults with his wife on important matters and respects her opinions, considers her a partner rather than an amusement, even to the point of being unable to apply esthetic categories of attractiveness to her—he simply does not see her 'objectively,' as an object, but only 'subjectively' as a subject.[34] Constantin the esthete says that man is 'absolute,' while woman is 'relational'; but the Judge's view is supremely relational as well; it is only the esthetic which strives to be 'absolute,' unconditioned by the other.[35]

Just as the esthetic chapter serves both to review and clarify key elements of the esthetic, so the ethical chapter repeats the Judge's key themes while further distancing his views from the esthetic and religious stages. There are two particularly telling references: one, where William claims that the individual relates to God 'through the universal'; and another, where he argues that man and woman come to the religious by different routes.[36] The first echoes William's comments on the religious in *Either/Or*, where he treats the religious as an adjunct to the ethical, and the God-relationship as impersonal.[37] One relates to God not as a singular individual, but as a member of the human race just like any other. In making the ethical resolution and having faith in its outcome, one relates to God, just as any other person can who likewise takes up the universal human task and embraces the essential human nature as free and responsible. This again echoes William's earlier writings; but it is much clearer than William's similar essay 'On the Esthetic Validity of Marriage.' There, the frequent references to God and the religious somewhat obscure the differences between the ethical and the religious; although the views there do not essentially disagree with the later essay, the number of references which intermix religious themes with ethical contexts tends to blur the distinction. Similarly, the 'Ultimatum' reflects William's own inability to distinguish his views from those of a genuine religious individual, and in doing so may render the distinction more obscure for the reader as well. What is obscured in *Either/Or*, the *Stages* is clearly stating about the ethical understanding of the God-relationship.

The claim regarding gender differences in the God-relationship is a little less clear. It is at variance with both *Fear and Trembling* (which specifically rules out gender differences) and Kierkegaard's direct writings.[38] The claim is linked to the Judge's belief that woman is less reflective than man, a belief that seems a little unclear itself since he does not seem to think her views are any less intelligent or worthwhile. But while he writes at length of how the man's falling in love should lead to ethical reflection, resolution, and faith, the woman is said to be transferred straight from the esthetic immediacy of erotic love to the religiously based love on which her marriage will rest. If by this William means essentially what Kierkegaard means when he distinguishes between the 'simple man' who knows the essential ethical and religious verities and the 'simple wise man' who knows that he knows, or knows that he does not know, then this would be a harmless (albeit clumsy) attempt at egalitarianism.[39] The reflective person arrives through reflection and striving where the unreflective person arrives more easily, the task matching itself to each one's particular abilities. But if he means that the religious is something which can be reached immediately, then this seems to be at variance with Kierkegaard's expressed views and those of his religious pseudonyms. We consistently see in Kierkegaard's writings (to this point) that the appearance of guilt-consciousness is treated as an essential prelude to the development of the religious consciousness, and that a consciousness of sin is an essential forerunner to Christianity. William's picture tends to eliminate the essentially moral nature of the God-relationship, as he depicts the woman as 'swooning' her way from the esthetic to the religious with the support of her ethically reflective beloved, as well as making the religious something of a substitute for the ethical—a condescension for the reflectively impaired. The egalitarian nature of the religious, which Kierkegaard takes pains to emphasize in his direct writings, is all but denied here.[40] And perhaps worst of all, the religious becomes more ambiguous, so that one is not sure whether it is one aspect of the ethical, or an eternal mood coloring the man's reflection and the woman's immediacy, or an independent relation to the eternal valid in its own right, which undergirds the ethical resolution. William's views on the religious are seen to be mistaken at some points, and simply muddled and undeveloped on many others. His God is vague, distant, and impersonal; and his theology is likewise as vague and ill-defined as its object. It is clear that he is in what Haufniensis called the 'first ethics'; he has not yet really come up against the problem of sin, and believes it is still possible to fulfill its requirements. He has not encountered the problem of sin, or felt the need of a 'second ethics.'

'*A Story of Suffering:*' The third and largest section of the *Stages*, which deals with the religious stage, clears up this confusion. The chapter is divided into two main parts: the first, an 'imaginary construction' known as 'Quidam's Diary,' chronicling a broken betrothal and its psychological aftermath for the young man who broke it; and second, the pseudonymous author's comments on the diary. Unlike 'The Seducer's Diary,' which is presented as the actual journal of a (fictitious) person, Quidam and his diary are claimed as an imaginary construction of the pseudonym Frater Taciturnus, a psychologist of the religious. Its material and style are reminiscent in many ways of *Repetition*; both deal with the case of a young man who breaks his betrothal, renounces the universal ethical principle of marriage for purely private reasons, and who now continues to wrestle with the question of his own guilt and whether he might find some higher justification beyond the ethical. He knows himself to be morally guilty for having broken his commitment, but he believes that he would also have been blameworthy to have carried through on his ethical commitment. He cheats his fiancée by breaking his promise, but he feels he would cheat her more by marrying, for he would be psychologically and spiritually incapable of the intimacy marriage partners should share. In both works, the young man wrestles with the guilt of being outside the ethical and unable to fulfill its infinite demands, and the suffering of having to renounce the joys of both the finite and the universal which normal human life offers, in order to follow a personal and private prompting in the direction of the religious. In both the theme of deception is prominent; in *Repetition*, the plan to deceive the girl out of the relationship is abandoned, and the young man simply leaves without a word, while in 'Guilty?/Not/Guilty?' he actually does carry through such a plan. In both works the theme of noncommunication is therefore prominent as well; whereas Judge William has claimed that it is an ethical duty to disclose oneself, these young men renounce disclosure and practice evasion. In both works, the young man is shattered by his experience, and turns to the religious for comfort, healing, and a reintegration of his personality—a new sense of wholeness and meaning. In *Repetition*, the subject finds a new life, a new beginning as a poet, which he proclaims to be just the repetition he needed; in the *Stages* by contrast the young man remains caught in a psychological trap of his own devising, endlessly worrying on his past actions and choices connected with the engagement and breakup.

Like the esthetic and ethical sections of this book, this chapter thus reworks and clarifies themes previously examined in earlier works. Whereas Constantin leaves his readers to puzzle out for themselves how or whether his subject attained the repetition he sought (or even what a repetition is), Taciturnus presents a subject who clearly remains caught in the demonic (though in the direction of the good), unable to find the newness of a true repetition. Whereas Constantin presents a subject who retains the religious as a mood within the esthetic category of the poetic, Taciturnus takes pains to separate them; in fact, he is the first pseudonym to clearly and directly lay out the theory of the stages which has structured the pseudonymous authorship, writing:

There are three existence-spheres: the esthetic, the ethical, the religious. The metaphysical is abstraction, and there is no human being who exists metaphysically. The metaphysical, the ontological, is, but it does not exist, for when it exists it does so in the esthetic, in the ethical, in the religious, and when it is, it is the abstraction from or a *prius* to the esthetic, the ethical, the religious. The ethical sphere is only a transition sphere, and therefore its highest expression is repentance as a negative action. The esthetic sphere is the sphere of immediacy, the ethical the sphere of requirement (and this requirement is so infinite that the individual always goes bankrupt), the religious the sphere of fulfillment, but please note, not a fulfillment such as when one fills an alms box or a sack with gold, for repentance has specifically created a boundless space, and as a consequence the religious contradiction: simultaneously to be out on 70,000 fathoms of water and yet be joyful.[41]

Either/Or discusses the esthetic and the ethical, the distinctions between them and the transition between them. It then goes on to hint at the transition from the ethical to the religious, although it does not clearly present this transition since the pseudonyms themselves are unclear about it. *Repetition* and *Fear and Trembling* most clearly deal with the transition to the religious, though again somewhat cryptically. Both present the transition as if it were somehow exceptional; only *Fear and Trembling* suggests that the transition might be triggered by a universal crisis such as guilt.[42] The esthete Constantin does not fully comprehend either the ethical or the religious, and hence fails to adequately present their interrelationship. Taciturnus uses an exceptional subject to present, in the clarity of exaggeration, guilt, sin, suffering, inwardness, repentance, and the search for meaning or justification, which are essential elements in the religious life; and highlighted by absence is redemption. Because Quidam cannot carry through his repentance before God and find a sense of forgiveness there, he is unable to let go of the guilt of his past. Because he does not let go, he continues to take responsibility for what can only be left to God: the fate of his beloved, the consequences of his actions once they have left his hand, the world and its reactions to him. He thus becomes his own demon, as he tortures himself more rather than accept divine forgiveness and restitution.

'Guilty/Not Guilty' is thus very different from *Repetition*, despite the fact that the former revisits themes of the latter. In its examination of guilt, suffering, sin, and the transition from the ethical to the religious, it draws together concepts from *Repetition, Fear and Trembling, Concept of Anxiety*, and the *Fragments*. And in doing so, it summarizes and structures a conceptual framework implicit in these earlier pseudonymous works. Quidam has found himself outside the universal through his own guilt. This guilt is largely unavoidable; once he has made the initial mistake of becoming engaged (a perfectly natural and even worthy act), he is unable to find a way out of his moral quagmire. Whatever he does is wrong; if he marries, he saddles his beloved with an unsuitable spouse unable to truly return her love or offer the openness a spouse deserves, while if he breaks off he betrays his word at least—and at worst, he will have a murder on his conscience, if the girl really does die of heartbreak as she has predicted. All of this shows the infinite demand of the ethical; it asserts itself even over acts done innocently (though carelessly), and continues to assert its claims until the subject reaches the breaking point.

His guilt has placed him outside the ethical and moves him toward the religious. What he needs to do is to repent, and then to release himself, the girl, and everything else into God's judgment and God's providence.[43] He lacks the sense of resignation, of renunciation, of the humility essential for faith. He simply does not trust God to take over, or at least he does not allow God to do so; therefore he devises and executes an elaborate plan of deception allegedly for the girl's sake, and continues to be obsessed with her progress afterwards. He will not relinquish control, and this works him more and more deeply into the demonic. Frater Taciturnus claims that the erotic relationship is of minor concern; what he is interested in is the religious in general.[44] Quidam has fallen into sin because of his unfaithful response to his own guilt. Or, in the language of Haufniensis, his anxiety about having (possibly) become guilty through becoming engaged breeds further anxiety, until he becomes caught up in his own inclosing reserve as a demoniac.[45] He loses his freedom to act or to disclose himself, although he remains obsessed with themes of hidden guilt versus open evil, and seems convinced that to reveal one's own guilt is itself morally (and religiously) good.[46] His loss of the originality of true repetition, and his enslavement to habit instead, marks his state as demonic.[47]

The 'suffering' in this 'story of suffering' is not simply the pain of a broken heart or worry over guilt; it is rather the suffering of having left the joys of erotic love and the universal validation of the marriage bond without being able to fully break with either immediacy or the universal so as to attain a purely eternal existence, free from the demands and claims finitude continues to press. This suffering grows from his essential heterogeneity with finitude; he has left the immediate and the universal behind, but cannot fully enter the infinite and eternal as long as he lives. He has died to this world, but still must live in it. He is caught between the life he would like to lead and cannot fully renounce—the life of a husband, with human passions, relationships, and a body such as anyone would consider normal for a human—and the life which now appears before him instead: an individual relationship to the eternal, infinite God. Even if he were to find faith, this suffering would remain as part of the essential human condition, though it would find some validation in being related to faith. As it stands, he keeps the suffering of the religious, but does not embrace the comfort of a full relationship to the eternal.

While the *Stages* and Frater Taciturnus deal extensively with the transition from the ethical to the religious, this book gives scant attention to how a religious person ought to live, make moral choices, and so on. In fact, the pseudonym claims not to be religious, and hence has no actual experience of what such a life would be like.[48] But while Taciturnus is vague on the content of a religious ethics, his experiment makes clear that there must be such a thing. Quidam's fall into the demonic results in his obsession with religious concerns, coupled with a total loss of concrete social relatedness. All the fruits of the ethical—responsibility, freedom, integrity—have vanished from his life. This makes him a particularly good case for Taciturnus, just as Freud found neurotics helpful for understanding healthy minds: the sickness exaggerates certain elements while suppressing others, so that parts of the structure become clearer. To see how the exaggerated elements should function, one need only consider how they would function in a healthy psyche, in proportion and integrated with the whole. Taciturnus uses Quidam to demonstrate religious disclosure, guilt, and so on by creating him as a demoniac for whom these issues are fixations, and for whom other potentially relevant but distracting issues (such as religious ethics) are conspicuous by absence.

C. *Conclusion*: Quidam fits earlier pseudonymous descriptions of the demonic quite closely. De Silentio said the demonic merman needed to confess and disclose himself if he were to be saved. Haufniensis likewise said the same, identifying the demonic with 'inclosing reserve.' Both pseudonyms claim that the individual becomes demonic through lack of faith. They describe the demoniac as a person who has failed ethically, and chooses self-punishment rather than repentance, confession, and faith. Haufniensis specifically identifies the demonic state as not just an aberrant reaction to sin, but itself a new sin.

The cure for Quidam is presented in Kierkegaard's discourse 'On the Occasion of a Confession.' Disclosure to his jilted beloved is the only way he can be reintegrated into the social world, and acceptance of grace is the only way he can be healed before God. Kierkegaard presents confession as the moment of isolation before God, but it is also a moment of community as each individual personally confesses before God.[49] And confession is not 'just religious'; it clearly involves the ethical as one confesses guilt, and it involves the esthetic in its passions (wonder, fear, earnestness).

Frater Taciturnus writes that the ethical is a transitional stage between the esthetic and the religious; if this is so, then the Judge is a case of arrested development. In one sense, he seems much healthier than Quidam, or the esthetes of the earlier speeches; but on the other, he has not realized something which Quidam has seen, and it is this ignorance which is his bliss. He has not recognized his own guilt, and hence has not had the sense of being excluded from the universal which is part of Quidam's suffering. But this is a delusion, for as the sermon he himself quoted in an earlier book says, 'in relation to God we are always in the wrong.'[50] He does not have as clear a conception of God or himself as he thinks he has. And in being unable to fully repent, he also has less community with his wife than he imagines; he cannot really seek her forgiveness as he should, nor can he fully grasp the essential equality between them, because he has not had the experience of being nothing before God. William is attempting to live in the 'first ethics,' which Haufniensis tells us is impossible; once one has sinned one fails to attain its ideality, and must begin over with faith and the 'second ethics' faith allows. William simply does not recognize his sin, and so does not see his need for salvation.

The discourse 'On the Occasion of a Wedding,' by contrast, shows a healthy ethical relationship, because it has been integrated within the religious. Only by having a true understanding of God can one have a true understanding of life and oneself; this is what the Judge lacks, and this weakens his marriage.[51] The ethical and the marriage relationship are completed in the religious life; again, what had been dysfunctional has become vitalizing by ceasing to stand on its own, and taking its proper place in the greater whole.

'At a Graveside' also captures the essence of its esthetic counterpart in the *Stages*, and cures it by integrating it into the religious life. The essential insight of the esthetic, as shown by the destruction of the banquet hall after the speeches, is this: Everything dies, and can never come back.[52] Immediacy must be grasped before it its too late, for that is all there is. Victor calls the banqueters to their places with a speech linking the night's festivities with 'the earnest thought of death.' And in truth, they are them-selves dead men; they speak of love, but are dead to its reality, and to the other. In all their talk of love, the reality of another person never arises; nor can it, in the esthetic view. Because they have seen that everything dies, they grasp after immediacy with the desperation of Tantalus, and with as much success. They must amuse themselves, to keep the realization of their own emptiness at bay. They must be drunk before they speak, for sobriety would allow reflection, and that might lead to awareness, which is what they dread.

The discourse, too, considers 'the earnest thought of death.' However, while the esthetes consider the coming death of everything else, the dis-course urges the reader to consider his or her own death. With that earnest reflection banquets, erotic affairs, speeches, and all else sink into the insig-nificance they deserve; and the earnest one is left with only the question: What more is there, which might prove truly real? The realization of the emptiness of finitude, which by itself leads to the perdition of the Seducer, can also be the first step in the religious life and is the constant foundation for all true religiousness.

It does seem that there are correspondences between these two books, and that the strongest correspondences connect the second chapters, and the first and third chapters of each book. There are esthetic elements in the 'Confession' discourse, for example, so there are grounds for dispute; but the most likely explanation is that when Kierkegaard writes in his own name and seeks to portray real life, the spheres are not so tidily separate. In the religious life, the esthetic and the ethical continue in harmony.

Haufniensis has said that to deny the reality of sin is itself a sin, once Christianity has revealed it. Therefore, all three of the 'stages on life's way' presented here are sinful, as none is faith. And one of the results of this sin is the fragmentation of the spheres of existence. When any one sphere is lived in isolation, it fails to produce a full individual. In the three discourses, Kierkegaard presents the esthetic and ethical as healed and integrated within the religious life. Faith is salvation, not just of the 'immortal soul' but also for the integrity and health of the living self.

Chapter Six

Sin and Salvation in the *Concluding Unscientific Postscript*

I. Nature of Subjectivity

The *Postscript* was intended to conclude not just the unfinished work left by the *Fragments*, but Kierkegaard's work as an author begun with *Either/Or*. Thus, at this point in his authorship Kierkegaard was going to 'clothe the question in its historical costume,' and show the practical implications of the esoteric and abstract meanderings of the pseudonyms. If, as he said in the *Point of View*, his authorship was a concerted stratagem to infiltrate, undermine and expose the fallacies of Christendom, here is where this strategy will be completed.[1] The *Postscript* not only refers back to the *Fragments*, but back even as far as the *Concept of Irony* to correct and explicate Kierkegaard's works. In doing so, it provides the fruits of these earlier labors, as well as of Climacus' own thoughts.

A. *The Objective Issue*: The *Concluding Unscientific Postscript* begins with a fairly straightforward argument:

a) There are two ways to approach the truth: the objective and the subjective;
b) The objective way fails; therefore
c) The subjective way is the only valid way to approach the truth.

Part One in particular depends on Climacus' first book, which has itself already begun the task of distinguishing the detached, rationalist approach to Truth from the passionate, faithful response of true Christianity. The issue in Part One is first to finish discrediting the objective approach and to firmly establish the sole validity of the subjective path for existing thinkers.

There are two alleged objective paths to the truth of Christianity, says Climacus: the historical and the speculative. The first concerns itself with

the historical facts of Christianity, and the historical succession leading
from the original events to the present; the second concerns itself with
the philosophical truths contained within the dogmas and beliefs of
Christianity.[2] The historical approach treats the origins of the Scripture or
the Church as certain. However, no historical knowledge can have true certainty, as Climacus argues in both the *Fragments* and *Postscript.* Speculative
philosophy takes Christianity as given and then seeks to permeate this given
historical phenomenon with thought, to uncover and grasp its inner ratio-
nality. But if all historical truths are contingent, and all historical belief
essentially decision rather than deduction, then the speculative approach
too is essentially wrong-headed. It treats its object as given, as if it were
certain that this church is the true Christian church, and all its members
are in fact Christians; or more accurately, it doesn't even concern itself
with questions of the Church's faithfulness to the original impulse, or the
individual's faithfulness to the message. The faithfulness of the individual,
the institution, and even of the speculator, are all irrelevant. But, if the
issue is one's eternal happiness, the state of the individual is precisely the
question; so speculative philosophy leads away from the truth, not toward
it. Climacus writes:

> What if this entire undertaking were a chimera, what if it could not be
> done; what if Christianity is indeed subjectivity, is inward deepening,
> that is, what if only two kinds of people can know something about it:
> those who are impassionedly, infinitely interested in their eternal hap-
> piness and in faith build this happiness on their faith-bound relation to
> it, and those who with the opposite passion (yet with passion) reject
> it—the happy and the unhappy lovers? Consequently, what if objective
> indifference cannot come to know anything whatever? . . . With refer-
> ence to a kind of observation in which it is of importance that the
> observer be in a definite state, it holds true that when he is not in that
> state he does not know anything whatever. Now, he can deceive one by
> saying that he is in that state although he is not, but if it turns out so
> fortunately that he himself declares that he is not in the requisite state,
> he deceives no one.[3]

The *Fragments* has already made clear that the 'requisite state' is faith;
even the (objective) eyewitness to a miracle, or to the God as Teacher,
gains nothing if he or she does not possess the eyes of faith; and one loses
nothing in missing the chance to see with physical eyes, provided one has
faith.[4] So speculative philosophy, far from comprehending the essence

of Christianity, is actually oriented away from the central message of Christianity.

So there are two objective alleged paths to the truth of Christianity. One makes Christianity into a purely historical fact, whose truth can be seen by historical investigation and its historical fruits. The other makes Christianity into a philosophical truth, to be known through rational inquiry. Both fail to truly understand Christianity's message. Thus, the only true approach to Christianity is through subjectivity.

B. *The Subjective Issue.* The second, larger part of the *Concluding Unscientific Postscript* is an exploration of the question raised by the first part: Given that the objective way is a religious and ethical dead end, how should the subjective thinker go about thinking, communicating, and living? If the ethical and the religious are not the objective phenomena which speculative philosophy (and more commonplace views) has assumed, then what are they?

1. *Theses Attributable to Lessing.* This investigation begins with Lessing, who is used as both a source and a role model. In both capacities, Climacus admits he uses Lessing rather freely; Lessing is presented as an archetypal subjective thinker, who concentrates his activity in existence rather than dry pronouncements.[5] Thus Climacus offers these theses '*attributable* to Lessing,' not simply quotes and instructions; the spirit of the subjective thinker is more important than the thinker's objective words. Together the theses (with commentary) sketch the distinction between the objective and the subjective, and what thinking (and the thinker) ought to be if the subjective way is in fact the truth.

In all this, the objective way is allowed full credit within its proper limits. Ordinary communication is largely objective; and rightly so, since most ordinary communication aims simply to exchange information or to obtain some concrete result.[6] But the subjective thinker works in the realm of existence, where both the knower and the known are in a process of becoming. Communication here must be understood as inviting the subject along a particular path of becoming, not as giving a particular result.[7] The subjective thinker may have some element of positivity, but always mixed with the negative, recognizing the essential uncertainty of knowledge.[8] Large portions of the *Fragments* have already been devoted to demonstrating this, so it is unnecessary for Climacus to belabor the point. What is new is discussion of how the subjective thinker thinks in the face of this uncertainty. This is not to say that the subjective thinker knows *nothing*, but rather that the subjective thinker *knows* nothing; there are a host of things which the thinker grasps in an approximation process, and a large realm where this is an appropriate form of 'knowledge.' In other words, Climacus' views do not dictate an absolute skepticism; the calculation of probabilities that goes on every day is fitting and necessary in most areas of life. But this sort of objective, probabilistic thinking is inappropriate when one is thinking one's own existence. Here, one needs to banish doubt, and act decisively—that is, one must make a decision and act on it, knowing that all existence is uncertain, that there is no smooth transition from calculations and reason to the choice, that there is always some sort of gap that must be bridged by a leap.

It is clear from this discussion that the 'leap' does not mean anything like 'believing the logically absurd.' While Climacus does use the phrase 'by virtue of the absurd,' this is taken to be the manner in which one decides to believe—believing beyond proof. The evidence or grounds for belief are conceded to be just as good as any other historical belief, which is clearly *not* absurd in normal parlance. The point is that the very nature of religious belief dictates that it is reached by a decision which is not determined by evidence or probabilities but is reached essentially by an act of will. While other sorts of belief may be held tentatively, as the evidence mandates, the decision on which one's eternal happiness rests must go beyond tentativeness. The only way a person can banish doubt and hold firm to such a belief is through a resolution.

It is equally clear that Climacus is not here addressing the concept of grace, as this is understood in the *Fragments*. While his original thought-project assumed that no one could ever want to come to the truth apart from grace, in this discussion Climacus claims that anyone who wants to believe can do so. How one comes to want to believe is left undecided for now.

All of this leads up to the fourth thesis attributable to Lessing: that if God could give one the choice, the eternal striving for truth (even if accompanied by incessant error) would be a more fitting request for an *existing* individual to make, than the request to actually *possess* truth.[9] An existing individual is in a constant process of becoming, finitude, temporality; and for such a being, *striving* for truth makes sense. On the other hand, for such a being to actually *possess* truth would be nonsense. Specifically, the claim of systematic philosophy to have grasped eternal truth and to have expressed it in time is ridiculous. The System is not finished, indeed cannot be finished in time, since it attempts to understand and comprehend with absolute certainty all of existence. Existence can only be understood with certainty after the fact. Even Hegel agrees with Climacus that the owl of Minerva flies only at dusk; or as Kierkegaard famously objected to

Hegel, 'It is quite true what philosophy says: that life must be understood backwards. But then one forgets the other principle: that it must be lived forwards.'[10]

This has a number of implications for philosophy, ethics, and religion. First, as Climacus says, a logical system is possible, but a system of existence is impossible. That is, completeness and certainty can only be obtained by completely eliminating any contact with actuality from one's system, reducing it to logical analysis alone.[11] Hegel's attempt to conflate logic and existence, as if pure thought discovers the dialectic in existence, is a 'mystification' and 'ventriloquism' which projects logical concepts onto actuality.[12] It does this by neglecting the fact that systematic philosophy is not carried out by Pure Thought, but by individual thinkers, trapped in existence, who must think under its constraints and must reflect, resolve, doubt, believe with either acknowledged or unwitting uncertainty. It is resolution that overcomes doubt, not reflection: will, not pure intellect.

On the other hand, while existence may be a system for God, it cannot be so for anyone under its rule. An existing individual needs to be a *subjective* thinker, who remembers that he or she is existing and that the truth he or she seeks is to be lived in existence, not thought in eternity. Even if one did somehow come to posses all truth, 'the repetition by which he must indeed fill out his existence, if he is not to go backward . . . will again be a continual striving.'[13] So striving, not reflection, is the fundamental category of existence, which philosophy ought to describe. No philosophical (or theological) system can be either true or healthy for its adherents if it neglects this or deludes people into believing they now have certainty and no longer need strive.

The implications for ethical theory are likewise far-reaching. Climacus thinks thinking must conform to the conditions of existence, a primary characteristic of which is separation.[14] Thought is separate from realization, hence the need to strive to achieve repetition in actuality. What one knows one ought to be is always different from what one merely is, so one must strive to actualize one's ought in life. One lives life forwards, not always knowing the good but always obliged to try to do the good; so one reflects and then chooses, and risks choosing wrongly. One must strive, looking beyond what one already is, and beyond whatever is simply given as an objective moral certainty.

In Hegelian terms, Climacus operates at the level of *moralitat*.[15] Hegel argues that thought should progress beyond such dualistic thinking, which opposes the good against the individual, or separates the individual from the whole of society. Thought should move beyond to the situation of *sittlichkeit,* where the good is finally expressed in social institutions, and one does the good by being a good citizen.[16] In such a situation, moral uncertainty is eliminated, as the good is to be found in objective reality. The subject-object duality is also to be overcome, so the picture of the moral individual struggling to recognize and live out the moral imperative will likewise be superseded.

In other words, the Hegelian judgment is that such thinkers as Climacus are stuck in a lower form of thought, while the systematic philosopher must move beyond such dualisms to realize the rational content expressed socially in the institutions of Christendom. By contrast, Climacus would say that the Hegelian/Christendom position has abandoned ethics and the whole ethical project, treating the question of what a poor, existing individual is to do as an immature preoccupation; while in fact Hegelianism lags far behind, returning to the premoral, esthetic detachment from one's personal existence. And this criticism can be leveled with equal force at any system which would try to shift the moral focus away from the individual and the individual's striving, and focus it instead on objective thinking and social engineering. The Soviet attempt to create a superior person by reshaping society, the liberationist claim that sin lodges primarily in social institutions, the civil religion of the fundamentalists who believe God condemns flag-burners and pacifists for such sins against the status quo—all who seek to locate the ethical-religious good in the objective order and to have certainty in fact fall far below the ethical, no matter to which of the many opposed socio-political or metaphysical systems they choose to surrender themselves.

2. *Becoming Subjective.* The bulk of the *Postscript* is contained in Section II of Part Two. Part Two is a discussion of 'the subjective individual's relationship to the truth of Christianity;' Section II examines 'how subjectivity must be constituted in order that the issue can be manifest to it.'[17] In other words, Part Two examines how one lives as a Christian; objective facts about Christianity are set aside for the most part. Climacus feels he has already established the validity of the subjective over the objective approach, and now seeks to examine the subjective in more detail. And while the discussion of Lessing has served to clarify the nature of subjective thinking, Climacus now proposes to devote the rest of the book to exploring the nature of subjectivity—that is, the nature of the self, the person.

Climacus begins his endeavor by further distinguishing the subjective and the objective, both by suggesting the negatives that would hold if the subjective were not the highest, and arguing that some supposedly essential things are in fact irrelevant to the ethical. In other words, he lays out what is lost or rejected if the objective, or the subjective, way is chosen. In the course of this discussion, Climacus makes some very significant, and at times surprising, comments on the nature of the ethical.

What might come as a shock to some readers of Kierkegaard is the description by Climacus of the 'deceitful lover' who 'does not want to understand that there is nothing between him and God but the ethical.'[18] One cannot help but be struck by the contradictory language of *Fear and Trembling*, where the religious is actually opposed to the ethical, the faithful person is defined by his willingness to do the unethical, and the ethical by contrast is precisely the route away from the religious. More surprising, Climacus himself makes several references to de Silentio's writings, always favorably, without mentioning this contradiction. The only explanation is that Climacus simply doesn't see a contradiction.

If Climacus doesn't see a contradiction, then either he is a fool, or there really is none. Given that Climacus and de Silentio share the same mind, it is more likely that Climacus does in fact see truly, although (either by accident or intent) the bridge between his language and de Silentio's has not been presented. In his discussion of *Fear and Trembling*, de Silentio regularly equates 'the ethical' with Hegelian, socially based ethics; so that 'the religious' represents the individual's search for validation in the eternal apart from social standards. In these cases, *Fear and Trembling* identifies 'the ethical' with the objective, whether the socially concrete or the rationally necessary.

Climacus, by contrast, equates the ethical with the subjective. He lauds the 'subjective ethical' over the objectifying tendencies of speculative philosophy.[19] The ethical is inwardness, having essentially to do with the individual, and the individual's intentions.[20] The ethical is the absolute.[21] The ethical is essentially the expression of freedom. As Climacus writes:

> In fables and fairy tales there is a lamp called the wonderful lamp; when it is rubbed, the spirit appears. Jest! But freedom, that is the wonderful lamp. When a person rubs it with ethical passion, God comes into existence for him. And look, the spirit of the lamp is a servant . . . , but the person who rubs the wonderful lamp of freedom becomes a servant— the spirit is the Lord.[22]

In other words, the ethical is freedom. When one truly lives by ethical passion, one is truly free. Furthermore, it is only as a truly, ethically free individual that one can come into any relationship to God. The irony of this dialectic is that the truly free person thus becomes the servant of the

Lord, and seemingly unfree; and likewise, the one who is free from the Lord is unfree, has not even experienced the wonderful lamp of freedom. At no time, it seems, is the person fully his or her own master.

The ethical is the category of repetition, wherein one actualizes whatever truth one has apprehended in one's life.[23] It is the subjective relationship to objective truth-claims such as the nature of God and the good. It is the continuity of the individual's life. And it is the individual's freedom, the stepping out of the individual from the bondage to the external world; it is the individual becoming an individual, a personality. And in this, the individual comes into relationship with God.

But despite his higher esteem for the ethical, Climacus has no esteem for one element which many would consider the essence of the ethical: actually doing good, helping others, using one's talents in a meaningful way. He writes:

> The deceitful lover . . . does not want to understand that there is nothing between him and God but the ethical; he does not want to understand that he ought to be made enthusiastic by it; he does not want to understand that God, without doing any injustice and without denying his nature, which is love, could create a human being endowed with capacities unmatched by all others, place him in a remote spot, and say to him, 'Now go and live the human life through with a strenuousness unmatched by all others, work so that one-half would be sufficient to transform an age, but you and I are alone in this. All your effort will have no importance whatever for any other human being, and yet you shall, do you understand, you shall be enthusiastic, because that is the highest.'[24]

Many people today would regard this attitude as immoral. A common criticism of Kierkegaard's writings in general has been that they unduly emphasis the inward and personal, needlessly and irrationally denigrating actual ethical acts. To some extent, it would seem that Kierkegaard came to agree with this view; his later works (particularly after 1848) place far greater emphasis on the external manifestations of one's inner dispositions. Here, however, my purpose is to focus on Climacus' reason for making this point. He has some clearly specified opponents: philosophers and theologians who make external works and standards the essential criteria of the value of a person's life. No objective criteria, says Climacus, are of ultimate ethical importance. One person may be remembered as a benefactor of humanity, another die unremembered and unmourned, without either differing one whit in their ethical efforts or intentions.

It all largely comes down to luck, or Providence, depending on your beliefs; external, nonmoral criteria decide the success of one's moral efforts, and how history will judge them. And if external, extramoral circumstances dictate the results of one's ethical action, while only internal moral criteria apply to one's ethical intentions, it is on the internal which ethics must concentrate.

Notice, however, that Climacus is not urging ethical passivity or quietism. The ethical person is to strive enthusiastically to do good, but he or she must not become attached to the results of these actions. One must do one's best, without looking back or looking around to see if a fickle world nurtures or rewards one's good works. The ethical viewpoint is thus also a blindness: sharp-sighted to inspect itself, sharp-sighted to seek the good to do, but blind to the fruits of all this ethical striving.

Climacus' critique can be directed against a variety of positions that seek objective criteria for ethical success, but his particular target is of course Hegelianism, most particularly as it was understood by his Golden Age contemporaries. Climacus repeatedly attacks the Hegelian claim that 'the inner is the outer,' that inner principles are only real or relevant insofar as they have concrete effects and manifestations, or that it is in some way inevitable that they do so.[25] In proposing this principle, Hegelian philosophy measured moral greatness by its effects on world history; the morally significant was the one whose acts made it into the history books. The category 'great' became more important than 'good.'[26]

Climacus is particularly concerned about the moral elitism this implies. While the king is included because he is a king, and the hermit because of his extraordinary particularity, the vast majority of people are treated as unimportant. They simply aren't relevant to speculative 'moral' philosophy; only the concretion of ideas in the history of societies and extraordinary individuals warrants the attention of the speculative philosopher. By contrast, ethics applies to each individual as an individual, equally. While speculative philosophy may see the millions of masses as little more than grist for the world-historical mill, the ethical judges each individual as infinitely important, because subjectivity is infinitely important, infinitely more important than any objectivity.[27]

Summary: The first chapter of the second section of the *Postscript* sets out to contrast the objective and subjective ways to approach the truth, seeking to establish whether the essence of human nature is to become more objective, reflective, detached, and 'rational'/or subjective, resolute, interested, and 'passionate.' It is widely assumed, and not just by Hegelians, that the mature and fully developed human will turn more toward the objective pole. This belief rests on the opinion that the 'subjective' indicates the selfish, eccentric, arbitrary, or other 'accidental' elements of a person, so that to become 'subjective' would be the same as becoming more childish, self-absorbed, quirky, or even delusional. But this, says Climacus, is not the true subjectivity. While both the Hegelian and Climacus agree that the essence of human nature is to grow beyond childish antics and whims, they disagree as to how this is to be done.[28] The objective thinker believes that the way to grow beyond such unhealthy subjectivism is to become objective, more detached from the world and oneself; whereas the subjective thinker believes that the way to escape subjectivism is to nurture a true subjectivity, a real concern and intentionality for the quality and direction of one's own development.

Thus there are two possible routes to escape the hazards of immaturity and subjectivism: which one is the true one? Climacus argues that the objective way actually distorts human nature and destroys all sense of the individual or individual worth. In the objective approach, only the race, or at most a few salient individuals who personify elements of the race, receive any attention or really matter. The subjective approach, by contrast, places everyone on an equal footing; everyone is infinitely important, and judged not by the comparative grading scale of history but the absolute individual judgment of ethics. In objectivity, the individual and the ethical cannot even come into view, whereas these are the essence of subjectivity.

Climacus concludes the chapter by demonstrating something of what the subjective approach to truth actually entails.[29] While objectivity seeks truth in general, abstractly, apart from particular persons or circumstances, subjectivity considers only those concepts which relate to existence, and then only as those concepts relate to the thinker's own life. The first writes and reads learned essays on death or the immortality of the soul; the second asks only, 'What does my mortality mean to me? What does it mean that I might have an immortal soul?' The first is so concerned about making a mistake that the thinker may spend his or her whole life examining the arguments *pro e contra*, until finally dying without ever answering the question. The second is so concerned about living badly that the thinker must have the question resolved (or rather, must resolve the question) so that he or she may begin to live in accordance to the doctrine he or she claims to accept.

The chapter ends with an autobiographical passage apparently intended both to ironically tease the reader, and to illustrate the true, subjective approach to life.[30] In contrast to the rather bombastic claim of a certain Hegelian to have been converted to speculative philosophy by a miracle,

Climacus depicts his own beginning as an author as quite arbitrary and even frivolous. Barely concealed in this description, however, is the essential seriousness that he is consistent with his own professed beliefs, particularly regarding the innate uncertainty of life and truth-claims. Whereas the speculative philosopher preaches the doctrine of the race, the rational, and the detached, the thinker (a certain Dr. Hjoretspring) is irrationally self-important; he and his doctrine are both so important that he comes to it by a violation of the rational order that appoints him spokesman for the doctrine that the rational is the real. Climacus, by contrast, claims that the utter uncertainty of life shows that what goes on in this world is not ultimately important, and his style, his form of communication, and even his life reflect this uncertainty and this sense that the world (and he himself) are not that important. Still, he is at least serious enough to be consistent, to judge himself by his own words, so that he repeats in his life what he claims as the truth. He allows what he claims as the truth to claim him, too.

It is generally assumed that moral maturity involves a process of becoming less self-centered, more able to see another's perspective, less dominated by irrational passions, and hence more objective. This chapter suggests, however, that the pursuit of objectivity can have highly immoral and inhuman results, many of which were mirrored in fact by the attitudes of Kierkegaard's contemporaries. The Golden Age had a decidedly 'mandarin' attitude: certain elite individuals were seen as the bearers of value, and the others could either gain value derivatively by aping their betters, or be essentially left out of the spiritual process of history and culture.[31] The vast majority was only partly capable of attaining the full human life. Instead of being directed to value the ethical tasks of their own lives, these people were encouraged to look to the elite for their values and morality. The elite for their part were not so much encouraged to look to morality either, but to their own self-expression and self-development; the exemplar of the spiritual elite was the poet, not the judge or preacher. So for both high and low, this objectivity militated against the ethical viewpoint of good/or evil, and in favor of a distinction of great/or plebeian.

3. *Truth is Subjectivity*: The second chapter of the second part of Kierkegaard's *Concluding Unscientific Postscript* surely ranks as one of the most controversial passages ever published in the history of philosophy. The title of the chapter invites shock, bemusement, and/or incredulity, an invitation that has been accepted repeatedly since it was first issued. The problem of interpretation is increased when this chapter is presented in

isolation from the rest of the book, let alone the bulk of the authorship, in some philosophical anthology or undergraduate survey class. Problems with this text are not limited to undergrads, however; plenty of informed, intelligent scholars have wondered what to do with it.

Too often, 'truth is subjectivity' is interpreted as meaning 'truth is subjective.' As long as the individual believes strongly enough, that person is said to be 'in the truth.' Questions of the reality of the object of belief are held to be irrelevant, and the answers arbitrary. Alasdair MacIntyre, for example, argues that Kierkegaard's whole program is to argue that persons ought to adopt authoritative principles '*for no reason*.'[32] The choice to be esthetic, ethical, or Christian is radical and criterionless, essentially arbitrary. Only the sense of commitment to these first principles gives them any authority for the individual. And this, says MacIntyre, is self-contradictory; any principle adopted for no reason can be abandoned for no reason as well, and cannot have any real authority.[33]

It is useful to begin by remembering that 'what is being discussed here is essential truth, or the truth that is related essentially to existence.'[34] That is, there is no question here as to physical realities or other objects of 'objective' truth-value, which Climacus would say are rightly treated in the approximation-process of ordinary historical belief.[35] The topic here is ethical-religious truth, those claims to truth that essentially relate to how one lives one's life. Those are the sorts of things that either one consciously decides or the drift of one's life decides for one, because merely living forces some sort of tacit choice.[36] One cannot live one's life as if it were equally probable that there is or is not a God, or a final judgment; one either lives as if one thought there were or weren't such things. Clearly, a large part of Climacus' maxim is simply a plea for consistency between what one claims is truly ultimate, and how one lives one's life.[37]

The sort of belief proportioned to the evidence (such as Hume's mitigated skepticism) is fine for matters that do not essentially touch one's existence or life-choices. But for other matters, simply living, deciding, valuing, all constitute either/or choices. One cannot decide to be partially faithful or good; to be partially faithful is not to be faithful at all. One must resolve any uncertainty, either by finishing the research and adding up the evidence to find the sum, or by a resolution that closes the books on further reckoning. Unfortunately, as Climacus has argued, while one exists the only option is to settle doubt by resolution, by faith, by a leap.

Defining the concept of 'truth' more closely has helped some; but we must furthermore define the concept 'subjectivity.' Here is where so many anthologies and survey courses fail, and even intelligent scholars can go astray. When Socrates is said to be 'subjectively in the truth,' Climacus discusses his passion and his consistency as elements of this.[38] But let us remember the lessons of the previous chapter of the *Postscript*: 'subjectivity' is above all *moral* subjectivity. One becomes more of a subject by becoming more ethical, by morally striving with passion, and by becoming morally self-aware. In the *Fragments* we saw that it was after serious self-examination and earnest ethical investigation that Socrates ran into the paradox that obscured everything for him, that he did not know whether he himself was something divine or monstrous, more good or evil—in short, his moral striving led him to the problem of sin.[39] This is true subjectivity: not just to will with passion what one believes, but to continue the process of willing with passion until (as William and Climacus have said) life shows one whether one has made (or is living) a mistake.[40]

This is the way one must interpret Kierkegaard's claim that in Christianity there is a 'how' which is also a 'what.' It is not, as Pojman suggests, that reason flails about until it hooks onto the most absurd object of faith it can find, so that it might find its own downfall.[41] While the cognitive repellence of Christianity may increase the primacy and purity of faith, it is not the main 'selling point' of Christianity, despite what parts of the *Fragments* may seem to suggest.[42] Rather, the true recommendation of Christianity, which turns it from an absurdity to a life-necessity for the believer, is the problem of one's own sin encountered as the problems of guilt and 'radical evil' when one's moral striving has been allowed to spend freely fulfilling one's moral debts, until it has bankrupted itself.

To be a subject or to be subjectively in the truth is not just to be fervent: it is to be ethically fervent. It is not just to fiercely and devotedly pursue what one believes, but to fiercely and devotedly pursue the good. If 'truth is subjectivity,' then truth is the lifelong pursuit of ethical and religious development.

Of the two relationships to the truth, the objective way pursues objective certainty as its guarantee against error and madness; but objective certainty is a chimera for any existing knower. Even if the object of knowledge is an eternal object (such as 'the good') the knower is not eternal, and hence is not finished; thus existential knowledge is always a striving, a struggle to attain and reaffirm one's realization. The objective pursuit of the truth turns the knower away from his or her own state to consider the object; objective truth is that which holds the same for any knower, for the knower-in-general. But just as objectivity demands the knower abstract away from his or her own existence, so the results of objectivity apply only to the abstract knower-in-general, who is finished and need not struggle to realize the results of his or her knowledge. For an existing knower, all essential knowledge is an unfinished result, since the knower is unfinished even if the object is finished and perfectly known (which are themselves pretty hefty assumptions).

Thus, the manner of relating to the truth should be one that recognizes that the knower is an existing individual, not an abstract knower-in-general or *sub specie aeternae*. The objective way deemphasized precisely this fact. Furthermore, the fact that the knower exists suggests that the proper object of knowledge should be one that essentially relates to existence, or what it is to exist. One's manner of life is unaffected by world history or molecular biology; but it is defined by what one takes as truly valuable or normative: the good, the true, and the divine.

The subjective truth-relationship accounts for these concerns. First, it is concerned solely with what is truly essential to the knower's existence: ethical and ethical-religious truth. Second, it directs attention toward the subject, and the question of whether the knower is in such a state that he or she could be said to be related to the object. The objective person might pursue knowledge of 'the good' as an object of theoretical curiosity; but the subjective person pursues knowledge of the good in order to do good. It is wrong to seek to know the good and not to seek to do it, even if the 'good' you know is right. The object of your own knowledge will condemn you, even if you fail to condemn yourself.

Thus it is 'in order to clarify the divergence of objective and subjective reflection' that Climacus redescribes subjectivity and the subjective approach to truth.[43] It is not, at least initially, the belief that paradox is superior in eliciting subjectivity that leads him to praise it. Rather, it is the fact that truth is a paradox, 'precisely in its relation to an existing subject.'[44] For an existing subject seeking to exist in the truth, this truth is inherently a paradox, an uncertainty that the subject resolves to believe despite its uncertainty. Said another way, one should define the truth as a paradox, not because it is better for truth to be so, but because the truth *is* a paradox—if one is the sort of knower one should seek to be. Contrariwise, if one defines truth as other than a paradox, one *eo ipso* defines the knower as something other than what he or she is (and should strive to be)—an existing individual.

This is the context for understanding Climacus' claim that it is better to be a sincere pagan than a 'Christian' without passion.[45] First, he argues that one must choose which to pursue: objective truth about God or a true God-relationship. An existing individual cannot simply 'choose' not to choose, or choose to be the mediation of God and human, or to pursue the mediation of subjectivity and objectivity. An existing person must choose whether to undertake the endless approximating deliberation of objectively investigating the truth about God, or to seek to have faith in God even knowing that this is uncertain. For the one who lacks passion, and lacks an understanding of what it is to exist, the objective way seems attractive; but for the one who knows what it means to exist and exists with passion, the question of God cannot be a matter of indefinitely extended debate. It is an ethical-religious question, not a philosophical-metaphysical one. The subjective thinker is trying to live as he or she ought, and hence cannot simply leave undecided a vital question that would truly dictate how one ought to live.

This explains Climacus' controversial claim that 'God is indeed a postulate.'[46] For the objective thinker, God is not a postulate; God is an open question, and God can have no real relevance to the objective person's existence until God becomes a confirmed reality that must be taken into account. The objective thinker does not face the necessity of deciding, because the objective thinker lacks passion. But the subjective thinker sees that God cannot be left an open question, nor can God ever be an objectively certain or closed question. Thus the subjective thinker must choose to live *as if* the question really were closed, when by its nature it can only be a paradox. Thus it is not so accurate to say that God is a postulate, as to say that postulating God is a necessity.[47] For the existing subject, God is a matter of essential truth, and the only way to ever relate to God is to recognize this, and to treat God as essential to one's existence. The objective way treats God as optional, and hence fails to really treat God at all.

The question, then, is whether God is a matter of intellectual investigation or moral-existential deliberation. The method of approaching the truth must fit the truth being approached, lest what the knower approaches and perhaps reaches will not be what was originally sought at all. You can no more approach God objectively than you can kill time by shooting it. Whatever the marksman hits will not be time, and whatever the objective thinker defines will not be God. The objective approach is a category mistake.

a. *Implications*: It is widely argued that 'subjectivity' is essentially tied to strength of will; since it takes willpower to believe the uncertain and none to believe the certain, the position which is more dubious will elicit the greater subjectivity. I concede the truth of this to a point; but even more essential to subjectivity is ethical-religious maturity. The truest subjectivity is the one that is the most moral, not just the most willful. The truest subjectivity produces the greatest passion because it is the most decisive;

but decision implies both uncertainty and significant stakes. If it doesn't matter what you believe as long as you are sincere, the decision is arbitrary and there is no real passion. The only *real* choice is one that acknowledges good and evil, real value and real loss, the outcome depending on how one chooses.

The question seems to be: what is it about Christianity that makes it an advance upon the Socratic position? It must be admitted that in some sections of the *Postscript* Climacus seems to argue that Christianity is better because it is more absurd.[48] The Socratic position, says Climacus, was that recollection was possible, but that the knower chooses not to leave existence through speculation, but to continue to exist and live out the truth he or she has believed. The next advance on this position, Climacus argues, is to suggest that the knower is in fact unable to recollect the truth, that the conditions of his or her existence have rendered this impossible. Such a person now *must* pursue a subjective route to the truth, since the objective way is not an annulled possibility but an impossibility. If making the *subject*'s existence decisive rendered an advance in subjectivity, then introducing existence into the *object* should render an even greater advance. Thus Climacus 'posits' that the eternal object has come into time, has been born, that God has lived as a poor existing human being just like one of us. This is 'the absurd,' hence the riskiest belief, and hence requires the most faith, the most subjectivity. In all of this 'advancing' beyond the Socratic position, the ethical is barely mentioned; even 'sin' is sketched in only the barest, most neutral terms.

It certainly appears that Climacus is arguing for the superiority of Christianity because it is absurd; or at least, that he is arguing that an uncertain belief is somehow better than a certainty, because the greater the risk the greater the faith, and a dubious or impossible belief is riskier and hence more passionate. I believe, however, that this is not in fact what Climacus is doing here. His purpose throughout his writings has not been to prove Christianity superior so much as to prove it to be something different from the speculative philosophy which has sought to appropriate it: 'Here the question is only how the speculative explanation is related to the Christianity that it explains.'[49] I believe that is his intent here as well: not so much to show Christianity superior, as to show that whether or not it is truer, it certainly is passionate, subjective, and the very opposite of speculative philosophy.

A careful reading of key parts of the argument will support my view; or at least, passages that appear to contradict it can be shown not to do so. Let us begin this process by examining two quotes from Climacus that seem to argue that certainty is simply 'bad' and uncertainty *qua* uncertainty 'good':

> In the same way a girl has perhaps possessed all the sweetness of being in love through a weak hope of being loved by the beloved, because she herself staked everything on this weak hope; on the other hand, many a wedded matron, who more than once has submitted to the strongest expression of erotic love, has certainly had demonstrations and yet, strangely enough, has not possessed *quod erat demonstandum.* [50]

This passage seems to suggest that the married person does not experience love because she has the certainty of it, whereas the young girl feels it precisely because she is uncertain, has no tangible 'proof,' and hence has greater passion. This would seem an odd thing for Kierkegaard to say (though perhaps not Climacus), since in *Either/Or* he has argued eloquently (albeit pseudonymously) that the task of marriage was precisely to preserve one's first love in a sustained relationship. If this really is impossible, then it would seem that a lasting faith-relationship would also be impossible. But in fact this is not what the passage is saying, as seen from its immediate context. Rather, the passage is suggesting that just as Socrates had a proper relationship to the concept of an 'immortality' despite his professed uncertainty, so too a young girl might feel love even though she has no proof, because she herself is such a person that she can feel love; and likewise, just as the modern Hegelians lack a true faith in immortality despite their proofs, so too a wife may fail to possess a love-relationship despite 'proofs' if she herself has not 'staked everything' on her love as the young girl did. The 'proofs' here are thus not so much the enemies of subjectivity, as simply irrelevant to it. They only become enemies if one relies on them instead of on subjectivity. Just as one's marriage can wither if one relies solely on objective criteria to measure its health, so too one's faith withers if one abandons subjectivity and instead substitutes the objective proofs.

Even stronger praise for uncertainty appears in Climacus' definition of subjective truth, or 'faith':

> Here is such a definition of truth: *An objective uncertainty, held fast through appropriation with the most passionate inwardness, is the truth,* the highest truth there is for an *existing* person. At the point where the road swings off (and where that is cannot be stated objectively, since it is precisely subjectivity), objective knowledge is suspended. Objectively he then has only uncertainty, but this is precisely what intensifies the infinite passion

of inwardness, and truth is precisely the daring venture of choosing the objective uncertainty with the passion of the infinite. I observe nature in order to find God, and I do indeed see omnipotence and wisdom, but I also see much that troubles and disturbs. The *summa summarum* of this is an objective uncertainty, but the inwardness is so very great, precisely because it grasps this objective uncertainty with all the passion of the infinite. In a mathematical proposition, for example, the objectivity is given, but therefore its truth is also an indifferent truth.[51]

I cannot think of a passage that better supports the reading I am arguing against than this one. Climacus appears to be arguing that an 'objective' definition of the truth aims at certainty, but a 'subjective' pursuit of truth aims at uncertainty, because uncertainty is what is helpful for provoking passion, and the more uncertainty the more passion. If this is true, then it would follow that the most uncertain view is the most passionate, the most 'true'; and Christianity, being 'the absurd,' would be the most true. But I believe one should first pay attention to the example given here of an objective certainty: mathematics. Climacus (and Kierkegaard) believes that the only truths where the objective certainty is 'given' are tautologies: the truth is given in the initial premise. So here Climacus would argue (against Kant) that a mathematical proposition is only an analytic truth, and hence not essentially related to existence. On the other hand (as we see in the 'Interlude' to the *Fragments*) any statement about *existence* requires belief. The only difference between the skeptic and most people is that the skeptic recognizes that there is an element of uncertainty in all knowledge of existence, whereas the 'ordinary' person fails to see this. The only difference between the skeptic and the believer is that while both recognize the element of uncertainty, one holds fast to the uncertainty and the other holds fast to the object despite the uncertainty. Both have become conscious of the uncertainty, and conscious of the passion of belief operative in even the simplest apprehension of existential truth; but their passion turns in opposite directions.[52]

The proper understanding of this passage must not suggest that 'uncertainty' is a gradual qualification. The old cliché about pregnancy applies: it is never 'just a little bit' true. What matters to the subjective definition of truth is not the degree of uncertainty, but the degree to which the individual recognizes this uncertainty versus the degree to which one fails to recognize it or holds to false certainty instead. Socrates, who passionately recognized the perhaps small degree of uncertainty involved in his belief in God, had more faith than someone who 'knows' the absurdity of

Christianity and continues to believe it, but has never let the full force of that absurdity to strike home to cause more than a mild uneasiness.

The idea that Christianity is somehow 'truer' because it is 'more uncertain' is thus false to Climacus on two fronts: it purports to 'prove' Christianity, while Climacus himself adopts an agnostic stance; and it makes the uncertainty a graduated characteristic when in fact it is a categorical predicate. I therefore read the 'deduction of Christianity' in this manner: The Socratic ignorance was the highest expression of subjective truth, because it renounced objectivity in order to live in passion. However, it preserved an element of objectivity within it through the doctrine of recollection. This doctrine understood the knower as essentially related to the truth, and capable of relating to it objectively, which opened the door to Platonic speculation. The 'only' problem Socrates believed he faced was that as an existing individual, he had the task of existing in the truth rather than speculating about it; Plato by contrast speculates himself out of existence in order to (objectively) draw closer to the truth, meditating on it rather than repeating it in his everyday life. In fact, Plato (in the *Phaedo*) has Socrates argue that philosophy is a kind of practice in dying, whereas Climacus' vision of Socrates is of a person who is supremely, passionately alive. Socrates accepts and embraces the conditions of existence; Plato seeks to escape or ignore them, but at least is conscious and honest about this. The professor who 'objectively' pursues the truth as if existence was irrelevant, but continues to embrace and pursue the goals of existence (such as a paycheck) has not even come as far as Plato.

What, then, could be more inward than Socratic ignorance? The elimination of the remaining element of objectivity. Thus Climacus denies the premise that the individual is still essentially *integer*, still essentially intact and uncorrupted, still capable of a direct relationship to the truth if only the conditions of existence allowed it. This is also what is denied by the doctrine of sin: the ability of the individual to come to the truth directly, apart from faith. The door of Recollection, which Socrates had left cracked open, is now shut and barred against us. It is not necessary for Climacus to fully spell out his doctrine of sin here; he need only show the role it plays in increasing subjectivity. It is therefore not terribly significant that he treats sin rather abstractly and superficially, although it is surprising at first blush.

What I find particularly significant is that nothing has been said up to this point about the nature of the *object* of knowledge. The existence of God is no more certain to Socratic ignorance than to religious belief, since 'certain' is an absolute category. What has changed is the *knower's* relationship to the truth. Whereas before the subject still held a slender thread which could have guided him or her back out through the labyrinth of existence into the sunlight, now that thread has been cut, and the knower has no hope of escape from the labyrinth, and no choice but to press onward to face alone whatever monsters might lurk therein. The sunlight is still out there, outside the labyrinth; but now the knower's immersion in the conditions of existence is total: is this not a 'more inward expression'?

In all three propositions—'objectivity is truth,' 'subjectivity is truth,' and 'subjectivity is untruth'—the object of knowledge is not itself inherently uncertain. As we saw in the *Fragments*, an existential claim must be an object of belief: but 'God does not exist, he is eternal.'[53] So none of the propositions Climacus has treated to this point have suggested that the actual object of knowledge partakes of the uncertainty of all existential belief. On the other hand, this is precisely what Christianity does: in claiming that the god became a man, it argues that the eternal, essential truth is also an historical fact, and partakes of the same uncertainty that inheres in any historical claim. Just as no historical belief comes about without some element of subjectivity, so here there is an element of subjectivity; but whereas most historical claims are not essential (only moral and religious claims are so), in Christianity the historical claim is also an essential claim, and Christian faith thus possesses the inwardness of historical belief and the inwardness of repetition.

This understanding of Climacus' meaning accords quite well with what we have seen up to now, both in the *Fragments* and in earlier passages in the *Postscript*. The 'absurd' in Christianity is not that it is ridiculous; rather, it is 'the absurd fact of coming into existence.'[54] 'The absurd' is that God, who is eternal, could have come into existence. All human understanding would proclaim that this is impossible. Of course, Christianity has already claimed that human understanding is corrupted by sin and knows nothing of what is possible for God, and has labeled this claim by the understanding as 'offense.' Also, the *Fragments* has argued that all coming into existence occurs through a free cause, not a necessary ground. God is eternal, and hence necessary and unchanging; any 'change' could only be a necessary unfolding of God's nature. But coming into existence occurs through freedom, and hence is ultimately incomprehensible and absurd. Subjectivity is thus not called upon to try to think this absurdity through, to strengthen its muscles by willing to believe this impossibility until it can lift the weight and run with it. Rather, it is called only to realize that this cannot be understood, cannot be directly related to, but can be indirectly, inwardly appropriated. It does this by willing to live as if Christianity is true, willing to express this truth in its life, willing to suspend the quest for certainty and simply deciding to live in such a way that it can be said to be in a God-relationship to the Christ. Again, the effect of the absurd is not to make Christianity harder to think, since in fact the ethical-religious task is never to think, but to live; rather, the effect of the absurd is to more tightly bar the door against any desire to retreat into objectivity, or to sneak into Christianity while avoiding the strait way of inwardness.

This understanding of the slogan 'truth is subjectivity,' and the relevance of this motto for Christianity, is much more consistent with the previous chapters of the *Postscript* we have examined than are other interpretations which neglect the ethical. It is also quite consistent with the later material in this chapter, where the primary thrust of criticism against Hegelian philosophers is not that they are not emotional or dedicated enough, but rather that they have inappropriately confused philosophy and Christianity to the detriment of both.[55] As Climacus writes:

> Whether Christianity is in the right is another question. Here the question is only how the speculative explanation is related to the Christianity that it explains. But if Christianity is perhaps in the wrong, this much is certain: speculative thought is definitely in the wrong, because the only consistency outside Christianity is that of pantheism, the taking of oneself out of existence back into the eternal through recollection, whereby all existence-decisions become only shadow play compared with what is eternally decided from behind. Like all *simulated* decision, the simulated decision of speculative thought is nonsense, because decision is the eternal protest against fictions.[56]

This does not sound like a person who has undertaken to prove Christianity the truth because it is the most subjective, or to prove that any position, no matter how absurd, is more valid than even the most logical thesis if only the absurd is embraced fully and deeply, in good faith. However, this clearly is the statement of someone who feels that he has successfully distinguished two separate things that had been confused, and now would use both ridicule and argument to lead others to make that distinction as well.

The issue is not, therefore, whether 'subjectivity' in the Climacan/ Kierkegaardian sense has an intrinsically ethical meaning; that much is clear. Rather, the issue is how that meaning relates to the passional element so often noted by the existentialists and other commentators. The point of contact is *concern*. The subjective thinker is always mindful of being an existing individual, and thinks about matters that concern an existing individual. He or she is also mindful of being a particular existing individual, and that what one concerns oneself with should also be what actually concerns one. That is, it's not enough to think about 'duty,' you must think about *your* duty. The subjective thinker concerns himself or herself with questions like, 'What ought I to do?' and 'Do I have faith, and what faith do I have?'

I have chosen the word 'concern' over Climacus' word 'interest,' because in today's parlance the latter suggests a lack of concern: 'I'm not really religious, but I'm interested in religion,' for example. The person who is concerned will, naturally, be passionate, and more passionate the more deeply one is concerned. Furthermore, the concerned individual must believe that the object of concern is inherently valuable; to say 'it only matters because I care' is like saying 'She's not really lovable, but I love her': which is at least to begin to stop loving her. So the concerned person by no means believes that the passion validates the object, but that the object calls forth the passion. And the concerned person believes that the choice matters, so that he or she must deliberate about choosing well, not just willing well after the choice has been made. And the ambiguity of the term 'concern' captures nicely what we really believe. What concerns us is (ideally) what we concern ourselves with. If I concern myself with the plight of the Bushmen, but ignore my own family, then I have missed the point because what happens across the globe to people I cannot affect and who cannot affect me does not really concern me; but what happens to those who I can affect and who rely on me does.

b. *Summary: 'Truth is Subjectivity.'* Climacus' slogan 'Truth is Subjectivity' is not to be understood as a battle-cry to embrace the meaninglessness of existence and to honestly endorse the absurdity of life. Only a detached, esthetic thinker could adopt such a position. Nor is it an attempt to prove Christianity the truest life because it is the most self-consciously absurd. What it is instead is a summation and development of the conclusions of the first part of the *Postscript*. The highest truth for an *existing* individual cannot be to seek the greatest objective knowledge. Objectivity lies precisely in detachment, in unconcern; but the existing person is concerned, and the most essential matters are precisely the ones that concern the existing person the most. So the existing person must accept and even embrace the inevitable objective uncertainty which existence imposes on the individual, and instead develop one's own subjectivity to truly repeat in one's own life the ideals one embraces. Such a person is concerned to act morally, to do whatever he or she believes is right; and such a person accepts the inevitability of error not because he or she believes the object of the choice is unimportant, but rather because he or she believes that the object is so critical that it is better to choose and possibly fail to hit the mark, than to never choose and hence inevitably fail.

Subjectivity is inevitably ethical: it believes that it must seek the right even in the face of uncertainty, and must live in the light of its choices and beliefs even knowing that it will fail and need to repent. It is inevitably religious because repentance goes beyond the ethical, and hence every subjective thinker is driven toward the religious even if he or she never actively embraces it. It is inevitably passionate since it is by definition concerned. It has interest in what it chooses, not in the pale manner of modern idiom but in the older, etymological sense of being essentially connected to its object. And the more a person embraces subjectivity, the more ethical, the more religious, and the more passionate that person will become; and contrariwise, the more a person embraces the opposite attitude, the less passionate, moral, and religious such a person will remain. It is thus essential to distinguish between the objective and the subjective approaches to ethical-religious truth, since the confusion of the two and the attempt to pursue essential truth objectively can only lead one further away from one's object of concern.

4. *Appendix: A Glance at a Contemporary Effort in Danish Literature:* One would think that the 'appendix' to this chapter would be just the thing to solve many of the exegete's problems. Here at last is a protracted discussion of Kierkegaard's writings from his own pen, even if published under a pseudonym. After the summary and review of the authorship up to the *Postscript* has been presented, what more could remain for the weary interpreter to analyze?

Plenty, given the nature of the authorship. Even though Kierkegaard's name appears on the title page as 'responsible for publication,' this is still a pseudonymous work. That being the case, it is dangerous even here to take the text too directly. The pseudonyms are more than pen names; they are fictional characters in their own rights, expressing views from their own perspective and according to their own temperaments. This appendix particularly reflects this fact. The entire review is set firmly within the fictional world Kierkegaard has created in his authorship: one pseudonym comments upon another as if speaking of a third person, commenting only on those aspects of the other's works that interest the commentator.

What is presented here, then, is not so much a simple commentary by the author on his authorship, but an edited commentary on the authorship by one of the fictional characters within it. The overall effect of Climacus'

redaction is to represent each of the pseudonymous works as quite distinctive, and yet as essential components of an overall strategy aimed at
the presentation of Christianity as the paradoxical religiousness. It also
describes the direct discourses, briefly, as important in that they keep pace
with the pseudonymous works and present the same themes in a religious
context, without the obfuscation of the pseudonyms. Elements where one
pseudonym might anticipate a later work are minimized, in order that the
shortcomings of each earlier position might stand out more clearly. This is
in keeping with the thesis proposed by Taciturnus (and apparently shared
by Climacus) that one sphere prepares the way for another by developing itself fully until its own limitations and finally its collapse demand the
spirit seek a higher form of existence. Movement from sphere to sphere is
reflected in the pattern Climacus sees in the pseudonymous authorship:
the earlier position appears, is developed fully, collapses and thus sets the
stage for the next, not by its foreshadowing and continuous development
but precisely by its fits, starts, stops, and leaps.

Nowhere is this clearer than in Climacus' discussion of the pseudonyms'
presentation of sin.[57] Climacus points to one particular category both
Repetition and *Fear and Trembling* share: the ordeal. The ordeal is a break
with the ethical, wherein the individual is thrust outside the ethical and
condemned by it, but is not himself or herself really heterogeneous with
it. Abraham is called to break with the ethical and to take Isaac to Mount
Moriah. This is, as Climacus says, a terror, a mortal danger, enough to turn
one's hair grey. But it is the nature of an ordeal to end. Abraham himself
is 'righteous.' There is nothing about Abraham that stopped him from fulfilling the ethical, except that they happened to come into collision. Once
the ordeal is over, once God gives the ram and sends Abraham back with
his son to their family, he is able to return to the ethical. It is true, as de
Silentio said, that the mere fact that this collision could happen is the decisive fact; but it is also true that the ordeal is the exception, a category for
unusual individuals and for unusual instances in their lives.

What makes the religious a distinct sphere of existence is that this 'teleo-
logical suspension of the ethical' is not merely 'a passing through,' but
rather an ongoing condition. Climacus writes:

> The ethical is then present at every moment with its infinite require-
> ment, but the individual is not capable of fulfilling it. This powerlessness
> of the individual must not be seen as an imperfection in the continued
> endeavor to attain an ideal, for in that case the suspension is no more
> postulated than the man who administers his office in an ordinary way is

suspended. The suspension consists in the individual's finding himself in a state exactly opposite to what the ethical requires. Therefore, far from being able to begin, every moment he continues in this state he is more and more prevented from being able to begin; he relates himself to actuality not as possibility but as impossibility. Thus the individual is suspended from the ethical in the most terrifying way, is in the suspension heterogeneous with the ethical, which still has the claim of the infinite upon him and at every moment requires itself of the individual, and thereby at every moment the heterogeneity is only more definitely marked as heterogeneity.[58]

Abraham is able to fulfill his ethical requirement; that is in fact his temptation. He could, at any time, take his son in his arms, say, 'That's enough walking,' turn around and go home. It is only his commitment to the absolute duty to God that blocks him; there is nothing on Abraham's side that prevents this. The merman is another story. While Abraham begins his relationship with Isaac through the ethical, the merman begins his relationship with Agnes in violation of the ethical. If he then turns around (in New Testament Greek, *metanoia*, usually translated 'repentance') and seeks to marry Agnes, he is already in the wrong for having first deceived her, and continues in the wrong as long as he does not confess and seek forgiveness. And even if she forgives him, he still began with criminal intentions. The ethical condemns him, and will continue to condemn him. We express this truth when we say that even if she forgives him, he ought not to forgive himself so easily, since he knows his own guilt. If he doesn't have a guilty conscience, we think this is itself another crime. He truly has become 'heterogeneous' with the ethical, by his own choice. As Climacus writes:

> The situation is different now. Duty is the absolute, its requirement the absolute, and yet the individual is prevented from fulfilling it. . . . The dreadful exemption from doing the ethical, the individual's heterogeneity with the ethical, this suspension from the ethical, is *sin* as a state in a human being.
>
> Sin is a crucial expression for the religious existence. As long as sin is not posited, the suspension becomes a transient factor that in turn vanishes or remains outside life as the totally irregular. Sin, however, is the crucial point of departure for the religious existence, is not a factor within something else, within another order of things, but is itself the beginning of the religious order of things.[59]

Climacus says that none of the earlier pseudonyms have dealt with sin, although he clarifies this by saying that while *Fear and Trembling* does discuss sin, it does so only in contrast to Abraham's suspension of the ethical, which was without sin. He does not discuss the three discourses Kierkegaard published on that same day, although two of these seem to specifically discuss sin. Technically, of course, they are not pseudonymous and therefore his statement is correct. Furthermore, they do not discuss sin in any great detail, but only discuss how the individual who loves much can 'hide' sin. This does not seem to be taking sin as seriously as Climacus has described it. But I believe the most likely reason he does not discuss a relationship between the pseudonymous books and the three discourses of 1843 is that Climacus is a third person. Kierkegaard lets his mask slip more than once before this, but he still strives to preserve the independence of the pseudonymous characters. It would be inappropriate to hint that the discourses may contain a key to deciphering the pseudonymous works. And furthermore, there is no need; Climacus can make his points while treating the pseudonyms in isolation from the discourses.

Climacus next discusses *Concept of Anxiety* as the pseudonymous discussion of hereditary sin.[60] Considering how important the concept of sin is, Climacus actually has very little to say about the contents of this book. He ignores Haufniensis' introduction, where he discusses how the 'first ethics' shipwrecks on the concept of sin, creating the need for the 'second ethics' that begins after sin and takes the sinner from outside the ethical back toward it. This discussion would have fit well with his discussion of sin in relation to Abraham, but perhaps that is why Climacus chooses to leave it out: his goals are better served by clearly distinguishing between books more than by bringing them together. Instead, he draws attention to the depiction of anxiety as the state of mind of the sinner, who recognizes his or her estrangement from the truth and yet still longs for it.

The summary in the 'appendix' thus preserves the pseudonymity of the authorship by refusing to reveal more than an outsider's perspective of the works it treats. At the same time, it does touch on the essentials of each of the pseudonymous works, as Climacus sees them. By downplaying those elements in the earlier Kierkegaardian authorship which hint at the problem of sin, Climacus both situates his work within 'contemporary Danish literature' and highlights the distinctive messages he is concerned to impart: the uniqueness of Christianity, the importance of subjective appropriation, and the patent falsity of the claims of speculative philosophy to have accurately appropriated the essential Christian message into its doctrines.

II. The Ethical, the Religious, and the Ethical-religious

A. *Actual and Ethical Subjectivity*: This chapter of the *Postscript* is short and fairly direct, perhaps making it more accessible. At the same time, it repeats the themes produced more thoroughly in earlier sections of the book, in the process confirming the main points of our exegesis. Furthermore, it raises issues first treated in *Either/Or*, revealing the strong connections between the various works of Kierkegaard's authorship and further clarifying the relationships between the esthetic, the ethical, and the religious.

The main theme of the chapter is the nature of 'actuality': that which exists in space and time. Much of what philosophy says about life, existence, and so on is general, abstract, and theoretical, not 'actual' and therefore not directly relevant to an existing individual. This is not to say that this is the only reality, however; for as Climacus writes:

> God does not think, he creates; God does not exist, he is eternal. A human being thinks and exists, and existence separates thinking and being, holds them apart from each other in succession.[61]

Clearly, 'God does not exist' does not mean there is no God; nor does 'he is eternal' necessarily mean 'he is,' he has being, he has reality. This aphorism is not so much a statement about the ontological status of God as a description of human existence. Humans have their thought and action separated, and their action and the results are temporally and essentially distinct, so that thinking, doing, and the results are all successive. For God, the 'It is' follows instantly and necessarily from the 'Let it be'; but actual human existence is neither instant nor necessary.[62] Human existence is constrained by the laws of time and space, while whatever is eternal is not.

Thus, the question about 'actuality' and 'existence' is about what has spatio-temporal reality. Climacus is not intending to discuss the conceptual definition of 'subjectivity'; a conceptual treatment is an ideal one, hence not actual subjectivity but an abstraction from the actual. He does not so much want to discuss 'human nature' as the nature of the particular, individual, existing human. Whereas Hegel and the Romantic poets discussed 'Spirit' in abstract, pantheistic, monistic, and/or world historical terms, Climacus wants to discuss the individual life of an existing person. And this sort of subjectivity, he says, is not speculative or poetic; it is ethical subjectivity.

To the twenty-first-century reader, it may seem strange to equate poetics and speculative philosophy the way Climacus does. To us, it seems clear that speculative philosophy really is 'objectivity': a dispassionate, detached, universalist standpoint, where the individual has only that sort of significance a grain of sand has to the beach. Poetry, by contrast, seems to us to be the height of subjectivity: personal perhaps to the point of idiosyncratic, passionate, imaginative, and supremely engaged with its object. But to Climacus, they are essentially the same in that they both treat possibility as higher than actuality. In both poetry and speculation, the progress is away from the actual, and toward the ideal.

The ethical makes the opposite move.[63] It appears when the individual reflects on such ideals as might be presented as the results of poetry or philosophy, and resolves to make an ideal actual in his or her life. The good may be eternal, and thus the good may be; but it does not *exist* unless someone chooses to be good, to live out goodness in the sphere of actuality. Said another way: imagination and thinking are important to the fully human life, because they present possibilities to the individual which one may choose to live out; and will is likewise essential, since without the will to carry out the work of repetition, the ideals remain merely ideal and not actual, and life dissolves into a series of disjointed and meaningless events with no higher meaning to give them continuity.

In two different senses, it can be said that actual subjectivity is ethical subjectivity. First, in the more technical sense of 'actuality,' ethical subjectivity is subjectivity expressed in the terms of actuality. Speculative philosophy treats actuality in abstract terms, essentially in terms of possibility or *sub specie aeternae*. Ethics deals with subjectivity as it actually exists, under the conditions of existence. Second, in a more general sense, the ethical understanding of subjectivity is the only one which deals with subjectivity as it actually exists; that is, in its completeness. The poetic life of imagination alone, or the speculative life of thought alone, both claim to be able to embrace all aspects of human subjectivity under their aegis, but in fact ignore large portions of the fully human life. The subjective thinker has (that is, lives) all the elements of a full, actual subject; the speculative thinker has reflection and lives only in reflection, and considers the other elements only as fuel for thought.

There is one important sense, however, which Climacus does not feel the subjective thinker worries about making the ideal 'actual': the sense of actualizing one's ethical commitment in social institutions or in externally observable actions. This sort of 'actuality' Climacus explicitly rejects. For Climacus, 'ideality is the actuality within the individual himself. Actuality is interiority infinitely interested in existing, which the ethical individual is for himself.'[64] The commonsense opinion might suggest that ideals are not really 'real,' since they exist only inside the subject. Only what can be seen and touched and experienced by others is actual or 'real.' Climacus says just the opposite: what is seen by outsiders may easily deceive, since outsiders may infer ideals which the subject does not in fact posses, or fail to perceive ideals the subject does passionately embrace. Furthermore, the third-person standpoint is not the ethical standpoint; what matters ethically is the subject's attempts to actualize his or her inner ideals. Therefore, the ethical actuality is that ideality which actually exists inside the subject, which the subject discovers by introspection and (more importantly) seeks to reduplicate in existence.[65]

Very well: so Climacus equates actual subjectivity with ethical subjectivity, and regards abstract interpretations of subjectivity (or spirit) as possibilities at best, and delusions at worst. What has thwarted consensus among Kierkegaard commentators is that Climacus is rather vague regarding 'the ethical.' He gives no concrete guide as to what is ethical, proposes no moral or legal code, rails against no social institution, nor does he even offer advice on etiquette. Some writers have taken this to mean that there really is no content to Climacus' notion of 'the ethical.' 'Ethical subjectivity' would thus seem to be a redundant term: 'subjectivity' meaning to be a self-conscious subject, passionately willing to be oneself, and 'ethical' meaning to choose responsibly to be oneself. In this view, Climacus is really saying that there is no reason to be Christian, or ethical, since everything is 'absurd'; but there still is a primary human responsibility to make a choice of some option and to passionately embrace it, while knowing it is no better than any other and that one's choice was by unmotivated will alone. Others, such as C. S. Evans, are not convinced that the apparent vacuity of Climacus' language really indicates that the ethical itself is a vacuous concept. Evans takes his cue from the claim Kierkegaard makes in his journals that there is a 'how' which, if correctly followed, generates a specific 'what.'[66] The correct manner of life will generate a specific moral content, or at least a specific range of content sufficiently specific that it is possible to judge that a particular individual is being immoral and unethical, regardless of how sincere and passionate that individual is. In that case, the necessity that the self pass through the ethical on its way to the religious might be more than simply the need to build up its will-muscles by lifting and toting heavy moral burdens. It may be that the self really does need to know the proper ethical content even as its entry into the religious stage moves it beyond the ethical *per se*.

There are some indications of the nature of the ethical life, although it may be threadbare by some standards. In a general and vague (although significant) sense, the emphasis on risk gives our first clue.[67] If the choices of the ethical life, or the choice to be ethical, were truly arbitrary there would be no risk. Risk only exists if there is a chance to be wrong, and a cost for error. This is suggestive of the overall debate between the two main pseudonyms in *Either/Or*, over their opposite uses of the title phrase. A sees all choices as equally meaningless and hence attaches no importance to the choice at all; since you will regret whatever you choose, it doesn't matter what or if you choose.[68] B (or William), the ethicist, attaches great importance to the choice; if you choose wrong you will have to repent, and may perhaps have quite a burden to bear or undo.[69] The stereotype of the existentialist reveling in the absurdity of life is close to A, but far from William and, it seems, from Climacus as well.

A second hint comes from Climacus' discussion of ideals and the eternal in the existing individual's life.[70] To an esthete, the possibilities that can be realized in life are themselves limited; hence the esthete's life can have no real continuity. Constantin, for example, despaired completely of repetition, as he could only aspire to esthetic repetitions such as a banquet or a trip to Berlin. The general formula of existence, of conceiving a possibility and then bringing it to actuality, is followed by the esthete; but the esthete's life lacks any larger unity because the possibility itself is limited. What gives a human life a true continuity, says Climacus, is an element of the eternal; but since the eternal is still abstract, it must then be actualized by the individual in his or her life. And while the list of eternal verities may include such things as mathematical axioms and logical rules, the eternals that Climacus cares about are the ideals such as the good, the true, and the beautiful. It is by having moral ideals, and then by living them out passionately and seriously, that one's life gains continuity.

The Socratic/Platonic nature of Climacus' views on the ideals likewise suggests another indicator of Climacus' views of the ethical. In his published works he shows a fascination with Socrates. And the Socrates of Climacus is not the Socrates of the later Plato, of whom Aristotle is said to have complained that all his lectures were mathematics. His fascination is with the Socrates of the earlier dialogs, who discussed morality with shopkeepers and saw his own trial and execution as chances to give ethical lessons to those around him. It is the Socrates who is absorbed in the question of whether he himself is a monster or the image of the divine who gives Climacus his cue to the dispute between immanence and Christianity.[71] It is the Socrates who wants only to know about the good who inspires and amazes him. His ideals are the ideals a person can live out; other abstract concepts simply don't absorb him, because he knows he must exist and that existence, not contemplation, is his task. But if Socrates knew that existence was his task, he also knew that existence truly was a task, a charge to be properly carried out. His highest aim was to live a good life, and his greatest gift to his neighbors was to try to persuade them to do so as well. Indeed, Socrates didn't even know whether the captain who delivered his passengers safely ashore had done them any good at all, but he knew that the person who helped another become morally better had given the chief and only benefit one person can give another.[72]

And finally, there is the complaint by Climacus that if thinking is really higher than existence, as the speculative philosophers claim, then the highest human life depends on the vagaries of individual talent.[73] Such a person is, he writes, a 'variant' on the human specimen who wants to be the norm, even the epitome.[74] This reminds one immediately of the discussion by William in *Either/Or* of the essence of the ethical: to realize the universal human.[75] The ethical person knows what the highest human life is, because it is that life which every human person can realize.[76] By contrast, the life that relies on special exemptions or talents, such as the wealth to enjoy leisure or the talent to imagine, are only offshoots of the essentially human. The only justified exception could be the person who truly loved the universal human, and yet had been unable to realize it despite every effort, and who continued to love it and acknowledge it as the highest.[77] In his disparagement of the idea that the highest human life could rely on a variant of talent, Climacus throws his lot in with William. The highest human life must be one to which any human can aspire who has the will to do so; variations of talent or resources can only affect how the universal human is to be realized, not whether it is or not.

When we begin to add up hints such as these, it become clear that Evans is right: Climacus does not discuss the content of the ethical because he assumes it to be already known, not because he believes there is none.[78] Climacus shares the moral universe of Socrates, of Christianity, and of the other Kierkegaardian writings. As far as he is concerned, the 'what' of the ethical life is not seriously in dispute: anyone who wishes to can easily learn it. What is in dispute in his day is the 'how.' Does one become ethical by attending to world history and the spirit of the times? By joining a political party? By attending lectures on moral philosophy, or writing them? Does one do good by wishing to be good, by joyfully meditating on how wonderful it would be to good? Or, does one become ethical by striving to actualize the ethical ideals one has in one's own life? To Climacus, the answer is obvious, although he realizes it may not be so to many of his readers.

Climacus wondered whether the appearance of speculative philosophers augured the coming day when the ethical and the religious might disappear.[79] Today, many would suggest that day has arrived; or at any rate, that the day when any meaningful sense of *the* ethical has passed, and that now we live in the babble of ethics where moralities are scattered over the face of the Earth, unable to communicate with one another. The question of the 'what' of the ethical seems more urgent to us, and a thinker who assumes in silence that his reader knows the good is taken to be one who simply has no good at all. But Kierkegaard thought that there was a 'how' which, if diligently followed, would give the correct 'what.' Evans relies on Kierkegaard's journals, which his contemporaries of course did not have: but what hints are there in the published words of Climacus to this effect? What sort of content to the ethical life might be generated by adhering to this pattern?

First, there are certain virtues demanded by this sort of ethic. Humility is paramount; one cannot carry out the moral inventory needed to do this work without it. The individual must closely consider what ideals he or she is living by, and how well those professed ideals match his or her real life choices. This is the sort of self-discipline lacking in the *privadocents* Climacus criticizes, who claim to prove there is an immortality while living perfectly philistine lives.[80] It is a humbling thing to admit to oneself that one does not come up to the standards one ought, but any serious attempt to live the ethical life must start with the recognition that one has oneself as a task, not a given.[81] The ethical task is to not just accept what one is, but to become better.

Humility is also required in the recognition that one cannot judge others; one can only judge oneself. Self-righteousness is impossible for the person who realizes that one's own ethical actuality is the only actuality that can be known: all other knowledge changes an actuality into a possibility.[82] Knowledge abstracts, looks for generalities and concepts with which to order and classify, and in the end must (according to Climacus) deal either in approximations or in purely logical truths without actual existence. Self-knowledge follows the opposite route, from existential possibilities conceived and appropriated as one's own ideals to the work of living them out, thus making them actualities. Ethical self-knowledge thus seeks to end with actuality, whereas all other sorts of knowledge start with actuality and end elsewhere. Therefore, no one can judge another, or say 'at least I am better than him,' or otherwise deflect ethical attention away from oneself and the absolute standard of the eternal.[83] One cannot console oneself or elevate oneself over others by a determination of moral righteousness compared to others, because ethically speaking there is no way to make the comparison.

Following from this virtue is another one: honesty, in the sense of the existentialists' 'good faith.' If being ethical means living out one's ideals passionately and seriously, then the ethical consists at least partly in being consistent. Hypocrisy would seem to be the cardinal vice, particularly hypocrisy toward oneself. The ethical life depends on honestly appraising oneself to see if one's actions are consistent with one's ideals, whatever they are. To have ideals one does not strive to live by is not to have ideals at all. It is not just to be morally weak; this would be to strive but fail. If one does not live out one's ideals to the best of one's ability, and strive to improve one's ability to actualize them despite obstacles and the temptations of comfort, then one simply is not ethical at all, according to Climacus.

There is furthermore a deep egalitarianism in Climacus' thought, a trait he shares in common with other Kierkegaardian creations. His oft-repeated refrain that 'the wise man and the simple man know the same thing' serves as a rebuke to those of his readers among the Danish elite who would be tempted to look down on the less-educated masses and their 'simple' faith. While the Golden Age salon circles tended to divide Danish society between the cultural and spiritual haves and have-nots, Climacus says that all have or have not the same essential things: either recollection is true and all have the essential, or Christianity is true and all lack it. There are thus no grounds for despising the uneducated peasant and his unreflective spirituality; it may be the same as the reflective person's, or even more developed, even though the peasant may not be able to articulate his spirituality as well. And this further implies that on some level at least, one must treat the other as equal. If 'the ethical' consists of living out one's ideals, and if the ethical person must admit that all human beings are essentially equal, then the ethical person—the only sort who can truly claim to be pursuing subjectivity—must treat all other persons as persons, with the respect that any individual deserves. This does not necessarily mean that all persons must be treated the same, nor is it likely that Climacus would see this as leading necessarily to any particular political arrangement; but it does mean that any treatment of another which dehumanizes the other, or treats the other as a means to one's own ends rather than as an end in himself or herself, must be rejected as unethical and a violation of the dictates of true subjectivity.

We can thus at least say that Climacus' views on the ethical do give some real guidance for action, and certainly has more connection with the moral than the anything goes, spontaneity-over-all mentality commonly associated with 'the father of existentialism' or the arch-postmodernist depicted by MacIntyre. But finally, it must be remembered that the 'how' of Climacus is not in fact primarily intended to simply generate a moral code; it is intended to ultimately lead to the breakdown of the ethical and to point toward the religious, and ultimately the Christian. It is Christianity which is the 'what' toward which Climacus believes his 'how' inevitably points. That being the case, it ultimately doesn't matter to him so much whether two ethical persons dispute over some moral choice; if they keep at the ethical quest long enough and passionately enough, they will eventually run into the issues of sin and repentance, that 'rock' upon which all ethics ultimately shipwrecks, forcing the individual to sink or to be cast up on the shore of the religious.

B. *The Issue in the Fragments*: It is to be expected from an author like Climacus that it is only after several hundred pages of his 'postscript' have passed through his pen that he finally gets around to writing a chapter discussing 'The Issue in *Fragments*: How can an Eternal Happiness be Built on Historical Knowledge?'[84] And it is also to be expected that relatively little space is devoted to really examining the *Fragments* at all, while vastly more attention is devoted to other questions. The central thrust of the argument of the *Fragments* is neatly summed up by Climacus:

> *The Importance of a Preliminary Agreement about What Christianity Is Before There Can Be Any Question of a Mediation of Christianity and Speculative Thought; the Absence of an Agreement Favors Mediation, Although Its Absence Renders Mediation Illusory; the Supervention of an Agreement Prevents Mediation.*[85]

That is, as long as there is no prior definition of the terms, speculative philosophy is able to redefine Christianity as suits it, reinterpret it as a philosophical doctrine to be thought and understood, and then to mediate and sublate as it pleases. But if the terms are allowed to define themselves, as they have historically been used most generally, then such mediation becomes impossible. Christianity defines itself not as a philosophical doctrine to be understood (that would be gnosticism) but as an existence-communication to be lived. This notion is easily misunderstood, as if it meant that Christianity had no noetic content, and was meant to uplift and inspire the individual in the same nonrational way a great symphony might. But that sort of interpretation undermines the central claim by Climacus that 'the individual's eternal happiness is decided in time by a relationship to something historical.'[86] Clearly there is some amount of objective, noetic content to the Christian existence-communication, such that if it were missing there would not be a *Christian* existence-communication at all. Rather, Climacus is instead making the point that Christianity is not to be *received* as one receives a philosophical doctrine. The proper way to receive a philosophical doctrine is to reflect upon it, criticize it, understand it. Until I can go through the steps in Hegel's doctrine backwards and forwards, until I can present it as if it were my own invention and even reinvent it myself from its constituent elements, I have not really received his doctrine. Unless I thus understand it, I only parrot it. But while there is a Christian message, it is a message that aims to affect the concrete existence of the individual, not just abstract reflection. It aims at the actual, ethical subjectivity of the individual.

To say that Christianity is an existence-communication thus is not to claim that it lacks any content, but rather to emphasize that the point should be to adjust one's life in response to whatever content there is, rather than getting lost in the process of reflecting on that content. If Christianity were a doctrine, then the proper way to deepen one's relationship to it would be to think about it more, explicate its concepts more clearly, spend as little time as possible thinking or doing anything else, even to the point of ignoring the conditions of one's own existence in order to devote all one's attention to the doctrine. But as Climacus has already argued, this 'objective' route actually leads away from any relationship to Christianity.[87] In the case of an existence-communication, the proper point of emphasis is on the individual, and his or her mode of existence. So rather than attempt to explicate Christian doctrines of grace, incarnation, and the like, Climacus turns to the individual, and the pathos and dialectic of the individual's relationship to the eternal. He never asks, 'What are the Christian doctrines that tell how God bestows upon the individual an eternal happiness?' Instead he concentrates on the subjectivity of the individual, and asks, 'What is the self such that it can be related to and saved by Christianity?' And to answer this question, he embarks on an exploration of the threefold nature of ethical-religious pathos: renunciation, suffering, and guilt.

A reader unacquainted with the *Postscript,* but knowing something of Kierkegaard's earlier pseudonymous works, could reasonably assume that if there is a threefold division of human pathos, it must parallel the three-fold stages of the self. In fact, this is not at all the case; rather, Climacus appears to undermine or at least qualify the entire theory of the stages. Climacus states that the self begins the religious life by a determination to relate absolutely to the absolute *telos.* This is pretty much what de Silentio describes in *Fear and Trembling* as 'resignation.' The self must give up the esthetic life of immersion in relative ends only, and 'die to the world.' The self exists in the finite world, and hence begins in a state of immersion in the relative. The self cannot simply say, 'Now I will relate absolutely to the absolute'; first it must tear itself away from the relative ends to which it has been absolutely devoted until now. The term Climacus uses for this process is 'renunciation.'[88] Clearly, this describes the break with the esthetic, where the self turns away from all the relative ends that have claimed absolute allegiance in order to pursue the eternal, ethical good. At the same time, this renunciation may be more accurately understood by the symbol of Isaac in *Fear and Trembling*, who represents not only the joys of esthetic happiness but also the reassurance and reward of social ethical responsibility. And as Climacus makes clear, this sort of renunciation is not something which can be done once at the beginning of the self's task, and then is finished; rather, 'The task is ideal and perhaps is never accomplished by anyone; it is only on paper that one begins summarily and is promptly finished.' So renunciation is an act and a process that commences the ethical life, and is practiced throughout the religious life. Not surprisingly therefore, Climacus begins eroding the apparently neat three-tiered scheme of the stages of existence by making references to the 'ethical-religious.' That is, the pathos of the ethical and the religious seem to be the same, and essentially different from the esthetic, so that there are really only two spheres of existence: the esthetic versus the ethical-religious, or immersion in the finite versus renunciation of the relative. So are there two 'stages on life's way,' or three?

1. *One Sphere, Two, or Three?* Like much of what Climacus writes, his understanding of the relationship between the ethical and religious spheres takes some teasing to reveal. At various times he both conflates and separates the ethical, the religious, and the ethical-religious.[89] He conflates the ethical and the religious in contrasting both together against the esthetic. The esthetic lives immersed in immediacy; the ethical, religious, or ethical-religious are said to be inwardness, detachment from externals and relativities, constancy in the face of time. And because they are inwardness, they comprehend suffering as essential. While the esthetic comprehends unhappiness as misfortune and thus as accidental, inwardness comprehends it as suffering, which is essentially related to the task of an existing individual living in the finite, but attempting to live for the absolute. Though Climacus writes of suffering as a specifically *religious* category, it in fact applies to the life of *ethical* inwardness as well. Any self which attempts to live unconditionally for that which is the highest, and give only relative worth to the many relativities which claim the allegiance of any existing

soul, will experience suffering as it attempts to carry out this task in time. It thus appears there are only two major spheres: either immediacy and the absolute valuation of the relative/or the ethical-religious, inwardness, and the absolute loyalty to the absolute alone; any further distinctions between types of inwardness appear to be just variations on a common theme.

At the same time, Climacus continues to advocate the theory of the *three* spheres of existence outlined by Frater Taciturnus.[90] His language elsewhere affirms that he thinks of the ethical and the religious as distinct, and of the ethical-religious as somehow distinct from the other two. If the ethical can be contrasted with the ethical-religious, and the purely religious contrasted with the ethical, then perhaps there are three spheres here, with immediacy being the fourth! Fortunately, this added complication does not appear to be the case; unfortunately, it is very hard to clearly distinguish the three 'spheres' of inwardness. The ethical arises as the self renounces the absolute claims of the relative, and chooses the ethical as the only absolute. This absolute must then, of course, be expressed in the concrete world of relativities; the self must disclose itself as far as humanly possible. The ethical person must, as Judge William said, have a vocation, a spouse, a friend, social relationships in which to express the good and disclose himself or herself. While even William would agree that the inner never becomes the outer, neither would he say the ethical person deliberately hides his or her essential nature from others to whom he or she is already committed in an ethical relationship. In this way, it can be said even of the ethical that the good 'exhausts itself' in the world of the relative.

When Climacus discusses 'the religious,' by contrast, he generally refers not to such abstract concepts as 'the ethical' or 'the good,' but to God, who is also conceived of as a person. An abstract concept must be given concrete material; a person already has content, and hence the religious self does not need to express the religious relationship in the concrete world to make it real. Thus when Climacus discusses such matters as prayer, which has no act and hence no 'ethical' import, he refers to the *religious*.[91] The fuzzy term is the 'ethical-religious.' This is not some border concept between the ethical and the religious, as if it were a lower, hybrid form of the religious. Rather, it reflects the hybrid nature of existence itself; the religious person must still act in and over time. When Climacus wants to refer to an aspect of life that includes both religious and ethical elements, such as a religious life that is acting in time, he can refer to the 'ethical-religious.' Climacus is continuing to use the three-tiered scheme found in the *Stages*. There, too, the ethical is both distinguished from the religious,

and essentially linked to it. However, he also alters the language to introduce new conceptual distinctions. Perhaps this is because the presentation
of the *Stages* is more ideal, concerned as it is with conceptually distinguishing between the spheres of existence. In actuality, a person needs all three,
and particularly needs the continuing ethical striving in the religious life.
The spheres are useful for thinking about existence, but in life they represent emphases or varying centers of gravity rather than absolutely distinct
alternatives.

In fact, Climacus goes so far as to make the mark of the ethical into
a defining characteristic of the religious: 'With regard to the religious,
the point is that this has passed through the ethical.'[92] Climacus criticizes
the religious poet who treats of spiritual themes, and perhaps even uses
Christian language, but whose work or life betray an orientation toward
esthetic categories of fortune/misfortune, fame/ignominy, and other
external criteria for determining the successful human life: 'To *celebrate* a
hero of faith is just as fully an esthetic task as to celebrate a war hero.' And
just as attention to externals may lead one astray in considering the hero
of faith (from imitating to celebrating), so too attention to the external talents and accomplishments of the poetic personality can easily lead a third
party to mistake such a person for a *religious* personality, 'even a *prominent*
religious individuality.' Again, one cannot help but think of the cult of
the poet observed by Kierkegaard's contemporaries in Denmark's Golden
Age. Such characters as Heiberg and Oehenschläger were regarded as the
heights of spiritual development by the cultured people of Copenhagen,
although their poetry and perhaps even their lives reflected little ethical
development, little acquaintance with renunciation, suffering, or actual
inwardness. Even more, Climacus (and Kierkegaard) may intend the reader
to think of Grundtvig as 'a poetic nature who by way of circumstances,
upbringing, and the like has taken a direction away from the theater to the
Church.' Whether invoking the spirituality of Pan or Christ, such a poet in
spiritual garb is still only an esthetic personality. It is by passing through
the ethical that the personality develops the detachment from immediacy
needed to attend to the true religious task of inwardness.

Renunciation, then, is the first movement of the pathos of inwardness,
where the individual determines to turn away from immediacy and toward
the absolute *telos*. Suffering is the expression of this pathos in existence, as
the individual finds that renunciation is something that must occur every
moment one is alive. Suffering can be said to flow from two distinguishable
sources. First, as the individual tears out the barbs of immediacy, existence
plunges new ones in just as fast. The finite person is absolutely immersed

in immediacy, is naturally attached unconditionally to the finite, and must tear these attachments out of his or her heart in order to live for the absolute; yet in order to live at all, the finite person must live in the world of immediacy. As long as the individual lives in space and time, he or she must orient toward this world and its demands; only someone who has moved body as well as soul out of the world could completely give up all attachment or attention to it.

Second, the would-be religious person suffers from a sort of homesickness, albeit for a home he or she has at most only barely glimpsed. The individual longs and hopes for an *eternal* happiness, but must live in temporality. This separates the individual from the fulfillment of his or her hopes, resolutions, and goals. As long as the individual sets his or her sights on the eternal, finitude can only be experienced as a separation, a drag on the self who would fly to its eternal home, but must instead plod along.

This may suggest why Climacus treats suffering as a peculiarly religious pathos. Clearly, suffering is part of the break with immediacy which the ethical and the religious share. However, the ethical can express its eternal in the world, in the attachments and commitments of life. The ethical person attempts to express eternal standards in the temporal world; while this may never occur completely, it is the ethical task to fight and win this battle against time. The goal and the objects are in this world, however. The married person who seeks to preserve first love in time expresses an eternal ideal toward a particular finite person, over time. By contrast, the religious person who prays or worships seeks an object that is essentially outside the world she or he lives in. The goal of this striving is entirely eternal; it cannot be adequately expressed in this world, since the object of the pathos is essentially and completely outside space and time.

At the same time, the pathos of suffering is not completely alien to the ethical; as we have seen, any sincere devotion to absolute values will involve some suffering. By contrast, when the inwardness of suffering deepens to *guilt*, the ethical is overthrown. Guilt represents the final development in ethical pathos, and the highest development of religious pathos. It is certainly an ethical concept; true guilt cannot exist in the esthetic world of relativities and equivocations. Within the esthetic there may be relative standards such as 'not so bad' or 'never convicted,' or 'not impeachable,' but not the absolute qualification 'guilty,' since within the esthetic there are no absolute standards. The person who sees himself or herself as guilty has admitted that there is a highest, unconditional good, which all persons ought to pursue. He or she has also taken responsibility for those actions and choices that do not reflect absolute commitment to the absolute *telos*.

Not only must the ethically aware person admit moral wrong when he or she fails to pursue the absolute *telos* he or she has recognized; the ethical person must also admit that he or she has not pursued the good at all until now, and hence began the task from a state of failure. It is not true that the person was innocent, outside of moral standards, and then suddenly acquired them and straightway began to pursue the good; rather the person first applies moral standards to himself or herself by recognizing that he or she is not what one ought to be, and is not becoming what one ought to become. And since the individual is to be good always, one cannot make up for any moral debt; one can never do more than one has to at every moment, so as to have a way to make satisfaction.[93]

As long as one's notion of the absolute *telos* is sufficiently abstract, one may decide that one is only accountable for what has happened since one decided to give absolute priority to the absolute. But of course, Climacus is not discussing the abstract, except to criticize it as an inhuman way to think about one's own existence. Rather, Climacus is discussing the pathos that arises when I begin to concern myself about my eternal happiness, my highest good. The more a person lets the question become personal in this way, the harder it is to accept evasions of responsibility. I realize that I did not first recognize the good by seeing it in myself, but by seeing it outside myself, as something beyond where I was. Even if I had been perfect from that point on, I would still have been guilty. I have not, and cannot, 'earn' an eternal happiness. One fully experiences the totality of guilt when one thus conjoins the notion of one's own guilt with one's own eternal happiness. In relation to the absolute, any failure is an absolute failure; therefore, even the good citizen, the philanthropist, and the churchgoer must recognize that he or she is absolutely guilty and that all 'more or less' is only an evasion. This assumes, of course, that the person has seriously and inwardly considered the notions of guilt and an eternal happiness; for the person who has not looked within rather than at others, or who has stopped short of fully allowing the thoughts to get hold of him or her, will never reach full guilt-consciousness.

But for the one who has thought his or her own guilt all the way through, this consciousness represents the end of the ethical *per se,* and the beginning of the religious proper.[94] The guilty person no longer finds final meaning in ethical striving, since this makes no progress out of guilt. The guilty person can only relate to the absolute by repentance; but this has no meaning within the ethical. If the guilty individual is to have any relationship with the absolute at all, it must be a religious relationship, one that hopes and trusts that the absolute justice of the ethical is tempered by mercy.

If there is only the ethical relationship to the absolute, then the moment one becomes aware of the absolute one is already infinitely far from it. One can only relate to the absolute by admitting that one has not related to it and is not relating to it: 'Guilt-consciousness is the decisive expression for the existential pathos in relation to an eternal happiness.'[95]

Thus, the person who chooses to relate absolutely to the absolute *telos* will first encounter the pain of renouncing the absolute claims of the relative, which arise naturally just because the existing individual is a finite creature and thus lives absolutely in the finite. Then the individual will encounter suffering as the work of this renunciation proves to last as long as time, and the infinite goal of an eternal happiness is still just as far away. Finally, as the individual continues to consider the gulf between his or her own state and the eternal happiness for which he or she hopes, the individual cannot help but recollect his or her own guilt.

2. *The Ethical in the Religious*: The passion of the absolute relation to the absolute can be seen as a process moving the self from the pre-religious stage of resignation through the ethical-religious suffering to the final state of guilt-consciousness, where the ethical has gone bankrupt. This scheme would be a neat way to reconcile Climacus' terminology with his adherence to the theory of the stages, if only it worked. However, the ethical and the religious can be seen manifesting in every level of the deepening existential pathos, although in different ways. At the price of further blurring the line Climacus seems to draw between the ethical and the religious, it is more illuminating to work with his description of existential pathos as basically religious, and examine how he presents the workings of the ethical even within the religious life.

a. *Renunciation*: That renunciation (or resignation) is a religious passion is easy enough to understand. The concept is first introduced by Johannes de Silentio, the poet of the religious, who describes it as the essential and final stage prior to faith. Climacus likewise describes it as the 'initial expression of the existential pathos,' the absolute respect for the absolute *telos*. Given de Silentio's treatment of the absolute *telos* as a religious concept, it would seem that resignation is the first glimmer of the religious, not the last ray of the ethical. It is thus perhaps less clear in what sense renunciation is ethical, or the ethical is manifest in renunciation. On the other hand, resignation is an essential part of the individual's actual life. As Climacus writes, ethical subjectivity is the only actual subjectivity. Climacus asserts that it is precisely in the world of concrete reality—responsibility and decision, interest, and passion—that the spiritual is to be located.[96] The speculative task of seeing matters *sub specie aternae* is not just irreligious arrogance;

Climacus usually describes it as a violation of the ethical, a refusal to live in the actual situation in which one in fact lives and ought to live.[97]

Similarly, it is clear that an 'eternal happiness' is a religious concept; but in fact Climacus seems to use the phrase just as much as an ethical concept, the absolute ethical good, gained through ethical striving and defined in terms of the ethical.[98] It is the ethical pathos of self-transformation that is most suited to the eternal happiness. Even Paul's testimonial of his career is recounted as an example of ethical striving.[99] Such content as the concept 'an eternal happiness' possesses is likewise to be defined solely in terms of the ethical; Climacus even seems to revel in the esthetic barrenness of the concept, which leaves the individual nothing to contemplate or dream about at all lest he or she be distracted from ethical action.[100]

How does the understanding of 'eternal happiness' as the 'absolute ethical good' relate to the claim by Climacus 'that it is that good that is attained by absolutely venturing everything'?[101] Does the ethical person 'venture everything,' or is this true only of the religious person? Arguments can be made both ways. On the one hand, the ethical person does not risk *absolutely* everything; he or she is still justified. Life may be a struggle, righteousness may go unrewarded, but at least the ethical person knows he or she has 'fought the good fight'; and since ethical standards are universal, any ethical person who knows the facts can also recognize the righteousness of another. And even if no one else knows it, the ethical person knows that he or she is justified. The ethical person does not venture everything, if one considers such intangibles such as pride, self-esteem, self-approval, and good conscience. The religious person, by contrast, gives up even these, and chooses to know only guilt. This person is not justified in his or her own eyes, but rather is condemned. And the approval of others doesn't concern the religious person. Only if there is an eternal happiness that can render guilt meaningful is the religious person justified; only if there is a transcendent power that can forgive might he or she find relief from guilt.

On the other hand, Climacus is not here contrasting the ethical versus the religious, but the sagacious versus the daring. Of the sagacious, 'serious man,' he writes:

> But someone, 'a serious man,' may say, 'But is it certain and definite that there is such a good, is it certain and definite that there is an eternal happiness in store?—because in that case I surely would aspire to it; otherwise, I would be lunatic to risk everything for it.' . . . I venture to have the opinion that if a person, trusting in the asseverations of all the

philosophers and the security-guarantee of the entire clergy, decides to
aspire to an eternal happiness, he still does not aspire to it, and his *trust*
in the asseverations of all the philosophers and the security-guarantee of
the entire clergy is precisely what hinders him (the pastor, of course,
believes that it is a lack of trust) and prompts him to want to be jolly well
included, to want to make an intellectual transaction, a profitable stock-
exchange speculation, instead of a daring venture, prompts him to make
a simulated movement, a simulated pass at the absolute, although he
remains completely within the relative, a simulated transition such as
that from eudaemonism to the ethical within eudaemonism. . . .[102]

The 'serious man,' then, does not really seek to venture at all; he seeks to
avoid risk. He wants to be related to an eternal happiness, but he wants
to know that he is; otherwise the price is too high. Why, then, should it
matter so much that the serious man seeks certainty? How could certainty
concerning an eternal happiness bar one from an eternal happiness?
Climacus continues:

> The point is this: the individual first becomes infinitized by the daring
> venture; it is not the same individual and the daring venture is not one
> among several undertakings, one more predicate about the one and the
> same individual—no, through the daring venture he himself becomes
> someone else. Before he has made the venture, he can understand it only
> as lunacy . . .[103]

So it is the very act of venturing which breaks the individual free from the
moorings of the finite. The 'serious man' is tied to the finite even when
he would most try to relate to something beyond it, precisely because he
relates to it in the same terms that he relates to everything finite. Climacus
further explains:

> . . . But what is it to venture? To venture is the correlative of uncertainty;
> as soon as there is certainty, venturing stops. If, then, he gains certainty
> and definiteness, he cannot possibly venture everything, because then
> he ventures nothing even if he gives up everything—and if he cannot
> find certainty, well, then, so says the serious man in dead earnestness,
> well, then he will not venture everything—indeed, that would be lunacy.
> In this way the serious man's venturing becomes a false alarm. If that of
> which I am to gain possession by venturing is certain, then I am not
> venturing, then I am *trading.* . . . But the question about certainty and

definiteness is sagacity, because it is a subterfuge in order to avoid the strenuousness of action and venturing and shades the issue into knowledge and nonsensical talk. No, if I, acting, am truly to venture and truly to aspire to the highest good, then there must be uncertainty and, if I may put it this way, I must have room to move. But the greatest space in which I can move, where there is space enough for the most rigorous gesture of infinite passion, is uncertainty of knowledge with regard to an eternal happiness, or that choosing it is lunacy in the finite sense—see, now there is room, now you can venture![104]

Only in uncertainty can a person truly venture, truly relate absolutely to the absolute *telos*. Where there is certainty (or supposed certainty) the individual only relates relatively, even to the absolute good. To demand certainty is to condition one's relationship to the unconditioned, which is nonsense. If the object is the absolute, the relationship to it must be likewise absolute.

In opposition to the 'serious man,' Climacus says that only the person who truly risks is actually related to an eternal happiness. He writes:

Therefore eternal happiness, as the absolute good, has the remarkable quality that *it can be defined only by the mode in which it is acquired*, whereas other goods, just because the mode of acquisition is accidental or at any rate relatively dialectical, must be defined by the good itself. Money, for example, can be acquired by work and can also be obtained without work, and in turn both are different in many ways, but money still remains the same good. Knowledge, for example, is acquired differently according to talent and outward circumstances and therefore cannot be defined by the mode of acquisition. But nothing else can be said of eternal happiness than that it is the good that is attained by absolutely venturing everything.[105]

An eternal happiness is the absolute, unconditioned good; only the person who is capable of treating the unconditioned as unconditioned (giving himself or herself over to it unconditionally) can even experience it. The one who is stuck in relativities does not even have the concept of the absolute; to that person such a commitment is lunacy.

Clearly, the opposition Climacus draws is not the same as the contrast de Silentio makes between the ethical Abraham and the Abraham of faith.[106] In de Silentio's scheme, 'the ethical' is a commitment to the universal *in opposition to* absolute commitment to the absolute *telos*. His ethical Abraham, in order to preserve his duty toward his son, would rather plunge the knife into his own heart than obey God's command to violate the moral law.[107] He thus in one sense has an absolute commitment beyond himself and his own relative ends, to the universal. De Silentio identifies this sort of understanding of the ethical with Hegel: 'but in that case, Abraham is lost.'

Climacus clearly does not identify the ethical with Hegelianism. He equates Hegel and mediation with the 'serious man,' and the esthetic; it tries to 'force its way into the ethical and the ethical-religious,' but ultimately it is 'left outside.'[108] So while it may be true that both de Silentio and Climacus seek to counterpoise Hegelianism and the religious, it is not true that they are (always) counterpoising the same concepts for the same reasons.

This shows that de Silentio and Climacus are working with subtly yet fundamentally different notions of the ethical. To de Silentio, the ethical represents a commitment to universal standards, in opposition to commitment to either esthetic relativities or the absolute *telos*. While Climacus has not fully clarified his notion of the ethical, it is obvious that he means something other than this. He is so far from trying to separate the ethical from the religious that at times even he seems unsure whether they can be separated (at least in some contexts). 'The ethical' is that life-view where the individual breaks with relativities and evasions, and recognizes its true nature as a self with both eternal and temporal elements. The ethical thinker is the subjective thinker, the self that reflects on and is interested in its own true nature. Only a life-view that essentially involves subjectivity can be said to be 'ethical.' At least at this stage of existential pathos, the religious appears almost as a subset within the ethical life-view (or better, within subjectivity).

All of this is not to deny that there is an essential difference between the ethical which rejects the religious, and the ethical which does not. Climacus accepts Taciturnus' description of the three spheres of existence, with the ethical as transitional.[109] If the essential nature of ethical pathos is to drive toward the specifically religious, then a self which rejects the religious is lacking in full subjectivity. For example, if the ethical tends toward the concept of an eternal happiness, but the self rejects the notion as irrational, then its commitment to subjectivity is not so absolute as its commitment to its own estimation of its rational capacities.

b. *The Ethical as Present in Suffering*: In suffering, the ethical continues to be active even as the self moves significantly beyond it into the strictly religious. The distinction between the ethical and the religious appears when Climacus describes marriage as a 'jest.' He writes:

> I see this when I put marriage together with the absolute *telos*, with an eternal happiness, and in order to be certain that it is the absolute *telos* of which I speak, let death as the arbitrator judge between the two— then I dare to say with truth: It is a matter of indifference whether one has been married or not, just as it is a matter of indifference whether one is Jew or Greek, free or slave. Marriage is still a jest, a jest that must be treated with all earnestness, except that the earnestness does not therefore inhere in marriage itself but is a reflection of the earnestness of the relationship with God, a reflection of the husband's absolute rela- tion to his absolute *telos* and of the wife's absolute relation to her abso- lute *telos*.[110]

The Kierkegaardian authorship consistently regards marriage as the par- adigm of the ethical; if marriage has become a jest, so has the ethical *per se*. Likewise, the ethical demand for disclosure is abrogated by the higher demands of the religious.[111] The absolute relationship to the absolute *telos* is capable of relativizing even the 'universal' and 'essentially human' of the ethical. As seen in the case of marriage, it must still be treated with 'ear- nestness,' though only as it reflects the earnestness of the individual's God- relationship. Of itself it has no seriousness for the religious person; only as it has been an occasion for the subject to live the God-relationship in the concrete context of a married life, is it of religious significance. As for the duty of openness, it still applies against an esthetic type of hiddenness. However, the absolute relationship to the absolute cannot be perfectly expressed in a finite life, and every direct attempt to do so only cheapens it. To make the inward religious relationship between the individual and God external and visible is only idolatry, as the god who can be defined and seen is only an idol. True religiousness is invisible.[112] Thus religiousness creates a new sort of inwardness which not only cannot be disclosed, but which it is a positive duty to hide. All of this reflects and amplifies what was said before in other writings: the ethical is oriented toward the universal human, the religious toward the god, and the difference in orientation means that at times a thing may be demanded by one which is forbidden in the other.[113] This disjunction did not appear in Climacus' writings about renunciation, but it does emerge in suffering.

At the same time, the ethical continues to be important in the religious life of suffering. This is not merely in the general sense that the actual is the ethical, and the religious takes place within the self's actual existence and hence within an ethical setting. It is also true in the stricter sense that the ethical as the individual's discipline of generating moral maxims and applying them to concrete particular situations continues even in religious suffering.[114] The religious person may desire to always exist solely in the light of the absolute, but human nature cannot sustain this.[115] At times even the most devout, enthusiastic sufferer must seek diversion. If the sufferer has determined 'after honest deliberation' that now is the time to enjoy a little recreation at the Deer Park, then he or she must disarm any further doubts (no matter how pious they may seem) with the 'ethical consideration . . . that when worst comes to worst it is worse to become maundering than with decisiveness to carry out what has been decided, which perhaps was less properly considered, because maundering is the absolute downfall of every spiritual relationship.'[116] This is specifically described by Climacus as an *ethical* principle, deriving from the universal and essential human, which is indeed serving the religious relationship but is not directly derived from any transcendent source. Thus, in the face of the 'piecemeal' nature of human existence, even when it would absolutely relate to the absolute, it must at times have recourse to the ethical to provide resolution, particularly when the demands of finitude and the absolute must somehow be reconciled within the individual's life.

But the most remarkable aspect of the *Postscript*'s treatment of the role of the ethical within suffering comes when Climacus writes:

Last Sunday, the pastor said, 'You must not put your trust in the world, and not in people, and not in yourself, but only in God, because a human being is himself capable of nothing.' And we all understood it, myself included, because the ethical and the ethical-religious are so very easy to understand but on the other hand so very difficult. A child can understand it; the simplest person can understand, just as it is stated, that we are capable of nothing at all, that we should give up everything, renounce everything. On Sundays it is understood terribly easily (yes, terribly, because this easiness often enough goes the same way as good intentions) *in abstracto*, and on Mondays it is so very difficult to understand that it is this little and specific thing within the relative and concrete existence in which the individual has his daily life, in which the powerful one is tempted to forget humility and the lowly one to mistake relative modesty toward people of status for humility before God, and yet a little bit is indeed something very specific, a mere trifle in comparison with everything.[117]

Or as he further explains:

> ... But that is just the trouble, and here is the suffering in dying to one-self, and although the distinguishing feature of the ethical is that it is so easy to understand in its abstract expression, it is so difficult to understand *in concreto.*[118]

How can what the pastor said be 'ethical?' After all, he is a *religious* authority speaking to *religious* believers about their relationship with God. It is a statement about the universal human: We *all* ought *always* to do this. It is a general maxim of action, not a particular injunction such as the one Abraham alone received once to sacrifice the very particular 'son whom you love.' Coming through a third party, it can only have authority if the listener yields to the authority of the speaker (an esthetic surrender of self-action) or if the statement itself has the impersonal authority of law (and hence is ethical). In an esthetic relationship, the relation is between the authority who speaks and the hearer who obeys. In the ethical the relation is between the hearer who responds and the moral principle pronounced; the speaker is only a mouthpiece for the ethical. In the religious, the relationship would be between the finite subject and the absolute; but this can never be a direct relationship, and hence no human can make a direct statement such as this and have it be religious in the strictest sense.

So this statement, that 'apart from God we can do nothing, 'and 'this is something which we must always remember,' is an ethical principle. And one who obeys an ethical principle is an ethical person. Wrong! Here is the truly remarkable thing: to actually obey this ethical principle is a religious task, or suffering. As Climacus depicts, to actually realize this maxim in concrete actuality requires more than ethical categories. The preacher's glib statement, when fully felt and lived out by an actual individual, requires the dying to immediacy, which is suffering. Then, if the sufferer is not to be completely paralyzed, he or she must again turn toward the absolute *telos*, this time for positive empowerment to go ahead and act. The same Scriptures to which the pastor refers also say, 'I can do all things through God who strengthens me.' The sufferer's task is thus twofold: to be absolutely humbled by the knowledge that apart from God we can do nothing; and then, having thus died to immediacy, to live again through God, who makes all things possible—even a trip to the amusement park.

Obedience to at least some ethical maxims inevitably leads out of the ethical into the religious proper. A universal maxim springing from and directed at the essentially human can lead to an encounter between the individual and the absolute, which leaves the individual unjustified and annihilated unless he or she either retreats from full conformity to the maxim/or is justified through a purely religious personal relationship to the absolute. There seems to be a contrast with Kant implied. He started with practical reason as the source of the moral law. However, obedience to the humanly derived ethical inevitably entailed postulating the religious concepts of God and immortality.[119] Likewise, Climacus has shown that the operation of existential pathos inevitably leads to an antimony of the ethical, where an ethical maxim is generated which cannot be concretely realized unless the individual adopts a religious standpoint.

However, for Kant the progression from the ethical to the religious is an operation of practical *reason*; and while this may not be quite as cold and detached as Climacus (and others) suggests reason is, it is still largely a cognitive matter. Action does not really require the religious concepts; in fact, to act on them rather than letting reason alone be your guide is both immoral and irreligious.[120] Climacus, by contrast, describes the progression from the ethical to the religious as an operation of existential *pathos*. The content of the pastor's ethical maxim and the sufferer's religious insight are the same: that apart from God we can do nothing. The difference between them is a matter of focus; the ethical focuses on the maxim, the religious on the absolute. The individual begins focused on the universal and his or her relationship to it; as the existential pathos deepens, the individual turns further away from immediacy and considers more concretely his or her relationship to the absolute ethical good (i.e. an eternal happiness). In relating to the absolute, the individual turns further away from immediacy, until living solely by the ethical becomes impossible. Because the need for the religious is not merely logical but also affective, it would be impossible for the sufferer to take Kant's advice and assume the religious to tie up loose ends of the ethical, while acting solely by the moral law. The sufferer knows and feels the deep need to relate to the absolute, to find comfort and justification in the God-relationship, and to live by this rather than the universal human.

c. *Guilt*: Compared to his prolix discussion of suffering, Climacus' discussion of guilt-consciousness is almost cryptically short. There is next to no discussion of what guilt is, and only slightly more as to its significance; most of the text is dedicated to penance as an inadequate expression of guilt-consciousness. Apparently Climacus considers the basic terms to be common knowledge, or at least already known to his reader. All that remains is to impress upon the reader the infinite nature of guilt-consciousness, and the importance of it in the spiritual life of the individual.

The infinity of guilt lies not so much in its enormity as in the interminability of guilt-consciousness. Once the individual has grasped the notion of an eternal happiness with existential passion (unless he or she arbitrarily breaks off again at some point) the individual cannot but be drawn toward a sense of guilt for which no satisfaction can truly prove adequate. If no other guilt exists, there is still the fact that 'even while the individual deliberates he is ethically responsible for the use of time.'[121] Once I commit myself to living absolutely for the absolute *telos,* I discover the difficulty of performing this absolute task in the conditions of existence, and the inevitability of suffering. But once I accept suffering as my lot and task, I discover a new concern. I have not lived as I ought to have up until now; I have lived absolutely for relative ends and relatively for the absolute. If there is an eternal happiness, I can know only one thing about it: I don't deserve it. The more deeply I feel my need for an eternal happiness, the more I must feel that my own actions have rendered my receiving it uncertain. One's guilt may seem utterly trivial to another person, but to the person in the grip of existential pathos one's own guilt is total.[122]

Paradoxically, the very guilt-consciousness which the individual feels thrusts him or her away from an eternal happiness is precisely the sign that he or she is in fact related to an eternal happiness.[123] If the fact that one thinks one can make (finite) satisfaction for one's guilt proves that one has essentially no relation to an eternal happiness, then the fact that one experiences one's guilt as infinite is the best indication that one is in fact relating to an eternal happiness. It is this absolute standard, and only this, which makes guilt-consciousness total and satisfaction impossible. Thus, if one does feel the infinity of guilt-consciousness, one has a pretty good sign that one is in fact relating to the absolute, or (put another way) that what one is relating to, in relation to which one feels guilty, is in fact truly the absolute. Thus the religious person experiences guilt-consciousness both as a barrier between him or her and the absolute, and the surest connection to the absolute; so as much as it may pain the individual and as much as it may make the individual feel unworthy and distant from the absolute, he or she knows it is the truest bond between them; thus the religious person will seek to preserve this feeling of guilt and relish the pain. The religious person will even fear a lessening of this pain, as this pain is the greatest assurance one has that one truly loves the absolute, and it is the absolute one truly loves; if the pain of guilt weakens, perhaps one's love is weakening or one's consciousness of the absolute is becoming unclear. Guilt is a repulsive force between the individual and the absolute, growing stronger the closer the individual comes to relating to it; so the more strongly repelled one feels, the closer one must be to the absolute.

d. *Guilt, Sin, and the Absolute Paradox*: Climacus devotes rather scant attention to his examination of specifically Christian pathos. He evidently feels he has discussed Christianity sufficiently in his earlier writings, and need add only a bit more to complete his comparison of Christian religiousness with religiousness in general. Likewise, the discussion here requires little more than a contrast of Christian religiousness (Religiousness B) with other developments of the existential pathos, and to examine the changes wrought on the ethical-religious dialectic by the appearance of specifically Christian categories.

Perhaps the most crucial point Climacus makes is that guilt is not the same as sin.[124] In this he is making a distinction not generally drawn in Christian language; for that matter, it does not seem to be terribly clear in his own earlier writings. In the *Fragments* one *repents* of one's sin.[125] Repentance would seem to be an ethical term, or ethical-religious; one repents that for which one feels guilty. One is in untruth by one's own fault, and one feels responsible and guilty.[126] In the *Postscript*, Climacus discusses the 'older orthodox theologians, when they defended eternal punishment in hell,' and following traditional Christian language he uses 'sin' and 'guilt' interchangeably. Guilt before God *is* sin.[127] However, this is not consistent with his overall project of distinguishing between generic religiousness (Religiousness A) and Christian religiousness (B). In guilt-consciousness, the guilty person still has an essential connection to the absolute; in fact, this very guilt is the sure sign of this connection. If I say I feel my guilt, then I know I have done wrong. I must know the absolute I should have sought, and know at least something of how I have failed to pursue it. In knowing I have done wrong, I know right from wrong.

I may be at the bottom of an impossibly deep pit I myself have dug, with no means to fill it in or climb out; but I know I am at the bottom, I am looking up at the light and seeing the contrast between the darkness I am in and the light above, and at least I can call up to the lighted surface for help (though there may be no answer). Even this situation is more positive than the one Climacus describes for sin. In sin, I am not only in the pit, but I also have no idea which way is up. The sinner is moving away from the absolute, whether he or she means to or not. If the hypothetical person in the pit of sin has made a wrong turn, and is now digging furiously downward; if that miner feels the rocks get warmer as he or she goes deeper and takes that as evidence that he or she must be approaching the Sun, is so certain of the direction that he or she rejects evidence of error in order to continue this misdirected course, then this would begin to be an analogy for the sinner, who 'is not merely outside the truth but is polemical against the truth, which is expressed by saying that he himself has forfeited and is forfeiting the condition.'[128]

In the case of someone who is blindly wandering away from safety, a voice from the proper direction may make one aware that he or she has gone astray, and that it is necessary to turn around. Otherwise, precisely the certainty, determination, and energy which the lost individual thinks is saving him or her will prevent that person from discovering the error. Likewise, the sinner is unlike the guilty person in that the guilty one knows he or she is lost from the absolute, whereas the sinner is so lost as to believe he or she is already moving toward salvation while actually fleeing the absolute. In this case, only a revelation from the absolute can enable the sinner to reestablish his or her existential bearings and recognize how completely lost he or she is.

In the *Fragments*, Climacus described sin as being in untruth through one's own fault and act. In the *Postscript*, he claims that there are countless ones who are excluded from salvation 'through no fault of their own but by the accidental circumstance that Christianity has not yet been proclaimed to them.'[129] While these writings seem contradictory, they flow from the basic description of Christianity as the revelation of the absolute in time. In the *Fragments*, Climacus argues that if the individual is in untruth, sin, it must be as a result of something the sinner has done to himself or herself; thus it would follow that the individual's sin flows from his or her own choice and action. On the other hand, since the individual was/is trapped in sin and God wishes to reach the sinner, God must come into existence as the Paradox, thus revealing the absolute in the medium of existence to those who have lost all sense of the absolute as absolute. Now that the absolute has done this, the way to the absolute must be through the Paradox. This paradox is a discrete occurrence in space and time, imposing the same epistemological restrictions as any other event. The absolute may be my source, but just as I would remain ignorant of my birth mother if I were separated from her at birth and never allowed to meet or hear of her, so too I will never know the absolute unless I am made to know of the Incarnation during the course of my existence. So while Climacus argues that the condition of sin could only be the result of one's own free action, he also argues that millions have been and still are born in sin and die without ever having the existential option of faith.

This apparent contradiction is a bit easier to understand with more understanding of his broader framework. First let us take time to examine a second important consequence of Climacus' description of sin: that free actions and ethical striving are largely irrelevant to one's salvation. In the consciousness of sin the individual realizes that he or she is something other than the essentially, universally human; being human is not essentially to be a sinner, but being a human who is a sinner is to have one's existence essentially qualified. To be a human (and not animal) is to be related to the absolute;[130] but to be a sinner who has the consciousness of sin is to be related to the absolute in time, the Paradox. Climacus continues:

> But inasmuch as the believer in his consciousness of sin will also become aware of the sin of the whole race, another isolation appears. The believer expands the consciousness of sin to the whole race and at the same time does not know the whole race to be saved, inasmuch as the single individual's salvation indeed depends on his being brought into relation to that historical event, which precisely because it is historical cannot be everywhere at once but uses time in order to become known to human beings, during which time one generation after the other dies. In Religiousness A, the sympathy is with all humankind, because it is related to the eternal, a relation of which every human being is assumed to be essentially capable, and because the eternal is everywhere, so that no time is spent in waiting or in sending a messenger for that which by being historical is prevented from being everywhere at once, and about whose having existed countless generations through no fault of their own could continue to be unaware.[131]

Climacus thus claims that the Christian is committed to the belief that anyone who is not a Christian, no matter how morally good or religiously enlightened that person may be, is lost. Or perhaps it is more accurate to say, the Christian cannot see how they can be other than lost. It is not really appropriate to think about eternal happiness in the third person, so it is not really the Christian's place to decide whether another person is saved; but the logic of sin-consciousness leads inescapably to the conclusion that there is no route to eternal happiness except through the God-Man. Thus the religious person (Religiousness A) feels a certain kinship and sympathy with all people, knowing that all are guilty and also that all are still children of the absolute; any person may feel the same pain and find the same balm in guilt-consciousness that the religious individual knows personally. The Christian by contrast knows that there are many who do not share the same relationship to the absolute which he or she knows, and indeed have no relationship to it as far as he or she knows; thus the Christian must

regard them as essentially different, and confess doubt or at least ignorance as to whether these others have any hope for salvation at all.

But while Climacus argues that Christianity necessarily claims that the
only route to the absolute *telos* is through the God-Man, he is equally insis-
tent that it is essential for the individual to pass through guilt-consciousness in order to experience Religiousness *B*. The primary reason for this is
that prior to Religiousness *A*, the individual lacks the concepts for understanding Religiousness *B*. He writes:

> Religiousness *A* is the dialectic of inward deepening; it is the relation to
> an eternal happiness that is not conditioned by a something but is the
> dialectical inward deepening of the relation, consequently conditioned
> only by the inward deepening, which is dialectical. On the other hand,
> Religiousness *B* . . . makes conditions in such a way that the conditions
> are not the dialectical concentrations of inward deepening but a definite
> something that qualifies the eternal happiness more specifically . . . not
> by qualifying more specifically the individual's appropriation of it but by
> qualifying more specifically the eternal happiness, yet not as a task for
> thinking but as paradoxically repelling and giving rise to a new pathos.
>
> Religiousness *A* must first be present in the individual before there can
> be any consideration of becoming aware of the dialectical *B*. When the
> individual in the most decisive expression of existential pathos relates
> himself to an eternal happiness, then there can be consideration of
> becoming aware of how the dialectical in second place (*secundo loco*)
> thrusts him down into the pathos of the absurd. Thus it is evident how
> foolish it is if a person without pathos wants to relate himself to the essen-
> tially Christian, because before there can be any question at all of simply
> being in the situation of becoming aware of it one must first of all exist
> in Religiousness *A*.[132]

By emphasizing that the change from *A* to *B* is not a matter for thinking,
he is again clarifying his claim that the distinctiveness of Christianity does
not lie in doctrines or theology which can become grist for the philosopher's mental mill. Rather, the distinctiveness of Christianity lies in the
understanding of the eternal happiness and how the individual can relate
to it. Whereas in *A* the relation was inward, and there was still an essential connection between the individual and the absolute, in *B* there is no
longer any connection save that which the god creates in existence. Even
if *A* and *B* had the exact same conceptions of the absolute *telos*, this would
still represent an essential difference between them. In *A*, as Climacus says

earlier, recollection is still possible; in *B* it is not and thus the entire under-standing of human existence has been altered.[133] Without any change in the concepts that could be said to be a matter for thinking, the entire basis for human existence is shifted.

Because Religiousness *B* entails a changed understanding of the relation-ship to an eternal happiness, a person who lacks knowledge of an eternal happiness obviously cannot understand Christianity either. The esthete may observe the working of existential pathos, but misunderstands it at every step. If the esthetic person tries to relate to the absolute *telos* (without understanding the ethical religious task) he or she will begin with a misre-lation, as Climacus writes:

> Esthetic pathos expresses itself in words and can in its truth signify that the individual abandons himself in order to lose himself in the idea, whereas existential pathos results from the transforming relation of the idea to the individual's existence. If the absolute *telos* does not absolutely transform the individual's existence by relating to it, then the individual does not relate himself with existential pathos but with esthetic pathos— for example, by having a correct idea, but, please note, by which he is out-side himself in the ideality of possibility with the correctness of the idea; he is not himself in existence with the correctness of the idea in the ideal-ity of actuality, is not himself transformed into the actuality of the idea.[134]

Climacus argues that a person may well feel very religious, and become quite emotional and agitated over religious issues or events; or a person may become so occupied with spiritual things that he or she thinks and writes incessantly about them; but if the person is not ethically transformed he or she is still esthetic. Whether such a person thinks of an eternal hap-piness as some fairy-tale happy ending for God's favored ones, or a more mystical *summa summarum*, or the consummation of the spiritual dialectic of existence, it is still a misunderstanding. And as the absolute *telos* is misun-derstood, so the Paradox that would reveal the absolute is misinterpreted, according to the peculiarity of the esthetic person. Whether one thinks of Jesus (for example) as the one who takes away our responsibility for the hard work of moral striving or as a symbol of the union between the divine and the human, one still thinks of oneself as essentially connected to the abso-lute, and hence in no need of a 'savior' as Climacus understands the term.

Esthetic religiousness first absolutely underestimates the enormity of the problem of relating to an eternal happiness, and then reduces the abso-lute paradox to something adequate to meet its own view of the problem.

The person who has passed through the full course of existential pathos to arrive at guilt-consciousness has seen that the problem of existence is insoluble, at least on its own terms. To such a person, Christianity's message of salvation may be seen either as an esthetic attempt to inadequately answer the problem, or as a paradoxical solution to a problem that certainly couldn't be solved without one. Thus the guilty one may respond with offense and insist that there can be no way back to the absolute; or, the guilty one may respond in faith, knowing that there seems no way back to the eternal happiness one has thrust away by one's own guilt, but believing the message that the absolute has changed the rules by entering into existence to make it possible again for an existing person to be related to the absolute. Climacus argues that Religiousness *B* requires Religiousness *A* in that Christian faith requires both that the believer recognize the impossibility of a (nonparadoxical) relationship between the individual and God, and then believe that nevertheless a relationship has in fact been created through the paradoxical incarnation of God in the particular person of Jesus.[135]

C. Summary: *so you call this a 'postscript'?* Is Climacus joking when he presents a six hundred page 'postscript' to a one hundred page book? If there is any meaning in calling this work a postscript, it would lie in the fact that Climacus considers the essential element to be the issue of the *Fragments*: the relationship between idealist philosophy and Christianity. Hegel, and his Danish successors such as H. L. Martensen, have conceded that Christianity is a significant spiritual advance on Greek philosophy. Climacus asserts, however, that idealism's interpretation of Christianity has presented it as not so much an advance upon Greek philosophy as simply another philosophical statement, perhaps not even as good as Plato's original. The *Fragments* presents its argument in the form of an experimental attempt to present a real alternative to philosophy, the only real alternative possible, which 'coincidentally' turns out to resemble New Testament Christianity (as opposed to the philosophically reinterpreted version so popular with Denmark's intelligentsia).

The *Postscript* abandons the fiction that Climacus is inventing his alternative, and seeks to present the issue in its 'historical costume.' In doing this the *Postscript* encounters a problem the *Fragments* had been able to avoid: the corruption of ethical-religious language. The terminology of the debate has been taken over by his opponents, and Climacus must struggle to reclaim the concepts so that he can state his case.

The essential error, as Climacus sees it, is found in such comments as Martensen's that the human's need for a visible God 'is so deep-rooted and engrained in the nature of the human race that one can say about God's incarnation in Christ that if it had not actually occurred, humanity itself necessarily would have invented it.'[136] Philosophy, even the somewhat humbled and rebaptized idealism of Martensen, assumes that the Incarnation either is in fact a human invention, or a realization of essential human nature such that humanity naturally receives it as the fullest development of its own aspirations. Climacus argues instead that Christianity is a violation of human expectations, which must have come from beyond the human and which even now can be believed only by a miracle (as Hume and Hamann agree). Apart from the miracle, the natural response of the individual to the Incarnation is offense. And without the revelation of the true nature of sin, the individual will naturally misinterpret both God and his or own human nature, making sin less than it is and thus also minimizing the Incarnation which removes sin.

Sin in the Postscript: Haufniensis, citing Constantin and de Silentio as predecessors, presented a fairly clear description of the development of sin-consciousness. When one strives to live ethically, one inevitably fails. The ethical is the ideal, and humans are not; as soon as a person fails even once, he or she has fallen outside the ethical. Knowing oneself to be guilty, one becomes caught up in anxiety and unable to work oneself out again. This is the bondage of sin. When one has sinned, one knows one cannot simply repent and start over with the ethical; one must find another way. In the 'second ethics' that follows after sin, the ethical standard becomes an ideal to be striven toward rather than a state of guiltlessness from which the sinner falls. In the religious 'second ethics' there is forgiveness; one strives to do good, fails, repents, and has the faith not to despair anxiously but rather tries again.

Taciturnus basically agrees with this understanding. He describes the ethical as a 'transitional' state, where one has left the esthetic but has not fully recognized sin. While he doesn't describe it in terms of a 'first' and 'second' ethics, it is clear that the realizations of the ethical are not forgotten in the religious. One strives ethically, and the ethical always goes bankrupt; the religious person is left out 'over 70,000 fathoms of water,' with no finite security or moral justification.[137] Without repentance and faith, the religious individual is driven toward the demonic; with faith, the individual can confess and be made whole, freed from the bondage to anxiety and guilt.

Climacus explores this further. The sinner cannot be redeemed unless God comes into time with the sinner, and there reveals Godself to the individual in a way that respects the individual's selfhood and restores the individual's freedom. God gives the freedom to choose faith, or offense. For the individual who chooses faith, existential pathos leads from resignation through suffering to guilt-consciousness. There is no discussion of the 'first' and 'second' ethics, but rather a more gradual transition or fuzzy boundary between the ethical and the religious. Where Haufniensis described the essential change in the ethical brought about by sin, Climacus goes further to describe a whole new religiousness, and a new existential dialectic for the whole of human existence. When God brings the knowledge of sin and its redemption through the Incarnation, human existence itself is essentially changed, and restored: restored to the wholeness it should have always had, and changed in that its essential human nature is now based on its relationship to the god incarnate in time. This restoration of what was lost in a way that makes it both the same and new is the true repetition.

Knowing the totality of sin, the Christian cannot see a way anyone could be saved apart from Christ, leaving the Christian to sorrow and fear for the many who could not or will not accept redemption. But at the same time, the truest relationship between one human and another is indirect; so even if the Christian wishes to 'save their souls,' he or she cannot simply preach or judge; it is necessary to work indirectly, so that the other can come to see the truth of the Incarnation for himself or herself.

Chapter Seven

Sin, Society, and the Individual
in the *Two Ages*

Kierkegaard began his review of the anonymous novel *Two Ages* in 1845, but set the project aside to finish the *Postscript*. At the same time it is quite distinct from the earlier works in some important respects, and thus serves as something of a bridge between that phase of his authorship that he 'concluded' with the *Postscript*, and the second phase with its greater emphasis on direct discourse and interpersonal/social themes. *Two Ages* has long been recognized as an important statement of Kierkegaard's social views, although its partial translation into English seems to have only delayed the full appearance of this work and thus obscured recognition of its significance for understanding the nature of the relationship between the ethical and the religious. The *Two Ages* offers a presentation of how the theories Kierkegaard has developed through both his pseudonymous and direct writings up to this point can be applied to the life of the individual in society, and to the understanding of society in general.

A. *The Two Ages, the Ethical and the Religious. Two Ages* threatens to seriously undermine the *Postscript*'s analysis of the relationship between the ethical and the religious. Climacus has presented an apparently straight and inviolate progression from the ethical to the religious. Everyone starts with the esthetic; some break with immediacy to pursue the ethical; those who pursue the ethical to the fullest discover guilt-consciousness and the religious, and the one who has done this is ready to make the jump to Christianity. While a person may freely choose to refuse to jump at any point along this progression, the order in which they appear in a person's life seems to be set, as the later ones are conceptually dependent on the earlier, more fundamental stages. If one moves from the esthetic to become a Christian, one must go through each intervening stage in order.

By contrast, in *Two Ages* Kierkegaard seems to suggest that it is possible to jump straight from the esthetic to the religious.[1] The *Postscript*, and the pseudonymous authorship as a whole, has apparently argued for a 'stages on life's way' understanding of the spheres of existence. However, to take this scheme at face value risks being deceived by the fictitious element of the pseudonyms.[2] They are dramatic characters in their own right, not mere masks for their author. Thus when dealing with a work written under Kierkegaard's own name, one must anticipate contradictions and be prepared to reconcile discrepancies with attention to 'the environment' of the seemingly contradictory remarks. As Lee Barrett writes:

> Viewed in the light of his total authorship, *Two Ages* is a puzzling book. Not only is the pattern of passional development atypical of his other works, but it is also difficult to harmonize with the description of the stages of life contained in Kierkegaard's pseudonymous literature. . . .
>
> Put starkly, the ostensible problem here is that *Two Ages* suggests an 'immediate' access to the religious life. Kierkegaard claims that the 'life-view' of the author of *A Story of Everyday Life* and *Two Ages* 'lies on the boundary of the aesthetic and in the direction of the religious' (TA, 14). Speaking in his own voice, Kierkegaard insists that this life-view is not ethical, but is aesthetic, and, as such, 'immediate' (TA, 39–40). At the same time he claims that genuine 'inwardness' is to be found here and that the religious life is not far away. He commends *A Story of Everyday Life* as a 'place of rest, or if you please, a place of prayer, for a certain religious tinge is unmistakable' (TA, 21). This opinion contrasts with the prevalent theme in the pseudonymous works that any 'inwardness' requires a decisive breach with immediacy, actuality, and the aesthetic life. . . . *Two Ages* seems to present a life-view that has close affinities with the religious life, but which is not characterized by any 'mediated' passage through melancholy, irony, guilt, or even ethical seriousness.[3]

I, like many commentators before, have assumed that there is a single underlying scheme within the pseudonymous authorship. In fact, however, the pseudonyms are not unanimous as to the actual relationship between the spheres of existence. While it is common to chalk this up to the fact that less advanced pseudonyms must have less insight than the later, more advanced ones, perhaps we should first reexamine those instances where the pseudonymous authors appear to assert a path to the religious other than the one Climacus describes.

Fear and Trembling uses the illustration of an impossible love of a young man for a princess as one example of an event which could lead an individual to become a Knight of Faith, seemingly by way of a direct leap from erotic love to the religious.[4] Barrett points out that this character seems similar in many respects to the heroines of *Two Ages*, particularly Marianne in her resignation.[5] Unlike the Knight of Resignation, however, neither woman finds contentment in preserving her love in its ideality alone: both prefer the satisfactions of actuality. In this they superficially resemble the Knight of Faith; but only at a glance, since neither expects to receive the actuality of love 'by virtue of the absurd.' The Knight has really renounced the realization of his actual love, has conceded its impossibility; the heroines of *Two Ages* continue to find comfort in what is possible. As de Silentio writes:

> Precisely because resignation is antecedent, faith is no esthetic emotion but something far higher; it is not the spontaneous inclination of the heart but the paradox of existence. If, for example, in the face of every difficulty, a young girl still remains convinced that her desire will be fulfilled, this assurance is by no means the assurance of faith, even though she has been brought up by Christian parents and perhaps has had confirmation instruction from the pastor for a whole year. . . . Her assurance is most captivating, and one can learn much from her, but there is one thing that cannot be learned from her—how to make the movements—for her assurance does not dare, in the pain of resignation, to look the impossibility in the eye.[6]

The pseudonym here claims that such a person as the heroines of *Two Ages* is not a precursor to the religious, but at best a precursor of the precursor. She indicates something of where the problem lies and what must be done, but until she faces the insurmountable nature of the obstacle finitude has placed before her wish, she does not become religiously instructive. Barrett would here urge us to pay attention to the environment of the quote. De Silentio is one who lacks faith, precisely because he has broken with actuality. Thus, he cannot imagine that a figure who has not done what he has can be instructive. In this he may be wrong. Why shouldn't a person like Claudine or Marianne, who has suffered a partial break with actuality but has been reconciled with it again, be at least a partial illustration of the faith which endures a complete rupture and then overcomes it? This is likely what Kierkegaard found so appealing in the novel.[7] At the same time, however, de Silentio makes a point if we are to take such a person as a role model for the religious. While the life-view exhibited by the heroines in *Two Ages* has some similarities to faith, it

also bears more than a passing resemblance to denial or wishful thinking. The life-view of *Two Ages* is not mere wishful thinking, of course;
it recognizes the obstacles and dangers finitude can present to human
fulfillment, and that some persons might be crushed. However, it does
not seem willing to think this all the way through; it continues to glean
the stubble of finitude for a few grains of happiness rather than strike out
for fresh fields. Such an attitude might just as well delay the leap into the
ethical-religious as prefigure it.

The young man of *Repetition* offers another example of one who seems
to come to the brink of the religious through an unhappy encounter with
the romantic. This case is all the more interesting because the young man
becomes a poet, which Kierkegaard apparently regards as a less developed
life-view than that of *Two Ages*. The poet is clearly a borderline case, at
least as described by Constantin. He is not 'religious,' yet he 'has the religious within him as a secret he cannot explain.'[8] Constantin describes his
young friend as an 'exception.'[9] He is an exception to the universal, a category already explored by William in *Either/Or*. And he is a transitional category to the 'true aristocracy' of the exceptional, the religious exceptions.
However, as we have seen, the young man fails to achieve faith, and hence
misses the true repetition he seeks.

Oddly, the one pseudonym who seems to most support Barrett's argument for alternative paths to the religious is one which he treats as a foil to
his position: Judge William. In his essay, Barrett cites William's writings in
Either/Or that specifically criticize the romantic choice unmediated by ethical categories.[10] In this William is consistent with his later writings on marriage in the *Stages*, which Barrett does not cite.[11] Through the resolution
to preserve the immediacy of love within the ethical bonds of marriage,
love is preserved against time and the 'spiritual trials' of doubt over love's
everlastingness. 'Finally, in the resolution (the lover) will, through the universal, place himself in relation with God.'[12] Through the ethical resolution
to marry, the individual encounters difficulties that the resolution alone
cannot overcome. William writes:

> In using his powers of thought and his concerned love to think this, he
> *eo ipso* thinks it [the danger] to be so terrible that he cannot surmount it
> by himself. He has run aground; he must either let go of love—or believe
> in God. In this way the wonder of falling in love is taken up into the won-
> der of faith; the wonder of falling in love is taken up into a purely reli-
> gious wonder; the absurdity of falling—in love is taken up into a divine
> understanding with the absurdity of religiousness.[13]

But this is not the only route to the religious William describes. The mediated, ethical route is only appropriate for a man, say William; a woman has an entirely different spiritual path. For the woman, the appropriate road leads straight from the esthetic to the religious. He writes:

> But now to her, for without resolution there is no marriage. A feminine soul does not have and should not have reflection the way a man does. Therefore, this is not the way she is to come to the resolution. But swiftly as a bird she comes from esthetic immediacy to the religious. . . . They meet in the religious immediacy as a married couple. But the man reaches it through an ethical development. . . . The highest understanding a woman has—and has it with honor and with beauty—is a religious immediacy. . . .
>
> Immediate love, then, is in the woman. Here is the common ground. But the transition to the religious occurs without reflection. That is, when an intimation of the thought, the content of which the man's reflection ideally exhausts, passes through her consciousness, she faints, and while her husband hurries off and, equally moved but also through reflection, is not overwhelmed; he stands firm, the beloved leaning on him until she opens her eyes again. In this swooning, she is transferred from the immediacy of erotic love into that of the religious, and here they meet again. Now she is prepared for the wedding, for without resolution there is no marriage.[14]

In the context of the *Stages*, William's claim appeared to be a misunderstanding to be 'corrected' by Taciturnus' comments about the ethical being the transitional stage to the religious.[15] However, the spiritual path William proposes for women seems the same Barrett finds in *Two Ages*: romantic love as 'an immediate way on the path to the religious life.'[16] Despite the similarities between *Two Ages* and William's views in the *Stages*, there seem to be significant weaknesses in William's understanding of the relationship between the ethical and the religious. For both man and woman in William's writings, God is Lord of the Gaps. Wherever the ethical is found lacking, the religious is evoked to provide the foundation, bridge, guarantee, or whatever the ethical needs. Woman is 'closer' to the religious simply because, being less reflective, she runs into difficulties sooner and must evoke the *deus ex machina*. However, William never really defines the religious; indeed, he seems to lack any distinct ideas about it at all. What he describes as 'the exception' (with all the hypothetical certainty of a biologist discussing unicorns) seems closer to what Kierkegaard himself means by 'the religious,' except that William seems to think such cases are rare anomalies or nonexistent possibilities; whereas Kierkegaard, like his creations Taciturnus and Climacus, holds this to be that which any individual can and should become.

All of this certainly impacts how we understand the relationship between the ethical and the religious in Kierkegaard's thought. A 'stages on life's way' approach would suggest that one must progress from the esthetic through the ethical to the religious, and from there (with God's grace) to the Christian. But such characters as the young man in *Repetition* and the heroines in *Two Ages* appear to skip the ethical and move 'immediately' into the religious. And William suggests that in fact many people make such a direct leap. And if it is true that one can move directly to the religious, that would further seem to suggest that the necessity of moving through sin-consciousness at all. If it is true that one can skip the ethical, then one could leap from the esthetic to Christian salvation without having to first repent of one's sin or even become aware of it.

But if we grant that there are multiple paths to the religious, the key question is: what would the next step be if one has been 'educated in resignation' by an unhappy love affair, as Barrett suggests? What is lacking in Claudine and Marianne, which leaves them in the esthetic rather than some higher sphere of existence? Ultimately, it seems to be the thoroughness of the break with actuality. They know 'actuality's way out,' which is to find support within actuality even while dealing with one's break with actuality, until the broken area heals again.[17] The image Kierkegaard uses of a broken twig which is splinted until it heals is telling, for the twig in his illustration is not broken all the way through. This appears to be the fundamental difference between the life-view of the *Two Ages* and the religious life-view: the religious life-view heals when the twig has completely broken. The religious categories are 'more decisive' than those of *Two Ages*, for they break completely with actuality.[18] The life-view of *Two Ages* is 'provisional,' and hence in a sense false even if it lasts all one's life.[19] It should be 'a place of rest,' but not the final rest. At the same time, it is instructive by being 'universally paradigmatic.' In expressing a break and reconciliation with actuality, Claudine and Marianne provide an image of the life of faith. However, in not completely breaking with actuality before being reconciled, each holds back from the complete healing of the religious. If the author had not intervened with a happy resolution, her heroines might have fallen into bitterness and despair as the futility of their wishes became undeniable.

Marianne's story is perhaps most instructive, reflecting as it does both the life-view of the novel and the envious reflection which Kierkegaard sees underlying his present age. Marianne is a person seemingly being destroyed by leveling. Reflection's constant criticizing, personified in her stepmother and the servants, has left her a withdrawn and largely defeated person. When her beloved declares that he cannot marry her because he has no money, this strikes her as reasonable. The romantic daring that believes that 'all we need is our love' has long since been ground out of her and Bergland. But still, the 'way out' she knows is actuality's way out, even if it is only the dream of how happy it would be to actually marry. She hides her love from reflection's criticism, thus surrendering her outer life to envy's oppression while seeking to preserve her inner life as a hidden treasure.

In thus exempting part of her life from reflection and its malicious envy, Marianne also denies herself the essential truth that is present here. The people around her live empty, trivial lives, and in their envy they seek to make Marianne feel empty and unimportant as well. The truth in this, as in all leveling, is that in fact all human actuality really is ultimately unimportant.[20] She hides her love, because she knows full well that they would tell her it is impossible; in this she fails to be a knight of faith who knows the love is impossible, and yet holds on in the face of reflection's mockery by virtue of the absurd.[21]

The difference and the similarity between Marianne and the knight of faith is that, as even William recognizes, faith is immediacy *after* reflection, whereas Marianne's love is immediacy that holds back from reflection. In this both are different from the poet or resignation, which despairs of actuality in order to grasp the eternal. And as Marianne has had her encounter with reflection and disappointment with actuality, her experience suggests the religious view as well. But where her view is one of a person who has been wounded by actuality, the religious life-view is of one who has died to actuality, yet lives again.

So the standpoint of Marianne is 'midway between the esthetic and the religious'; it has partly broken with immediacy, but still holds tenuously to actuality.[22] This would of course be a new route from the esthetic to the religious, bypassing the ethical as a middle step. So where is the ethical, if anywhere, in this new scheme? The only genuine escape from the vitiating power of leveling, Kierkegaard says, is when 'the single individual has established an ethical stance despite the whole world.'[23] When the individual has accepted reflection's verdict on the meaninglessness of actuality and relative unimportance of the individual, and yet has been religiously redeemed from despair to find the second immediacy and a reconciliation with actuality in virtue of the absurd over reflection's objections, then that person must be prepared to act despite the legion's voice of envy. Such an individual must be able to act out of resolution; but this is an ethical task. So even a religious individual who has come to the religious via reflection's cruel tutelage rather than the discipline of the Law must still integrate the ethical into his or her life.

What this shows is that, while Taciturnus and Climacus may be right in outlining the three spheres of existence and the interactions between them, it is wrong to interpret this as a temporal progression. The ethical is foundational to the religious life, and the religious life essential to enable and complete the ethical task; but this does not prove that they must follow one another sequentially. Climacus writes (dare I say it?) abstractly; concrete existential realities may differ. But while the esthete may progress directly to the religious, there can be no religious life without the inclusion of the ethical. The broad division of esthetic/or ethical-religious holds; and thus too the existential pathos described by Climacus of resignation, suffering and guilt, leading toward sin-consciousness and the need for salvation.

Religious Ethics, Envy and the Need for a Life. *Two Ages* offers a route from the ethical to the religious that differs from the dialectic laid out in the pseudonymous works. At the very least, this warns us not to take the dialectical structure of the pseudonymous arguments too strictly, as if they were meant to apply absolutely and invariably as a developmental roadmap for each individual. *Two Ages* introduces a number of concepts which significantly alter the description of the ethical-religious task, concepts themselves vulnerable to misinterpretation but which, once clarified, throw new light on the whole ethical-religious project.

In his conclusion to his review, Kierkegaard returns to a theme emphasized repeatedly in his pseudonymous works: passion. 'The age of revolution is essentially passionate, and therefore it essentially has *form*.'[24] It is a definable something, and those who are part of it likewise are definite persons with an essential inward relation to the idea of the age. This is a highly illustrative concept, though not the normal way of speaking in this postmodern, nominalist, materialist culture we live in now. In fact, read a certain way (somewhat selectively, and filtered through the lens of existentialism perhaps) this discussion can reinforce the image of Kierkegaard as an asocial or antisocial individualist whose view of an ideal world would be millions of disconnected individuals existing solely before God and aware only of the Absolute *telos*. We can see this in passages such as this:

> When individuals (each one individually) are essentially and passionately related to an idea and together are essentially related to the same idea, the relation is optimal and normative. Individually the relation separates them (each one has himself for himself), and ideally it unites them. . . . Thus the individuals never come too close to each other in the herd sense, simply because they are united on the basis of an ideal distance.[25]

It would be easy to come away with the impression (particularly if one came to this text with that impression already) that Kierkegaard envisions an ideal society like a theater, where each individual indeed is united in an experience shared in common with each other, but each does it individually, with no essential relationship to the others. Indeed, for every word about the idea uniting individuals, one seems to find two words about it distancing them; and this distancing seems to be the crucial thing. If we have the relation to an idea without separation of the individuals, we have the mob rule of The Terror in the French Revolution; and if we have no idea and no separation, we have crudeness and philistinism. On the other hand, an 'individually separating essential inwardness' seems to be ideal, as if just keeping people apart and introverted should be enough to protect them from both anarchy and triviality.

Kierkegaard's meaning here does not need to be interpreted so atomistically, and I believe it is a mistake to do so. In fact, oddly perhaps, the slang of our own pop culture can give us a useful clue to a truer reading of Kierkegaard, and I suggest, a truer understanding of the ethical task in general. The phrase I have in mind is 'to get a life.' The teenage boy shouts a crude comment to the pretty girl on the sidewalk; she responds disdainfully, 'Get a life!' The boy sees the businessman hurrying into his office building as his lunch hour ends; he says, 'That dude should get a life!' Stopping on the way home, the businessman sees the girl hanging around the mall with her friends; he wonders, 'Don't those kids have a life somewhere?'

It is a curious phrase, as most idioms are. The person to whom it refers is alive, and so has life, but does not have *a life*. So this is an implicit recognition that human life should be more than just biological continuance, and perhaps even more than biological satisfaction. It should have some meaning, some purpose, something more than just animal existence.

At the same time, it is not clear at all what this 'more' is. The boy, who was said by the girl to need to get a life, thinks he has one and even looks down on the busy stuffed suits in their offices; the businessman in turn thinks the young don't know what life is, but is sure enough that he does to look down on their irresponsible pursuit of happiness. So one identifies 'a life' with happiness or satisfaction of impulses or freedom from constraint and conformity, the other identifies it with responsibility and purposeful activity. But in each case, the root meaning of the injunction is the same: You have missed what is of most importance or value in life, you live a less than fully human life, your life is not 'a life.'

If 'a life' is taken to mean 'a human life lived in relation to that which is of highest value,' then this would seem to be what Kierkegaard means by a life lived in relation to the idea. It might even be possible to translate Kierkegaard's language into the more modern idiom, thusly:

> When individuals (each one individually) essentially have a life, and together have essentially the same sort of life, the relation is optimal and normative. Individually the relation separates them (each one has his own life), and ideally it unites them. Where each one has his own life, there is a decent modesty between man and man that prevents crude aggressiveness; in the relation of unanimity of life-view there is the elevation that again in consideration of the whole forgets the accidentality of details. Thus the individuals never come too close to each other in the herd sense, simply because they are united by each having his own life. . . . On the other hand, if individuals have a life merely *en masse* (consequently without the individual separation of inwardness), we get violence, anarchy, riotousness; but if there is no life for the individuals *en masse* and each personally has no life either, then we have crudeness.[26]

This paraphrase demonstrates that there is an essential similarity between Kierkegaard's phrase and our own. At the same time, the paraphrase makes clearer the social aspects of Kierkegaard's thought. There is clearly nothing antisocial in saying that each individual should have a life, or live his or her own life. At the same time, it can hardly be 'optimal and normative' for every individual in a community to have such a private vision of what life is that they cannot even discuss it with each other. It would be better for people who are to relate to each other to each have the same or similar views on what 'getting a life' means. Otherwise, as in my example of the slackers and the suits, they most likely won't have a real relationship at all.

What do we expect from people who need to get a life? For one thing, we expect conformity, mass gatherings, attempts to find an individual purpose by submerging into a collective. One might join an authoritarian religious sect that gives all its members a shared, rigidly defined world-view and a strict code of behavior, relieving its members of the need to think or choose as free individuals. Those outside the group say that those inside need to get a life, a real life they personally have chosen, rather than just taking the one handed to them. Another person who has no life may find a sense of meaning and belonging by becoming a sports fan, attending all the games, painting his or her body in team colors, screaming at the referee, and otherwise forgetting self in the participation in the crowd of spectators. Still another might submerge his or her personal identity in a race-based hate group, or a political movement. In every case, when we see a person who apparently has no life outside the collective, we are likely to judge that that person had no life before joining the group and still has no life as a free, self-conscious individual.

What about the person who has no life, and has not submerged into a collective either? This is the person of whom we most often and truly say, 'There's one who needs to get a life.' How do we claim to recognize the person who needs to get a life? First, we say this about the person who seems to live a life of pure animal self-indulgence, without 'higher aspirations'. As a poet said:

What in the world ever became of Sweet Jane?

She lost her sparkle you know she isn't the same.

Living on reds and vitamin C and cocaine,

All her friends can say is ain't it a shame.[27]

Sweet Jane has no life. Perhaps she did once, or thought she did. Perhaps she had a lover who left; perhaps she followed a rock band around until she lost her personal identity in a haze of drugs and mass ecstasy, and stopped caring anymore. When we see a person who is so caught in selfish animal satisfactions that he or she no longer cares about more rational, sophisticated, or social pursuits, we may say that person has no life. With a bit more perception, we may see that the greedy corporate raider, or the connoisseur who lives only on caviar, champagne, and opera are not essentially different from Sweet Jane. In the truest sense, each has no 'culture,' to use Kierkegaard's term. Each has lost essential elements of his or her full humanity by being caught up in egocentric pleasures; and each got that way because he or she had no life, no higher ideal or pressing responsibility or object of interest that could turn that one's attention to something besides self-indulgence.

The second way we may claim to recognize the person who needs to get a life is by the way that person treats others. The girl claimed to know that the boy needed to get a life because he had the free time and free attention to notice and harass her. The businessman who is obsessed with doing better than his coworkers, perhaps even sabotaging their efforts, needs to get a life. The old woman who spies on her neighbors and gossips should get out and try to get a life. As Kierkegaard writes of the world in which individuals have no relation to an idea:

> Then people shove and press and rub against each other in pointless externality, for there is no deep inward decency that decorously distances the one from the other; thus there is turmoil and commotion that ends in nothing. No one has anything for himself, and united they possess nothing, either; so they become troublesome and wrangle. Then it is not even the gay and lively songs of conviviality that unite friends; then it is not the dithyrambic songs of revolt that collect the crowds; then it is not the sublime rhythms of religious fervor that under divine supervision muster the countless generations to review before the heavenly hosts. No, then gossip and rumor and specious importance and apathetic envy become a surrogate for each and all. Individuals do not in inwardness turn away from each other, do not turn outward in unanimity for an idea, but mutually turn to each other in a frustrating and suspicious, aggressive, leveling reciprocity. The avenue of the idea is blocked off; individuals mutually thwart and contravene each other; then selfish and mutual reflexive opposition is like a swamp—and now they are sitting in it. Instead of joy there is a kind of sniveling discontent, instead of sorrow a kind of sullen, dogged tenaciousness, instead of enthusiasm the garrulous common sense of experience.[28]

In a society where people have no relation to an idea, where individuals have no life, each has no grand vision to look toward; and so they look at each other instead. When each has no glorious goal that beckons, they instead want what they see the others have. A society where none has an essential and passionate relation to an idea, where none or few have a life, is a society driven by envy. As Robert Perkins points out, envy in Kierkegaard's thought is not just a personal character flaw; it is a social force as well.[29] A single envious man wishes that no one have anything better than he has. In a society made up predominately of envious people, each watching the others to make sure that no one has or does anything better, this envy quickly becomes a superpersonal social force of its own. Any time an individual shows any excellence not possessed by the others, whether it be intellectual, social, or possibly even physical, that one will be set upon by the others until he or she is properly humiliated. Once everyone feels that the point has been made that the so-called excellent one really isn't any better than the rest of us, they can all relapse again into a state of mutual suspicion, a cold war of envy, until the next one tries to break with the standards of the group. While engaged in tearing down someone else, each feels vindicated and powerful; but in fact they are neither. Each is convicted because to envy another is to admit one's own inferiority in some way; each is impotent because each is in the bondage of the social envy of the group, and cannot break with it without becoming its target as well. Indeed, the whole society is united by this mutual suspicion; none dares try to break with the herd lest the fury of the group single him or her out. As Kierkegaard writes, envy is thus a negative unifying force.[30] Kierkegaard refers to this social envy, with its aggressive enforcement toward all who would strive for something better, as *leveling*.

As insidious and destructive as leveling is, it also contains an essential truth: each person really is essentially no better than any other. Thus, while it may be evil and destructive when envy says of another, 'You're no better than me,' it is positively upbuilding when one says to oneself, 'They're right, I am no better than anyone else.' However, this realization alone is not enough to save the individual from the effects of leveling upon his or her sense of self. This leads us to the essential divergence of our typical use of 'a life' from Kierkegaard's notion of 'a life lived in relation to an idea.' To most of us, the phrase 'to get a life' may have quite various meanings; Kierkegaard's prescription for an inoculation against leveling is quite specific.

One of the commonly recognized signs that someone needs to get a life is when that person has time to bother or judge others; a second would be when a person is simply sitting around bored. In such cases, the prescription is likely to mean, 'That person needs something to do, something to occupy the mind, to fill time.' In this our unsophisticated reaction begins to sound like the 'Rotation of Crops.'[31] Boredom is the root of all evil, we must banish boredom and the envious person will be too occupied to turn on neighbors in a destructive, leveling way. So for many of us, if the envious person has found the joys of stamp collecting, the problem is solved; and it seems that if every individual had some such pursuit, leveling could be eliminated.

The problem is that even the stamp collector's passion is not immune to the judgment of leveling. Ultimately, all such goals are trivial, and are judged so by the others in the dispassionate, impersonal reflection of leveling. This life is still a life of despair, in the language of *Either/Or*. It cannot give the individual a sense of meaning or worth; at best it can distract one from feeling the meaninglessness of existence or the worthlessness of oneself. The forces of leveling are all around one, and quash any sense or claim of uniqueness by the individual. The only sense of individuality such reflection will leave alone is the abstract mathematical fact that this is *one* person. To feel some personal value, persons in the age of reflection join together into groups, factions, parties, and thus take on a derivative value as part of something bigger than themselves. Reflection can recognize that two is bigger than one, and has no objections to this sort of claim to worth. Leveling has nothing to say against it, because the individual is not claiming any personal value but rather is acknowledging that personal worth derives from the herd, in which we sheep are all equal.

This is not the only possible escape from the corrosive power of leveling on the individual, however. There is a sense in which an individual may claim worth as an individual apart from the herd, without making any finite claim to superiority that would call down the justified condemnation of leveling. That sense is the infinite worth of each individual before God.[32] The person who lacks this sense may wish to confirm his or her own wisdom by always agreeing with 'the public,' as if agreeing with the prevailing opinion insured that one might always remain in the right. However, the public is an abstraction, a creation and tool of leveling; and so it can as easily condemn tomorrow what it praises today. We may say public opinion shifted, but we don't say it ceased to be the public opinion; and one who seeks to be guided by it may quickly find himself or herself publicly condemned for what was done in obedience to public opinion. This can destroy the individual's sense of meaning, leaving a cynical herd mentality; but Kierkegaard writes:

. . . if the individual is not destroyed in the process, he will be educated by this very abstraction and this abstract discipline (in so far as he is not already educated in his own inwardness) to be satisfied in the highest

religious sense with himself and his relationship to God, will be educated to make up his own mind instead of agreeing with the public,
which annihilates all the relative concretions of individuality, to find rest
within himself, at ease before God, instead of in counting and counting.
And the ultimate difference between the modern era and antiquity will
be that the aggregate is not the concretion that reinforces and educates
the individual, yet without shaping him entirely, but is an abstraction
that by means of its alienating, abstract equality helps him to become
wholly educated—if he does not perish. The bleakness of antiquity was
that the man of distinction was what *others could not be*; the inspiring
aspect [of the modern era] will be that the person who has gained himself religiously is only what *all can be*.[33]

These considerations raise two more questions: First, if this is the situation Kierkegaard's reader is in, what should that individual do? And
second, does this again point the way to another alternative route from
immediacy to the religious? Addressing the first of these questions may
give us a clue to the second. Kierkegaard does in fact have a scheme for
the improvement of society, although it is unlike the usual plans for social
reform. After all, the usual strategy would be to form an organization, or
maybe even a political party, to combine like-minded individuals into a
group which could grow into a social movement. However, this process is
itself in the service of leveling. Kierkegaard writes:

> In our age the principle of association (which at best can have validity
> with respect to material interest) is not affirmative but negative; it is an
> evasion, a dissipation, an illusion, whose dialectic is as follows: as it
> strengthens individuals, it vitiates them; it strengthens by numbers, by
> sticking together, but from the ethical point of view this is a weaken-
> ing. Not until the single individual has established an ethical stance
> despite the whole world, not until then can there be any question of
> genuinely uniting; otherwise it gets to be a union of people who sepa-
> rately are weak, a union as unbeautiful and depraved as a child-
> marriage.[34]

It is clear then that there is still a place for the ethical, although
Kierkegaard doesn't spell out here what that means. It certainly includes
commitment to duty for its own sake, just as William would have wanted
it. Specifically, its primary commitment seems to be to 'the principle
of individuality.'[35] The true individual, the one who has become 'an

essentially human being in the full sense of equality' under the cruel tutelage of leveling, will be so committed to this that he or she will even accept condemnation from society rather than give up working for the personal individual development of self and others.[36] Individuality is something only the individual can develop; no one can do it for another. Thus the individual must refuse the help of the herd, which would advise any number of ways to self-fulfillment except actually becoming a self. And the individual must stand back from those actions that a reflective society considers the truest help for others, because these very acts undermine the individuality of the one helped. Thus the individual will likely be condemned as arrogant, selfish, and antisocial simply for being unwilling to collaborate with leveling.

To say that the ethical individual's primary commitment is to fostering individuality does not rule out social action. In fact, Kierkegaard comments extensively on the reflective age's analog to the hero and reformer of earlier times.[37] It can easily be admitted that society needs changing; even society says so, provided no one actually *acts* on the claim other than to schedule meetings and make speeches.[38] And while it may be true that all society is in the service of leveling, some institutions seem to be particularly corrupting: the press, for example.[39] But to raise oneself up as a leader, even in so noble a cause as the reform of the press, is to become another tool and then victim of leveling. Instead, anyone who would wish to combat leveling must do so from a position of weakness. Such persons don't claim to act from a special calling or duty, but simply 'because of their apprehension of the universal in equality before God.'[40] They are thus without authority or importance, and in fact only doing what anybody could (and should) do. Kierkegaard writes:

> The unrecognizables recognize the servants of leveling but dare not use power or authority against them, for then there would be a regression, because it would be instantly obvious to a third party that the unrecognizable one was an authority, and then the third party would be hindered from attaining the highest. Only through a *suffering* act will the unrecognizable one dare contribute to leveling and by the same suffering act will pass judgment on the instrument. He does not dare to defeat leveling outright—he would be dismissed for that, since it would be acting with authority—but in suffering he will defeat it and thereby experience in turn the law of his existence, which is not to rule, to guide, to lead, but in suffering to serve, to help indirectly.[41]

One immediately thinks of Kierkegaard's own experience with *The Corsair*, where he set himself up as a victim in order to call attention to its injustice. It would not take much to develop a doctrine of civil disobedience from this, particularly as seen in Thoreau's personal choice to go to jail rather than support an unjust war. In fact, any individual who consistently and consciously seeks to oppose leveling and avoid (as far as possible) becoming its instrument will find ample opportunity to oppose social forces and structures, through being their suffering victim.

Even in martyrdom, the 'unrecognizables' act within the limits of the ethical alone. That is, they only seek to instantiate the universal duty incumbent upon the essentially human. Passionate commitment to their own selfhood and the selfhood of others is enough to turn them into covert crusaders. And yet the work of the unrecognizable is in fact a religious one, seeking to bring others to a personal God-relationship. Being unrecognizable, they do not cry out or preach necessarily; yet as Kierkegaard writes, because of their work

> Then it will be said: 'Look, everything is ready; look the cruelty of abstraction exposes the vanity of the finite in itself; look the abyss of the infinite is opening up; look, the sharp scythe of leveling permits all, every single one, to leap over the blade—look, God is waiting! Leap, then into the embrace of God.'[42]

The religious, then, provides the motivation, the energy, the foundation, the goal, the meaning of this cultivation of selfhood; but when the religious person acts out of this religiousness, he or she relies on ethical categories and manners of acting. Without the ethical, the religious would have no plan of action, except perhaps to claim direct inspiration and thus again to fall under the sway of leveling; and without the religious the ethical self could not sustain itself against the power of leveling to undermine and dissipate it. The lived ethical life is thus also religious, and *vice versa*. Here in his own name Kierkegaard repeats the confusing usage of Climacus, who both distinguishes the ethical and the religious only to recombine them in the ethical-religious.

B. *Conclusions: Postscript and Two Ages*. *Two Ages* makes no explicit references to the theory of the spheres of existence, or to the pseudonymous works which present this theory. As presented in the *Stages* and *Postscript*, there are three distinguishable stages of existence, though the leap from the esthetic to the ethical seems to be qualitatively different from the transition from the ethical to the religious. The esthete cannot even be properly said to be a subject. The esthete is really more of an animate object adrift in the currents of immediacy, reacting and conforming to the world but never actually choosing a direction or plan for his or her life. The ethical person by contrast begins to consider the question of value and choice that the esthete never raises. This individual begins to consider the issue of his or her own subjectivity, how it is developing, what goals to pursue, and so on. This is an essential difference in one's life, roughly analogous to changing from a piece of driftwood to a motorboat with compass and captain. While the esthete drifts through life, simply accepting whatever immediacy hands him or her, the ethical person chooses to captain his or her own boat—and more than that, the ethical person must even fashion a ship to captain from the collection of driftwood random chance has given him or her up to that point.

The religious person does not abandon the ethical task or essentially change it. The task still remains to take the talents and circumstances immediacy has handed one, and fashion these into a purposeful, meaningful life. The difference is that the ethical person sees this task as possible, as self-justified, and as self-sustained; the religious person believes otherwise, and seeks to ground his or her life in a personal relationship to the divine. As de Silentio says, repentance is the rock on which the ethical founders. The ethical life may be like a steamship, but once it goes off course it strikes a reef and is broken. The only option is to once again assemble the pieces, but the motor is irreparable; there is no choice but to fashion a sail, and let another power propel the craft. Similarly, once the moral law is broken it can only condemn; if the individual is to find justification and meaning again, it must come from outside the individual. With that new external grounding, the task of living returns to something very much what it was before, though not so self-reliant.

Kierkegaard does not discuss the three spheres in *Two Ages*, though he continues to employ much of the same language. In particular, he echoes Climacus in finding the essence of human existence in passion, and in regarding reflection divorced from existential passion as a deadly threat to the self. It is from passionate concern for the self that the self acquires motivation, direction, and focus. As this self-reflective passion is directed toward different ideals of self-realization, the self becomes religious, ethical, or esthetic. But there are two ways in which Kierkegaard seems to deviate from the views expressed by Climacus, which (if we wish to harmonize them) significantly affect how we can understand the meaning of the *Postscript*.

First, while the pseudonymous works generally depict the esthetic as something immature, pathetic, and tending toward the demonic, Kierkegaard presents it as (at least in some cases) something noble and with the potential to reach toward the religious. In his discussions of Claudine and Marianne, Kierkegaard suggests that it is possible for a person to have a partial, though real, break with actuality, thus gaining something of the transcendence over immediacy that the religious person enjoys, without ceasing to seek one's ultimate validation from the finite. This suggests that it is possible to move from the life of pure immediacy to the religious without passing through the transitional stage of the ethical first. On the other hand, there is nothing in *Two Ages* to suggest that the religious person could bypass the ethical and live completely without it. In fact, he continues to accept the close connection between the ethical and the religious that Climacus assumes when he hyphenates the terms. It is therefore probably better to interpret Climacus' dialectic of subjective passion nontemporally. That is, the ethical is essentially prior to the religious, in that the religious life must assume the ethical from the outset (or else it remains merely esthetic) whereas the ethical need not assume religious categories until it has bankrupted itself. However, this does not mean that the religious can appear only in a person who has in fact exhausted the possibilities of the ethical. One may in fact make the break with immediacy, 'leap into the arms of God,' and undertake the religious life straight away. Then, having embraced the religious already, one will find oneself growing ethically and religiously at the same time, as the task of living responsibly requires ethical categories and passion as well as the religious sense of the infinite.

Second, Kierkegaard presents principles that dramatically expand the realm of social-political ethics. Climacus discusses in detail the role of the subjective author, and the need to employ indirect communication and other such stratagems to assure that the author builds up the reader's subjectivity rather than just becoming an authority for the reader to admire submissively. Kierkegaard's discussion of the moral secret agent in an age of reflection shows that such concerns are not in fact for authors alone. Every ethical-religious person is called upon not only to develop his or her own subjectivity, but also the subjectivity of others whenever possible. This principle could justify social reforms, where institutional or economic structures are found to be dehumanizing. At the same time, it limits how such reforms might be pursued. Kierkegaard seems to have thought well of the abolition of peasant bondage in his country; but if liberating the peasantry meant turning them into a mean-spirited revolutionary mob driven by class envy and worship of a leader figure, then this would be perhaps worse than doing nothing. The leveling process may be more comfortable than slavery, but it is not necessarily less corrupting to the spirit; and bondage to the herd is more subtle than bondage to one's lord, but may for that be more pernicious. At the same time, to free the peasants in a manner consistent with their own selfhood and destiny as responsible individuals would be the true fulfillment of the ethical principle, Kierkegaard claims in *Two Ages*. Thus the ethical principles of *Two Ages* need not result in rigid social conservatism. Still, they must not result in political factionalism or revolutionary violence, as these undermine the individuality of the people ostensibly helped, the helpers themselves, and those who are designated the 'oppressors' or 'enemy.'

Two Ages and *Concept of Anxiety:* Kierkegaard writes, 'The present age is essentially a sensible, reflecting age, devoid of passion, flaring up in a superficial, short lived enthusiasm and prudentially relaxing in indolence.[43] The present age is formless; 'therefore in contrast to lunacy and stupidity it may contain truth, but the truth it contains can never be essentially true.'[44] Haufniensis describes spiritlessness as 'a sum of rational creatures . . . transformed into a perpetual muttering without meaning. . . . It may possess truth, but mark well, not as truth but as rumor and old wives' tales.'[45] He continues, 'Man qualified as spiritless has become a talking machine, and there is nothing to prevent him from repeating by rote a philosophical rigmarole, a confession of faith, or a political recitative.'[46] Climacus describes the person without inwardness as 'perhaps a "walking-stick," an artificial contrivance.'[47] It seems pretty clear that these three 'authors' are all describing the same thing. The present age and modern society is reflective, objective, and spiritless; its ideal citizen is passionless, able to parrot ethical-religious truth but with no real sense for its meaning or significance; and this lack of individual inwardness or spirit takes on a social force of its own, as true spirit is suppressed as lunacy and arrogance. And this spiritless, envious age is sin. The sin of individuals becomes something more; it becomes envy, leveling, the herd mentality, as each one seeks the security of the crowd. Anyone who would present the spiritless with the possibility of becoming spirit will awaken their anxiety toward the good; even by being an individual one presents the possibility of selfhood, calling others to freedom and thus to greater anxiety. For those in the grip of the demonic, this is an unbearable threat; no wonder they seek to suppress the individuals among them!

The unrecognizables whom Kierkegaard describes are not just moral secret agents; they are covert evangelists. They are not just trying to oppose dehumanizing social institutions; they are calling their neighbors to each 'leap into the arms of God.' Anyone who does is saved, both from his or her own anxiety and from the spirit-crushing force of leveling. Being saved, each will be made part of that society that Kierkegaard describes as 'having form,' where each one relates to each other through God, as individuals. As far as this community spreads, society itself is redeemed from the bondage of sin.

Chapter Eight

Conclusion

Kierkegaard believed that thought, faith and action must be intimately connected if any of these is to have validity; hence he wrote about ethics, religion, Christianity, and how these should be related in life. His argument is that an ethics that refuses to take sin seriously has failed to attain its full fruition, and one that does take it seriously has transcended its own categories and must pass into religion. As long as the esthetic, ethical and religious are treated as opposing spheres, human life remains self-contradictory and self-destructive. Only through faith in God as revealed in the Incarnation can the individual bring these elements together.

In this first phase of his authorship, Kierkegaard never directly discussed his famous 'spheres of existence' in his own name. This was presented to his readers solely through the pseudonyms, indirectly and piecemeal. And the pseudonyms do not always agree with each other. Haufniensis distinguishes between the 'first ethics' before sin, and the 'second ethics' after sin. Taciturnus refers to the ethical as a 'transitional' phase, suggesting that it is left behind when the individual enters the religious. Climacus offers a new term, the 'ethical-religious,' which blurs the line between the ethical and the religious almost to vanishing, turning the 'spheres of existence' into a continuum. And as the relationship between the ethical and the religious is obscure in the pseudonymous works, so too is the concept of sin. As we have seen, there are several reasons why his writings should be unclear and contradictory. His direct writings steer clear of the 'decisively Christian' understanding of sin, and his pseudonyms do not fully understand it themselves. More importantly, though, 'existence is not a system,' belief is 'by virtue of the absurd,' and Christianity gives 'offense.' Even the realities of existence cannot be fully put into words; how much more the mysteries of Christianity, which are far beyond the grasp of reason! Kierkegaard does not use the 'theory of the spheres of existence' as a roadmap from the esthetic to Christian salvation, but more as a tool-kit of concepts, images and relationships to point the reader toward the existential realities of guilt, belief, faith, grace, sin and salvation. There is a general framework that undergirds the pseudonymous authorship and is even reflected in the direct discourses; but the pieces do not fully mesh, allowing the framework to move a bit to accommodate the unfinished nature of actual life.

Kierkegaard is remembered as an apolitical, asocial writer, who was so fixated on the concept of 'the individual' that he wanted those words on his tombstone. In fact, there is a running social commentary throughout Kierkegaard's authorship, often covert and intermittent. As early as *Either/Or* there is recognition that the actual, concrete individual is not *sui generis*; rather, the concrete individual is the product of a history and society.[1] Thus any discussion of what the individual should be also implies a certain relationship to others, and a certain society to nurture and support the individual. *Concept of Anxiety* makes this criticism more overt, with its discussion of paganism within Christianity. In a self-declared Christian society, the attack on spiritlessness was also an attack on the culture. The upbuilding discourses generally show less overt social criticism, but still have social implications. They stress the spiritual equality of all individuals, while Kierkegaard's contemporaries generally believed themselves to be the spiritual elite and arbiters of value for the uncultured masses. And Kierkegaard wrote about virtues such as love, which obviously imply a social life for the religious individual.

More generally, the clarification of Christianity and what it means to be a Christian also implies a certain sort of 'Christian society.' There is a certain way a Christian should relate to others, a certain way to encourage others to become Christian individuals and to avoid thwarting them, a certain ideal society that would result if everyone related to others as Christian individuals. And the 'present age,' with its leveling, envious mass culture rather than true community, is identified as not just dysfunctional or immoral, but as reflecting sin as spiritlessness. So sin is not just an individual crisis, but also a social force, with certain institutions particularly reflecting this sinful spiritlessness. The spread of true Christianity would not just redeem individuals, but society as well.

Kierkegaard presents his conception of sin and salvation through a series of books written under multiple personae. Reading these books as they were written, in chronological order and with signed and unsigned works side-by-side, reveals aspects of Kierkegaard's thought that are obscure or invisible to other approaches. This is still a controversial and complicated process. His original readers were unsure how to interpret the connections between Kierkegaard's various works, when they bothered about it at all;

and even today we can disagree despite hindsight, access to journals and other advantages. I would not be a very good reader of Kierkegaard if I said I was certain I had everything right; my hope is that there is enough that is correct, useful and/or provocative to aid the reader of Kierkegaard and to steer our conversation down productive paths.

Notes

Chapter One

[1] Søren Kierkegaard, *The Point of View for my Work as an Author: A Report to History*. Translated with introduction and notes by Walter Lowrie, edited with a preface by Benjamin Nelson (New York: Harper & Row Publishers, 1962), pp. 19–20.

Chapter Two

[1] Søren Kierkegaard, *The Concept of Anxiety: A Simple Psychologically Orienting Deliberation on the Dogmatic Issue of Hereditary Sin*, edited and translated with an introduction and notes by Reidar Thomte in collaboration with Albert B. Anderson (Princeton, NJ: Princeton University Press, 1980), pp. 17–18, 21.

[2] Søren Kierkegaard, *Concluding Unscientific Postscript to Philosophical Fragments*, edited and translated, with an introduction and notes by Howard V. Hong and Edna H. Hong (Princeton, NJ: Princeton University Press, 1992), p. 268.

[3] Søren Kierkegaard, *Eighteen Upbuilding Discourses*, edited and translated, with an introduction and notes by Howard V. Hong and Edna H. Hong (Princeton, NJ: Princeton University Press, 1990), pp. 49–101.

[4] *Eighteen Upbuilding Discourses*, pp. 67–68.

[5] *Eighteen Upbuilding Discourses*, pp. 69–78.

[6] *Eighteen Upbuilding Discourses*, pp. 67–68, 78–79.

[7] Søren Kierkegaard, *Either/Or*, v. II, edited and translated with an introduction and notes by Howard V. Hong and Edna H. Hong (Princeton, NJ: Princeton University Press, 1987), pp. 214–219.

[8] *Eighteen Upbuilding Discourses*, p. 97.

[9] *Eighteen Upbuilding Discourses*, p. 98.

[10] Søren Kierkegaard, *Fear and Trembling/Repetition*, edited and translated with introduction and notes by Howard V. Hong and Edna H. Hong (Princeton, NJ: Princeton University Press, 1983), pp. 216–219.

[11] *Eighteen Upbuilding Discourses*, p. 98.

[12] *Repetition*, p. 229.

[13] *Repetition*, p. 136.

[14] *Repetition*, pp. 200–201.

[15] *Fear and Trembling*, pp. 94–99.

[16] *Fear and Trembling*, p. 94.

[17] *Fear and Trembling*, p. 96.

[18] *Fear and Trembling*, p. 98.

[19] *Fear and Trembling,* p. 99.
[20] *Fear and Trembling,* p. 98.

Chapter Three

[1] For example, see Louis P. Pojman, *The Logic of Subjectivity: Kierkegaard's Philosophy of Religion* (University, AL: University of Alabama Press, 1984), pp. 84–86.

[2] Pojman, pp. 101–102.

[3] Or at least, the pseudonym Johannes Climacus did; see *Concluding Unscientific Postscript,* pp. 268, 270.

[4] *Eighteen Upbuilding Discourses,* pp. 242, 272; see Søren Kierkegaard, *Philosophical Fragments/Johannes Climacus,* edited and translated with an introduction and notes by Howard V. Hong and Edna H. Hong (Princeton, NJ: Princeton University Press, 1985), pp. 39–44; and *Postscript,* p. 106.

[5] *Eighteen Upbuilding Discourses,* pp. 275–289.

[6] *Eighteen Upbuilding Discourses,* p. 288.

[7] *Fragments,* p. 9.

[8] *Fragments,* pp. 9–13, 109–111.

[9] *Fragments,* pp. 13–21.

[10] *Fragments,* p. 15.

[11] *Fragments,* pp. 30–35.

[12] C. Steven Evans, *Passionate Reason: Making Sense of Kierkegaard's Philosophical Fragments (Indiana Series in the Philosophy of Religion)* (Bloomington, IN: Indiana University Press, 1992), p. 61.

[13] W. M. Alexander, *Johann Georg Hamann: Philosophy and Faith* (The Hauge: Martinus Nijhoff, 1966), p. 72; also Ronald Gregor Smith, *J. G. Hamann 1730–1788: A Study in Christian Existence; with Selections from His Writings* (New York: Harper & Brothers Publishers, 1960), pp. 214–217.

[14] Thomas Aquinas, *Summa Theologiae,* v. 1, part 1, question 2, article 3.

[15] This particular portion of the *Fragments* has provoked much and varied critical attention. For three examples of the divergent views that have been offered, see: Nielsen, H. A. *Where the Passion Is: A Reading of Kierkegaard's Philosophical Fragments* (Tallahassee, FL: University Presses of Florida, 1983), pp. 61–87; Robert C. Roberts, *Faith, Reason, and History: Rethinking Kierkegaard's Philosophical Fragments* (Macon, GA: Mercer University Press, 1986), pp. 68–78; and Evans, *Passionate Reason,* pp. 63–71.

[16] *Fragments,* pp. 44–45.

[17] *Fragments,* pp. 45–46.

[18] *Fragments,* p. 46.

[19] *Fragments,* pp. 46–47.

[20] *Fragments,* pp. 49–54.

[21] *Passionate Reason,* pp. 86–91.

[22] *Fragments,* p. 16.

[23] *Fragments,* pp. 14–19.

[24] *Fragments,* pp. 23–36.

[25] *Fragments,* pp. 55–59.

26 *Fragments*, pp. 59–61.

27 For more on this, see W. Glenn Kirkconnell, *Kierkegaard on Ethics and Religion: from Either/Or through Philosophical Fragments* (London: Continuum Press, 2008), pp. 123–136.

28 *Fragments*, p. 62.

29 *Passionate Reason*, p. 119.

30 *Fragments*, pp. 75–76.

31 Roberts, pp. 106–108.

32 *Fragments*, p. 75 (italics author's).

33 *Fragments*, p. 76.

34 Hence repetition is a problem for persons, not for nature; a fact largely lost on Kierkegaard's contemporaries. See *Repetition*, p. xxviii.

35 *Fragments*, p. 77.

36 For example, see *Philosophy of Right*, esp. pp. 138–140.

37 *Fragments*, p. 77.

38 *Fragments*, pp. 18–19.

39 There is also a long and intriguing footnote to this section on the past; intriguing particularly because Climacus finally drops the pretense that his concern is to offer an alternative to the Platonic-Socratic epistemology, and attacks Hegel by name (*Fragments*, p. 78). Fredrick Sontag (in 'Strange Interlude,' *Man and World*, v. 27, 1994, 15–21) sees the Interlude, and even this footnote of the Interlude, as the center of gravity for the entire book.

40 *Fragments*, pp. 79–86.

41 *Fragments*, pp. 79–80.

42 *Fragments*, pp. 41–42.

43 *Fragments*, p. 78.

44 David Hume, *An Enquiry Concerning Human Understanding*, sections I–VII.

45 Hume, *Dialogues Concerning Natural Religion*, pt. I.

46 W. M. Alexander, *Johann Georg Hamann*, pp. 165–200; Smith, *J. G. Hamann*, pp. 39–102, 175–236.

47 *J. G. Hamann*, pp. 207–231.

48 It is significant to remember that though Kierkegaard had limited knowledge of Hume, Climacus himself is depicted as knowing Hamann and building on him. Hamann, in turn, had extensive knowledge of Hume's philosophy, and relied on it heavily.

49 *Fragments*, pp. 81–82.

50 *Fragments*, p. 83.

51 *Fragments*, pp. 82–83.

52 *Fragments*, pp. 83–84.

53 *Fragments*, p. 85.

54 *Fragments*, pp. 86–88.

Chapter Four

1 Vanessa Rumble, 'The Oracle's Ambiguity: Freedom and Original Sin in Kierkegaard's *The Concept of Anxiety.*' *Soundings*, 75/4 (Winter 1992); 605–625.

2 Lee Barrett, 'Kierkegaard's "Anxiety" and the Augustinian Doctrine of Original Sin'; in Robert Perkins, ed., *The International Kierkegaard Commentary, v. 8: The Concept of Anxiety* (Macon, GA: Mercer University Press, 1985), pp. 35–62.

3 *Concept of Anxiety*, pp. 8–16.

4 *Concept of Anxiety*, pp. 16–20.

5 *Concept of Anxiety*, p. 17.

6 *Concept of Anxiety*, p. 16.

7 *Concept of Anxiety*, p. 20.

8 The 'first ethics' seems to correspond to Luther's notion of the Law as tutor, convicting us of sin and driving us to accept grace; the 'second ethics' suggests the 'third use' of the Law, to guide the repentant believer to live rightly. See, for example, *The Formula of Concord*, VI.

9 *Eighteen Upbuilding Discourses*, pp. 125–127; *The Concept of Anxiety*, p. 37.

10 *Philosophical Fragments*, pp. 13–20.

11 *Eighteen Upbuilding Discourses*, pp. 127–139.

12 *Concept of Anxiety*, pp. 85, 92–93.

13 *Philosophical Fragments*, p. 75.

14 *Concept of Anxiety*, pp. 111–118.

15 *Concept of Anxiety*, p. 117.

16 *Concept of Anxiety*, pp. 93–95.

17 *The Concept of Anxiety*, pp. 118–154.

18 *Fear and Trembling/Repetition*, pp. 94–112; *The Concept of Anxiety*, pp. 118–154.

19 Ronald L. Hall, 'Language and Freedom: Kierkegaard's Analysis of the Demonic in *The Concept of Anxiety*'; in the *International Kierkegaard Commentary*, v. 8, pp. 153–166.

20 *Fear and Trembling/Repetition*, pp. 94–99.

21 Søren Kierkegaard, *Stages on Life's Way: Studies by Various Persons*, edited and translated with introduction and notes by Howard V. Hong and Edna H. Hong (Princeton, NJ: Princeton University Press, 1988), esp. pp. 232–234.

22 Romans 5:8, 8:38–9.

23 *Prefaces: Light Reading for Certain Classes as the Occasion may Require, by Nicolaus Notabene*, trans., with introduction by William McDonald (Tallahassee, FL: The Florida State University Press, 1989), pp. 51–55.

24 *Prefaces*, pp. 57–61.

25 *Prefaces*, pp. 66, 70–76.

26 *Concept of Anxiety*, p. 117.

27 *Eighteen Upbuilding Discourses*, pp. 305–310.

28 *Eighteen Upbuilding Discourses*, p. 352.

29 *Eighteen Upbuilding Discourses*, pp. 340–346.

30 *Eighteen Upbuilding Discourses*, pp. 328–342.

31 *Eighteen Upbuilding Discourses*, pp. 377–401.

32 *Eighteen Upbuilding Discourses*, pp. 399–400.

33 *Eighteen Upbuilding Discourses*, p. 379; *Either/Or*, v. 1, pp. 34–35.

34 *Eighteen Upbuilding Discourses*, p. 380; *Repetition*, p. 216.

35 *Eighteen Upbuilding Discourses*, pp. 382, 395–396; compare *Fragments*, pp. 10–12, 55, 37–71, 105.

36 *Eighteen Upbuilding Discourses*, p. 387.

[37] *Eighteen Upbuilding Discourses*, p. 386.

[38] *Prefaces*, pp. 51–55.

[39] *Fragments*, pp. 13–20.

[40] *Fragments*, pp. 99–100.

[41] *Fragments*, pp. 13–18.

Chapter Five

[1] *Stages on Life's Way: Studies by Various Persons*, p. xi. Contrariwise, see *Three Discourses on Imagined Occasions*, edited and translated with introduction and notes by Howard V. Hong and Edna H. Hong (Princeton, NJ: Princeton University Press, 1993), p. x.

[2] Andrew J. Burgess, 'The Relation of Kierkegaard's *Stages on Life's Way* to *Three Discourses on Imagined Occasions*,' in *The International Kierkegaard Commentary, v. 11: Stages on Life's Way*, edited by Robert L. Perkins (Macon, GA: Mercer University Press, 2000), pp. 281–283.

[3] Søren Kierkegaard, *Three Discourses on Imagined Occasions*, p. 12.

[4] *Discourses on Imagined Occasions*, p. 18.

[5] As, for example, in the *Phaedo*, p. 114.

[6] *Discourses on Imagined Occasions*, pp. 31–32.

[7] *Discourses on Imagined Occasions*, p. 23; cf. *Philosophical Fragments / Johannes Climacus*, pp. 9–22.

[8] *Discourses on Imagined Occasions*, p. 25; cf. *Fragments*, pp. 102–104; and *Concluding Unscientific Postscript*, pp. 28–30.

[9] *Discourses on Imagined Occasions*, p. 29.

[10] *Discourses on Imagined Occasions*, pp. 28–32; *Fragments*, pp. 15–20, 46–47.

[11] *Discourses on Imagined Occasions*, p. 10.

[12] *Discourses on Imagined Occasions*, pp. 43–44.

[13] *Discourses on Imagined Occasions*, pp. 52–63.

[14] *Discourses on Imagined Occasions*, pp. 63–67.

[15] *Discourses on Imagined Occasions*, p. 64.

[16] In several of his 'Diapsalmata,' from *Either/Or*, v. 1, for example.

[17] Søren Kierkegaard, *Either/Or*, v. 1, edited and translated, with introduction and notes by Howard V. Hong and Edna H. Hong (Princeton NJ: Princeton University Press, 1987), p. 37.

[18] *Either/Or*, v. 1, p. 137.

[19] *Either/Or*, v. 1, pp. 18–43.

[20] *Discourses on Imagined Occasions*, p. 83.

[21] For example, see Robert C. Roberts, 'The Socratic Knowledge of God,' in *International Kierkegaard Commentary, v. 8: The Concept of Anxiety*, edited by Robert L. Perkins (Macon, GA: Mercer University Press, 1985), p. 136.

[22] *Stages*, pp. 7–19; *Either/Or*, v. 1, pp. 292–295.

[23] *Stages*, p. 21.

[24] *Either/Or*, v. 1, p. 64, for example.

[25] *Stages*, pp. 22–26.

[26] *Stages*, p. 28.

27 *Either/Or,* v. 1, pp. 47–49.

28 *Stages,* pp. 27, 81.

29 *Kierkegaard on Ethics and Religion,* pp. 11–15.

30 *Stages,* pp. 71–80.

31 *Either/Or,* v. 1, p. 146.

32 For example, Constantin applies ethical categories to woman, only to make her more amusing; *Stages,* pp. 48–49.

33 Plato, *Symposium,* 199c–201d.

34 *Stages,* pp. 102–143.

35 *Stages,* p. 48.

36 *Stages,* pp. 164–167.

37 *Either/Or,* v. 2, pp. 250–260.

38 *Fear and Trembling,* p. 45; see also Søren Kierkegaard, *Eighteen Upbuilding Discourses,* p. 142.

39 *Postscript,* p. 160; *Upbuilding Discourses,* pp. 141–145.

40 Gene Outka, 'Equality and Individuality: Thoughts on Two Themes in Kierkegaard' (*The Journal of Religious Ethics,* v.10, no. 2, Fall 1982); 171–203.

41 *Stages,* pp. 476–477.

42 *Fear and Trembling,* pp. 98–99.

43 Compare *Fear and Trembling,* pp. 94–99.

44 *Stages,* p. 399. The breakdown he describes is not unique to his subject; the same failure is described more algebraically by Climacus in the opening chapter of the *Philosophical Fragments* as the untruth of the learner, offense, and sin.

45 *The Concept of Anxiety,* p. 123.

46 *Stages,* pp. 232–234.

47 *Concept of Anxiety,* p. 149.

48 *Stages,* pp. 485–487.

49 *Three Discourses on Imagined Occasions,* p. 38.

50 *Either/Or,* v. 2, p. 339.

51 *Discourses on Imagined Occasions,* p. 63.

52 *Stages,* pp. 23, 28, 81.

Chapter Six

1 *Concluding Unscientific Postscript,* p. 124. While Climacus is here referring to the work of undermining Hegelianism, not Christendom, the two are essentially one piece.

2 *Postscript,* p. 21.

3 *Postscript,* pp. 52–53.

4 *Fragments,* pp. 57–60.

5 *Postscript,* p. 72.

6 *Postscript,* pp. 74–79.

7 Note that this does not mean that the subjective thinker has no interest in communicating a particular view; it even assumes it (*Postscript,* p. 77).

8 *Postscript,* p. 81.

9 *Postscript,* p. 106.

10 G. W. F. Hegel, *Philosophy of Right*, translated with notes by T. M. Knox (New York: Oxford University Press, 1967), p. 13; Søren Kierkegaard, *Journals*, IV A 164. Sadly, Kierkegaard's contemporaries had no access to this gem from his journals.

11 For parallels with Hamann, see Smith, *J. G. Hamann 1730–1788*, pp. 214–217.

12 *Postscript*, pp. 110–111.

13 *Postscript*, p. 121.

14 *Postscript*, p. 123.

15 G. W. F. Hegel, *Philosophy of Right*, pp. 105–141.

16 *Philosophy of Right*, pp. 142–149.

17 *Postscript*, pp. vi–vii.

18 *Postscript*, p. 137.

19 *Postscript*, p. 144.

20 *Postscript*, pp. 134, 143, 153.

21 *Postscript*, p. 142.

22 *Postscript*, pp. 138–139.

23 *Postscript*, p. 121.

24 *Postscript*, p. 137.

25 *Postscript*, pp. 54, 138. Compare *Either/Or*, v. 1, p. 3.

26 *Postscript*, p. 134.

27 *Postscript*, pp. 158–159.

28 *Postscript*, p. 131.

29 *Postscript*, pp. 160–188.

30 *Postscript*, pp. 182–188.

31 Bruce Kirmmse, *Kierkegaard in Golden-Age Denmark* (Bloomington and Indianapolis: Indiana University Press, 1990), pp. 245–247.

32 Alasdair MacIntyre, *After Virtue*, 2nd ed. (Notre Dame, IN: Notre Dame University Press, 1984), p. 42.

33 Pojman also argues that Kierkegaard's project is self-refuting, although for slightly different reasons. See *The Logic of Subjectivity*, pp. 118–126.

34 *Postscript*, p. 199.

35 In other words, questions such as whether the tower is square or round, or the stick is bent, or the billiard ball caused another to move.

36 *Either/Or*, v. 2, pp. 163–164.

37 *Postscript*, pp. 201–202, for example.

38 *Postscript*, pp. 201–202.

39 *Fragments*, pp. 37–39.

40 *Either/Or*, v. 2, pp. 157–158; *Fragments*, pp. 13–15.

41 *Logic of Subjectivity*, pp. 118–126.

42 Particularly the entirety of Chapter Three.

43 *Postscript*, p. 198.

44 *Postscript*, p. 199.

45 *Postscript*, pp. 199–201.

46 *Postscript*, p. 200, footnote.

47 *Postscript*, p. 200, footnote.

48 *Postscript*, pp. 204–210.

49 *Postscript*, p. 226.

50 *Postscript*, p. 200.

51 *Postscript*, p. 203.

52 *Philosophical Fragments*, pp. 79–86.

53 *Postscript*, p. 332.

54 *Postscript*, p. 211 (Indeed, all 'coming into existence' is absurd, in that it cannot be rationally explained, predicted or known with certainty; this is the point of the 'Interlude' in the *Fragments*.)

55 *Postscript*, pp. 211–234.

56 *Postscript*, pp. 226–227.

57 *Postscript*, pp. 266–269.

58 *Postscript*, pp. 266–267.

59 *Postscript*, pp. 267–268.

60 *Postscript*, pp. 268–269.

61 *Postscript*, p. 332.

62 It seems that this is intended as mere definition; see *Fragments*, pp. 39–44.

63 *Postscript*, pp. 314–315.

64 *Postscript*, pp. 324–325.

65 The Hegelian approach could easily concede all of this as relevant and true for spirit at the stage of *moralitaät*, but when it has fully matured it will reach the stage of *sittlikeit* where the interiority of the subject will be fully expressed in outer reality. This is a recurring theme throughout Kierkegaard's authorship; see *Fragments and Postscript*, pp. 281–287.

66 *Kierkegaard's Fragments and Postscript*, pp. 130–131.

67 *Postscript*, pp. 204–210.

68 *Either/Or*, v. 1, pp. 38–40.

69 *Either/Or*, v. 2, pp. 157–167.

70 *Postscript*, pp. 312–313.

71 *Fragments*, pp. 37–39.

72 Plato, *Gorgias*, 511d–512b.

73 *Postscript*, pp. 303–304.

74 *Postscript*, p. 393.

75 *Either/Or*, v. 2, pp. 260–264.

76 *Either/Or*, v. 2, pp. 265–266.

77 *Either/Or*, v. 2, pp. 327–332.

78 *Fragments and Postscript*, p. 81.

79 *Postscript*, pp. 306–307.

80 *Postscript*, pp. 201–202.

81 *Either/Or*, v. 2, p. 178.

82 *Postscript*, p. 316.

83 *Postscript*, p. 322.

84 *Postscript*, p. 361.

85 *Postscript*, p. 369.

86 *Postscript*, p. 385.

87 *Postscript*, pp. 31–34, for starters.

88 *Postscript*, p. 431.

89 *Postscript*, p. 434.

90 *Postscript*, p. 501.

91 *Postscript*, pp. 486–489.

92 *Postscript,* p. 388.
93 *Postscript,* pp. 525–526.
94 *Postscript,* p. 537.
95 *Postscript,* p. 532.
96 *Postscript,* pp. 389–391.
97 *Postscript,* p. 411.
98 *Postscript,* p. 424.
99 *Postscript,* p. 390; II Cor. 11:24–33.
100 *Postscript,* p. 393.
101 *Postscript,* p. 427.
102 *Postscript,* pp. 422–423.
103 *Postscript,* p. 423.
104 *Postscript,* pp. 424–426.
105 *Postscript,* pp. 426–427.
106 *Fear and Trembling,* pp. 10, 13.
107 *Fear and Trembling,* pp. 20–21, 59.
108 *Postscript,* pp. 395–396.
109 *Stages,* pp. 476–477; *Postscript,* pp. 294, 501.
110 *Postscript,* p. 456.
111 *Postscript,* pp. 499–500 footnote.
112 *Postscript,* p. 475.
113 See also *Postscript,* p. 476.
114 *Postscript,* p. 488.
115 *Postscript,* p. 491.
116 *Postscript,* p. 497.
117 *Postscript,* p. 467.
118 *Postscript,* p. 472.
119 Immanuel Kant, *Critique of Practical Reason;* translated by Lewis White Beck (Indianapolis, IN: The Bobbs-Merrill Company, Inc.1980), pp. 114–153.
120 Immanuel Kant, *Religion within the Limits of Reason Alone,* translated with an introduction and notes by Theodore M. Greene and Hoyt H. Hudson, with a new essay by John SR. Silber (New York: Harper & Row Publishers, 1960), pp. 139–190.
121 *Postscript,* p. 526.
122 *Postscript,* p. 529.
123 *Postscript,* pp. 528–537.
124 *Postscript,* p. 532.
125 *Philosophical Fragments,* p. 19.
126 *Fragments,* pp. 14–15.
127 *Postscript,* p. 530.
128 *Fragments,* p. 15.
129 *Postscript,* pp. 582–583.
130 *Fragments,* p. 15.
131 *Postscript,* p. 584.
132 *Postscript,* pp. 556–557.
133 *Postscript,* pp. 204–209.
134 *Postscript,* p. 387.
135 *Postscript,* pp. 559–560, 572.

[136] Hans L. Martensen, from *Between Hegel and Kierkegaard: Hans L. Martensen's Philosophy of Religion*, translated by Curtis L. Thompson and David J. Kangas, with introduction by Curtis L. Thompson (Atlanta, GA: Scholars Press, 1997), p. 18.

[137] *Stages*, p. 444.

Chapter Seven

[1] Lee Barrett, 'Kierkegaard's Two Ages: An Immediate Stage on the Way to the Religious Life'; in *Two Ages: The Present Age and the Age of Revolution, A Literary Review. v. 14, International Kierkegaard Commentary*, edited by Robert L. Perkins (Macon, GA: Mercer University Press, 1984), pp. 53–55.

[2] Barrett, p. 54.

[3] Barrett, pp. 54–55.

[4] *Fear and Trembling*, pp. 41–50.

[5] Barrett, pp. 62–65.

[6] *Fear and Trembling*, p. 47.

[7] Barrett, pp. 62–63.

[8] *Repetition*, pp. 228–229.

[9] *Repetition*, pp. 22–29.

[10] Barrett, pp. 66–69.

[11] *Stages*, pp. 100–103.

[12] *Stages*, p. 164.

[13] *Stages*, p. 163.

[14] *Stages*, pp. 166–167.

[15] *Stages*, p. 476.

[16] Barrett, p. 53.

[17] *Two Ages*, pp. 15, 20.

[18] *Two Ages*, p. 21.

[19] *Two Ages*, p. 65.

[20] *Two Ages*, pp. 92–112.

[21] *Fear and Trembling*, pp. 41–42, 46–47.

[22] *Two Ages*, p. 39.

[23] *Two Ages*, p. 106.

[24] *Two Ages*, p. 61.

[25] *Two Ages*, pp. 62–63.

[26] From *Two Ages*, pp. 62–63.

[27] Robert Hunter, '*Truckin*,' *Grateful Dead*. Ice Nine Publishing Co. Inc., 1973.

[28] *Two Ages*, p. 63.

[29] Robert L. Perkins, 'Envy as Personal Phenomenon and as Politics,' from *The International Kierkegaard Commentary*, v. 14, pp. 113–128.

[30] *Two Ages*, p. 81.

[31] *Either/Or*, v. I, pp. 281–300.

[32] *Two Ages*, pp. 86–89.

[33] *Two Ages*, p. 92.

[34] *Two Ages*, p. 106.

[35] *Two Ages*, p. 89.

36   *Two Ages*, pp. 88–90.
37   *Two Ages*, pp. 88–89, 106–109.
38   *Two Ages*, pp. 104–105.
39   *Two Ages*, pp. 90–95.
40   *Two Ages*, p. 107.
41   *Two Ages*, p. 109.
42   *Two Ages*, p. 108.
43   *Two Ages*, p. 68.
44   *Two Ages*, p. 100.
45   *Concept of Anxiety*, p. 94.
46   *Concept of Anxiety*, p. 95.
47   *Postscript*, p. 196.

Chapter Eight

1   Søren Kierkegaard, *Either/Or*, volume 2, edited and translated with introduction and notes by Howard V. Hong and Edna H. Hong (Princeton, NJ: Princeton University Press, 1987), pp. 216, 262–263.

Bibliography

Primary Sources

Aquinas, Thomas. *Summa Theologiae*, v. 1, part 1.

Hegel, G. W. F. *Philosophy of Right*. Translated with notes by T. M. Knox. New York: Oxford University Press, 1952.

Hume, David. *Dialogues Concerning Natural Religion* in *The Empiricists*. Garden City, NY: Anchor Press/Doubleday, 1974.

—*An Enquiry Concerning Human Understanding* in *The Empiricists*. Garden City, NY: Anchor Press/Doubleday, 1974.

Kant, Immanuel. *Critique of Practical Reason*. Translated, with introduction by Lewis White Beck. Indianapolis, IN: Bobbs Merrill Educational Publishing, 1956.

—*Fundamental Principles of the Metaphysic of Morals*. Translated by Thomas K. Abbott, with an introduction by Marvin Fox. Indianapolis, IN: Bobbs-Merrill Educational Publishing, 1949.

—*Religion within the Limits of Reason Alone*. Translated with an introduction and notes by Theodore M. Greene and Hoyt H. Hudson; with the essay 'The Ethical Significance of Kant's *Religion*' by John. R. Silber. New York: Harper & Row Publishers, 1960.

Kierkegaard, Søren. *The Concept of Anxiety: A Simple Psychologically Orienting Deliberation on the Dogmatic Issue of Hereditary Sin*. Edited and translated with introduction and notes by Reidar Thomte in collaboration with Albert B. Anderson. Princeton, NJ: Princeton University Press, 1980.

—*Concluding Unscientific Postscript to Philosophical Fragments*. Edited and translated, with an introduction and notes by Howard V. Hong and Edna H. Hong. Princeton, NJ: Princeton University Press, 1992.

—*Eighteen Upbuilding Discourses*. Edited and translated, with an introduction and notes by Howard V. Hong and Edna H. Hong. Princeton, NJ: Princeton University Press, 1990.

—*Either/Or*. Edited and translated with introduction and notes by Howard V. Hong and Edna H. Hong. Princeton, NJ: Princeton University Press, 1987.

—*Fear and Trembling/Repetition*. Edited and translated with introduction and notes by Howard V. Hong and Edna H. Hong. Princeton, NJ: Princeton University Press, 1983.

—*Journals*, IV A 164.

—*Philosophical Fragments/Johannes Climacus*. Edited and translated with an introduction and notes by Howard V. Hong and Edna H. Hong. Princeton, NJ: Princeton University Press, 1985.

—*The Point of View for my Work as an Author: A Report to History.* Translated with introduction and notes by Walter Lowrie; edited with a preface by Benjamin Nelson. New York: Harper & Row Publishers, 1962.

—*Prefaces: Light Reading for Certain Classes as the Occasion may Require, by Nicolaus Notabene.* Translated, and introduction by William McDonald. Tallahassee, FL: The Florida State University Press, 1989.

—*Stages on Life's Way: Studies by Various Persons.* Edited and translated, with introduction and notes, by Howard V. Hong and Edna H. Hong. Princeton, NJ: Princeton University Press, 1988.

—*Three Discourses on Imagined Occasions.* Edited and translated, with introduction and notes by Howard V. Hong and Edna H. Hong. Princeton, NJ: Princeton University Press, 1993.

—*Two Ages: The Present Age and the Age of Revolution, A Literary Review.* Edited and translated, with introduction and notes by Howard V. Hong and Edna H. Hong. Princeton, NJ: Princeton University Press, 1978.

Martensen Hans L. *Between Hegel and Kierkegaard: Hans L. Martensen's Philosophy of Religion*; translated by Curtis L. Thompson and David J. Kangas, with introduction by Curtis L. Thompson. Atlanta, GA: Scholars Press, 1997.

Plato. *Gorgias.*
   Meno.
   Phaedo.
   Phaedrus.
   Symposium.

Secondary Sources

Books

Alexander, W. M. *Johann Georg Hamann: Philosophy and Faith.* The Hauge: Martinus Nijhoff, 1966.

Evans, C. Stephen. *Kierkegaard's 'Fragments' and 'Postscript': The Religious Philosophy of Johannes Climacus.* Atlantic Highlands, NJ: Humanities Press, 1983.

—*Passionate Reason: Making Sense of Kierkegaard's Philosophical Fragments.* Bloomington & Indianapolis: Indiana University Press, 1992.

Ferreira, M. J. *Kierkegaard (Blackwell Great Minds).* Malden, MA: Wiley-Blackwell, 2008.

Green, Ronald M. *Kierkegaard and Kant: The Hidden Debt.* Albany, NY: State University of New York Press, 1992.

Kirkconnell, W. Glenn. *Kierkegaard on Ethics and Religion: From Either/Or through Philosophical Fragments.* London: Continuum Press, 2008.

Kirmmse, Bruce H. *Kierkegaard in Golden Age Denmark.* Bloomington & Indianapolis: Indiana University Press, 1990.

MacIntyre, Alasdair. *After Virtue*, 2nd. ed. Notre Dame, IN: University of Notre Dame Press, 1984.

Nielsen, H. A. *Where the Passion Is: A Reading of Kierkegaard's Philosophical Fragments.* Tallahassee, FL: University Presses of Florida, 1983.

Perkins, Robert L., ed. *International Kierkegaard Commentary*. Macon, GA: Mercer University Press.

> v. 8: *The Concept of Anxiety*, 1985.
> v. 11: *Stages on Life's Way*, 2000.
> v. 14: *Two Ages: The Present Age and the Age of Revolution, A Literary Review*, 1984.

Pojman, Louis P. *The Logic of Subjectivity: Kierkegaard's Philosophy of Religion*. University, AL: University of Alabama Press, 1984.

Roberts, Robert Cambell. *Faith, Reason, and History: Rethinking Kierkegaard's Philosophical Fragments*. Macon, GA: Mercer University Press, 1986.

Smith, Ronald Gregor. *J. G. Hamann 1730–1788: A Study in Christian Existence; with Selections from His Writings*. New York: Harper & Brothers Publishers, 1960.

Articles

Hunter, Robert. Truckin' *Grateful Dead*. San Rafael, CA: Ice Nine Publishing Co. Inc., 1973.

Outka, Gene. 'Equality and Individuality: Thoughts on Two Themes in Kierkegaard.' *The Journal of Religious Ethics*, v. 10, no. 2, Fall 1982; pp. 171–203.

Rumble, Vanessa. 'The Oracle's Ambiguity: Freedom and Original Sin in Kierkegaard's *The Concept of Anxiety*.' *Soundings*, v. 75, no. 4, Winter 1992; pp. 605–625.

Sontag, Fredrick. 'Strange Interlude.' *Man and World*, v. 27, 1994; pp. 15–21.

Index